FREEI
THE BALTIC

GEOFFREY BENNETT

Birlinn

This edition published in 2002 by
Birlinn Limited
West Newington House
10 Newington Road
Edinburgh
EH9 1QS

www.birlinn.co.uk

First published in 1964 by Collins, London as
Cowan's War

ISBN 1 84341 001 X

British Library Cataloguing-in-Publication Data
A catalogue record for this book is available
from the British Library

Printed and bound by
Antony Rowe Ltd, Chippenham

Contents

Preface to the Birlinn Edition

WHEN THIS BOOK first appeared thirty-five years ago under the title *Cowan's War*, the three Baltic states of Estonia, Latvia and Lithuania were firmly entrenched in the Soviet Union, where they had been since their occupation during World War II. Any chance of their regaining the independence they had had between the World Wars seemed remote. It was to be almost another three decades before this even started to become a reality, but as it now has, a further edition is very welcome.

While this new edition was being prepared I learnt that in at least one of these states the events recounted here are remembered and respected. I had an opportunity to visit the Estonian capital Tallinn (called Reval, its old German name, in this book). Walking around the charming 'old town' I entered the historic Church of the Holy Ghost and spotted a white Ensign at one end. Beneath this a new plaque, placed there in the year 2000, records Britons who have been honoured by Estonia for their contribution to freedom. High on the list, just below Winston Churchill, is Sir Walter Cowan.

Then, at the edge of the old town, there is a well-appointed maritime museum in a castle tower known as 'Fat Margaret'. By the side of the entrance another clearly recent plaque, black marble topped with the silhouette of a destroyer, records in both English and Estonian:

IN MEMORY
of the officers and seamen of the British Royal Navy
who served and gave their lives in the cause of freedom
in the Baltic during the Estonian War of Independence
1918–1920

The following Admirals were decorated
with the Estonian Cross of Liberty for their distinguished services:

Admiral Sir Edwyn Alexander-Sinclair G.C.B. M.V.O VRI/I
1865–1945

Admiral Sir Walter Cowan of the Baltic Bart. K.C.B. D.S.O. M.V.O. VRI/I
1871–1956

Admiral Sir Sydney Freemantle G.C.B. M.V.O. VRI/I
1867–1958

Admiral Sir Bertram Thesiger K.B.E. C.B. C.M.G. VRI/I
1875–1966

On behalf of the grateful people of Estonia

Clearly a lot of care has been taken with this though a pedant might say there should be an asterisk * after Cowan's D.S.O. as he was awarded a bar — forty-eight years after the original award.

The sixtieth anniversary of the Soviet occupation was also being remembered with clear disfavour in a special exhibition recounting how the neighbouring colossus forced its way in 1941.

In addition the present prime minister, Mart Laar, has given his personal endorsement with a pamphlet in both Estonian and English, published through the British Embassy, recounting the events, which concludes:

The British were among those who gave their lives in the fight for Estonia's freedom in the Baltic in 1918–1919. The losses of the British fleet in the in the Estonian War of Independence amounted to one light cruiser, two destroyers, one submarine, two sweepers and eight torpedo boats. The presence of the British fleet and its operations eliminated the Soviet Baltic Fleet and, moreover, assured young democracies that they were not alone in their fight. And this is something we should not forget.

The decision to rename the book reflects that today the name of Walter Cowan will mean little except to a very few, but the position and past problems of the now free Baltic states are widely appreciated, so the story told has a broader impact than just the activities of a single man.

As it was not mentioned in the original edition, it may be helpful to know a little about the author — my father — and the background to this work.

A Dartmouth trained naval officer, and son of a naval officer, he qualified in Signals and spent a significant part of his early career as a flag lieutenant on various admirals' staffs. His main World War II appointments were in Freetown and then the Mediterranean, where he was awarded the D.S.C. for, the citation said, '...leadership, zeal and skill while serving as signals officer on the staff of Flag Officer Force H since April 1943 in operations which finally led to the surrender of the Italian Fleet'. From his early career he wrote articles and he was awarded the Royal Untied Services Institution gold medal for an essay on three occasions.

Promoted to commander at the end of the war he continued for a while in the Mediterranean commanding HMS *St Bride's Bay* and then served at the Admiralty in Bath, where he was promoted to captain in January 1953 (when the writer of this preface was training to be a national service midshipman in the carrier HMS *Indefatigable* in Portland harbour).

Later that year he became naval attaché in Moscow, also covering Warsaw and Helsinki, where he had good opportunities to acquire a knowledge of the Soviet Union, its history and its growing navy. This was shortly after Stalin's death, when it was still a very closed and suspicious society; the cold war was only just coming off full freeze. He was responsible for the Soviet end of the Royal Navy's historic 1955 visit to what was then called Leningrad.

By this time he had also established a reputation as a writer for his naval yarns published under the pseudonym 'Sea Lion', as a serving officer he could not use his own name, producing more than a dozen novels as well as scripting a number of radio plays. His interests were broad; he loved theatre and music and after his Moscow stay he gave two substantial talks on the Bolshoi Ballet, then little know in the West, on the BBC Third Programme and championed the cause of Prokifiev's wonderful opera *War and Peace*,[1] then unknown outside the Soviet Union, which he had had an opportunity to see in Leningrad.

---

[1] First performed in Britain by the then Sadler's Wells Opera (now English National Opera) at the London Coliseum in 1971. It was also the first work to be performed at the new Sydney Opera House in Australia three years later.

Returning from Russia he joined the staff of C-in-C Portsmouth, but the navy was entering a period of retrenchment, so when he was offered a post in the household of the Lord Mayor of London, along with the opportunity of generous 'golden bowler' retirement, he accepted.

After three years there he became secretary to the Mayor, later Lord Mayor, of the City of Westminster, where he became an authority on civic protocol. Now permanently shore-bound he had more opportunities for research and turned to naval history under his own name, producing a series of studies on a variety of topics including Jutland, Nelson, Coronel and the Falklands and a biography of Admiral Lord Charles Beresford. He retired from Westminster in 1974 and went to live in the beautiful Shropshire town of Ludlow, where he died in 1983.

For the story in this book he was still close enough to the Royal Navy and Russia when he wrote to get much help and, as his list of credits shows, to talk with quite a few who had been directly involved in the events portrayed. Two who assisted deserve a further mention. Lieutenant-Commander 'Jamie' Davidson, a fluent Russian speaker who assisted with translations, and who had been his very able assistant in the first part of his Moscow stay and become a good friend. He was for four years, 1966–70, the Liberal MP for West Aberdeenshire and a noted Scottish farmer. I have also been able to recall the writing of this book in her Lake District retirement with Mary Rundle C.B.E., my father's cousin, who was Superintendent of WRNS at the end of World War II, and who indexed this and all my father's histories.

This new edition is mostly a direct reproduction of the original text, but I have taken the opportunity to make a number of minor alterations, in particular to the concluding pages, re-captioned two photographs and added two supplements, one based on the significant number of informative letters sent to my father after the original publication and the other dealing with Sir Walter Cowan's release from being a POW in Italy in unusual circumstances. The details of this have only surfaced quite recently.

One point concerns the city my father, quite correctly, calls Petrograd, as this was its name at the time of these events. Now it is once again known by its original name of St. Petersburg. In 1914 Tsar Nicholas II changed it to the more Russian sounding Petrograd, when Germany declared war. Then it became Leningrad after Lenin's death in 1924 but, following a plebiscite, reverted to its original name in 1991. (The majority for this was quite modest; not apparently because of any great reverence for Lenin but from those from the older generation who did not want the horrendous siege of World War II forgotten).

I have my own acknowledgements to add to my father's. I am grateful in particular to Hugh Andrew at Birlinn for believing there is still interest not only in this but also in my father's *Coronel and the Falklands*, which he published again last year.

Thanks also to the staff at library at the Imperial War Museum, in particular Angela Wooten, for ferreting out the rare magazine *World War II Investigator*, which contains details of Cowan's repatriation, and to the helpful staff at the Caird Library at the National Maritime Museum which holds my father's papers, catalogued as MS 85/132 and MS 85/098. I also had useful help from Rear-Admiral Gueritz, Ken Oakley and Bill Mellow of the Royal Navy Commando Association. My thanks also to Reg Kennedy in Helsinki for assistance in making contacts and to Estonian historian Martti Turtola.

Any son having the temerity to make any changes in or additions to his father's work must wonder if he is perhaps looking down to see if his high standards are being maintained. I have done all I can to ensure they are and can only hope I have his blessing.

Rodney M. Bennett
August 2001

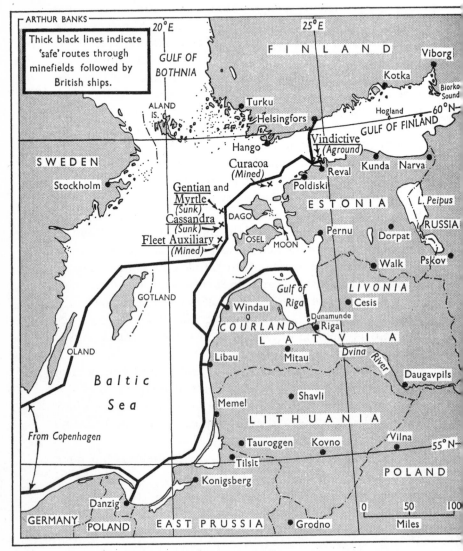

The Baltic in 1919

Chapter One

THE BALTIC SCENE

But soon will shine the sun of liberty,
And from the west a wind will warm the land—
Will the cascade of tyranny then stand ?

From a Polish poem by A. Mickiewicz

THE STORY which this book aims to tell cannot be better summarised than in the slightly bowdlerised words of an anonymous contributor to the first (and only) issue of *Baltic Bits*, the journal which emanated from the wardroom of H.M.S. *Delhi* in the autumn of 1919:

Now the days following the Great Peace were troublous days. There were wars and rumours of wars, famines and pestilences in divers places. Of all the lands, no land was more sorely distressed than the Land of Russ. For there arose a band of thieves and murderers who called themselves the Bolshevites, and their hand was against every man and every man's hand against them. Then said the Great Men of the Land of Brit, these Bolshevites have troubled the world overlong. We will utterly destroy them. But we dare not do it openly, for we fear the people, who have a great love for these Bolshevites, not understanding them. Let us therefore send The Ships, and in order that no man may gainsay us, we will call it A Summer Cruise. . . . So The Ships came and cast anchor in the place which is called Biorko of the Land of the Fin and close by the Isle of Kron, a fortress of the Bolshevites of exceeding great strength. And they besieged the Bolshevites by sea while the Lettites, the Finnites and the Estonites besieged them by land. But the Bolshevites fled before The Ships and hid in their harbours, refusing to give battle. So The Ships tarried at Biorko, waiting and watching. And the men passed their time in the pursuit of arms and with games, The Ships competing one with the other. But many sighed for the fleshpots of their own land, and for their wives and children. . . . Now the chief of all the Captains was a mighty man of valour, not great of stature but cunning in battle. . . .

Ridentam dicere verum quid vetat ?

*   *   *

From the North Sea east of Aberdeen the wide mouth of the Skagerrak, immediately to the south of Norway, rounds the Skaw and contracts into the Kattegat between Sweden and Denmark. Thence it narrows into the Sound and the Great and Little Belts. These three channels lead into the Baltic which is seldom more than 100 miles wide—in some places only half this figure—which runs 900 miles north into the Gulf of Bothnia, a distance less than that from London to Gibraltar. The eastern shore is punctured by the balloon-shaped Gulf of Riga; and by the Gulf of Finland, 30 miles wide, extending nearly 250 miles up to the mouth of the Neva. To set the scene for our story we must first recall something of the history of the countries bordering this almost landlocked sea in July 1914.

Of these, Denmark held the door, but she was in no position to turn the key. Though the Sound and the Belts were in her territorial waters, she lacked the force with which Nelson had had to deal a century before. Sweden, another monarchy with a strong democratic tradition, bordered the whole of the western side of the Baltic; but though the paramount power in the time of Gustavus Adolphus (1594–1632), she had grown self-centred and pacific since Peter the Great (1672–1725) determined to gain " *la fenêtre par laquelle la Russie regarde continuellement l'Europe.*"

Germany, whose low-lying coast confined the Baltic to the south, was a new and upstart country: it was only half a century since Bismarck had created a nation strong enough to challenge France. Since sea power had played no part in compassing the surrender of Napoleon III, the Prussian ruling caste accepted Moltke's dictum that their country could never claim to command the sea; in 1872 Germany had five iron-clads to Britain's fifty. But the arrogant Wilhelm II, who ascended the throne sixteen years later, initiated an aggressive foreign policy. France, fearing Germany's massive army, reacted by signing an alliance with Russia in 1892. Eight years more and the Kaiser began to build a navy intended to wrest the trident from Britannia's hand. Britain responded with the *Entente Cordiale* which enabled her to concentrate her fleet in the North Sea. Germany could not, however, risk a war before August 1914: the *Dreadnought* forced Tirpitz to build battleships of comparable size, and the Kiel Canal had to be deepened to allow them to pass freely between the Baltic and the North Sea. But when this was finished, Germany held the key to the Baltic; if there was to be war, no British ships could enter it, or Russian leave it, so long as the High Seas Fleet remained " in being."

The eastern coast of the Baltic, from the Swedish frontier in the Gulf of Bothnia around the Gulfs of Finland and Riga so far as the boundary of Prussia, was bordered by the powder magazine which Tsar Nicholas II inherited in 1898. Six years later he made the mistake of plunging Russia into a disastrous war with Japan. This—and " Bloody Sunday "—provoked what Lenin called the " dress rehearsal " for 1917—a wave of industrial strikes, nation-wide peasant disturbances and mutinies in the Baltic and Black Sea Fleets. To pacify his people, Nicholas was obliged to allow them their first elected government, but the Duma's franchise was so limited and its power so circumscribed that it had little more than the trappings of democracy. In the summer of 1914, the superficial observer might detect few signs of coming chaos. It was supposed that, in time, the Tsar would allow a measure of liberalism to his country. Moreover, since his army was admired and steps had been taken towards rebuilding his shattered fleet, Russia appeared a worthy ally. The truth was very different. The few with wealth and influence might be the most charming people in the world, but, like Chekhov's Gayev and Madame Ranyevskaya, they were rotten to the core. Though the Tsar could mobilise an army of more than five million men, his corrupt, pleasure-loving War Minister had done nothing to ensure that they were properly equipped. The Baltic Fleet was only large enough to contain a small part of Tirpitz's navy. And for the workers and peasants whom Gorky called " the countless pawns on the endless road of Russia," the only escape from the " tangle of cowardice, blindness, craftiness and stupidity " [1] by which they were governed was the path that Lenin urged them to follow.

In the course of centuries Muscovy had engulfed many states around its periphery into an amalgam of peoples with varied characteristics, language and customs. The most distinct was Finland, whose people came from Asia and settled in this " land of a thousand lakes " more than two thousand years ago. But they brought none of the oriental traits inbred in the Russians; their national character mirrored by their country's coast, " low, reddish granite rocks emerging from the pale blue sea, solitary islands of a hard, archaic beauty inhabited by hundreds of sea birds," [2] they had a greater affinity with the Germans and the Swedes. Indeed, from the second half of the twelfth century they were vassals of Sweden until Peter the Great and the next two Tsars annexed their country (1721–1809) and it became a Russian grand-duchy. Alexander I allowed the Finns to retain their Swedish constitution with an elected Diet, and his successors tolerated this single example of democracy within their empire until Nicholas II mounted the throne. In 1899 he abrogated the Diet's right to enact legislation and invested a Russian governor with dictatorial powers. This led to the assassination of the Governor-General in 1904, and a national strike which brought

---

[1] So wrote Count Witte of " this insane régime " when he was Prime Minister at the time of the Russo-Japanese war.

[2] Bengt de Torne's description.

14

the Finns into such bloody conflict with their oppressors that the Tsar was frightened into restoring the *status quo ante*.

The Finns made good use of this victory; they remodelled their constitution on the basis of universal suffrage with complete freedom of speech, and adopted a programme of far-sighted social reforms. But the Tsar was not to be deterred for long from wielding absolute power over this corner of his empire. In 1909 he imposed a crippling annual contribution to his coffers. A year later, in obedience to his wishes, the Duma cried, "*finis Finlandiae.*" The Diet retaliated by refusing to pass imperial laws and denied civil rights to Russians resident in Finland. When the Governor-General then dismissed the Diet, every provincial governor left his post, judges resigned and other officials went into exile. Nonetheless, by 1914 the Tsar had imposed his oppressive rule, so that four million Finns were as ripe for a struggle that would give them freedom as the Russians were ready for a revolution that would rid them of a despotic Throne.

The Estonians came to the most northerly of Russia's provinces on the opposite side of the Gulf of Finland centuries before the Christian era. Elements of the Ugrian tribe, from which came the Finns and the Hungarians, with both of whom the Estonians share an affinity of language, migrated from the Volga and Ural Valleys to settle in this small corner of Europe with its 700-mile coastline to the west of Lake Peipus.[1] Invaded by the Vikings in the ninth century, and by the crusading Prince Yaroslav of Kiev a hundred years later, they were divided by conquest at the end of the fifteenth century. The northern half became a Danish province, whilst German

---

[1] Also known as Lake Pepsi. In any English book about the Baltic, proper names present problems. Many, especially Latvian ones, should bear accents; but since few English readers know how these affect a word's pronunciation, they have been omitted here. As many may be spelt in more ways than one; this is especially true of geographical names, some having two or more different versions according to the language used, or because a change has been made for political reasons. Here, therefore, the names by which places were commonly known at the time have been used. But, to assist the reader in identifying them, the more important variants will be found in Appendix C.

Knights of the Sword, once crusaders for the Catholic faith, now aggressive colonists, added the southern half to Livonia. The Estonians thus gained Christianity but lost their land and freedom. They did not, however, remain divided; in 1346 the Danish king sold his Baltic province to the Germans, when all Estonia was embraced by Livonia. But before the Germans could unite Livonia with Prussia, Lithuania, which lay between, joined with Poland to destroy the military might of the Teutonic Knights at Tannenberg (1410), after which Livonia accepted the suzerainty of the Polish Crown (1561). Before this, however, Livonia had become a battleground; attacks by Tsars Ivan III (1502) and Ivan IV (1558) were unsuccessful, but a later seaborne invasion secured this province for the Swedish Throne (1660). These successive changes in the fortunes of their country were, however, of little interest to the Estonian people; they remained serfs of the German Barons who held the estates into which their forebears, the Knights, had divided the land.

Swedish domination lasted less than half a century: having defeated Charles XII at Poltava (1709), Peter the Great seized this " land of the Virgin " at the end of the Great Northern War (1721). As slaves of the Tsar, the Estonians gained one benefit: to weaken the dominant position of the Barons, Alexander I abolished serfdom in Livonia fifty years before the Russian peasants were granted their freedom. Subsequent liberalisation allowed an Estonian national conscience to awaken, though the administration of the country had again been divided into two. The Estonians likewise welcomed Alexander III's abolition (1881) of the local autonomy which his predecessors had allowed to the Baltic States because this further restricted the Barons' power. Indeed, by the end of the century the latter had been forced to return nearly two-fifths of a largely low-lying country, physically very similar to Finland, to those to whom it really belonged. Later Russification was not, however, so acceptable; the Estonians responded to the 1905 " revolution " with demands for political autonomy, the unification of all areas with an Estonian ethnic majority, the abolition of the special privileges still enjoyed by the Barons, and the distribution of Crown lands to the peasants. Though Nicholas II's troops suppressed this revolt, its aims remained strong in the minds of nearly a million people who retained the rural interests of their ancestors, despite a measure of industrialisation centred on the ancient capital of Reval and the smaller port of Narva.

Immediately to the south of Estonia, and as large as Belgium and the Netherlands, lay Latvia, a country of sand and swamp sprinkled with thin forest, much of its 350-mile coastline bordering the Gulf of Riga. A Slav race from the Carpathian mountains, the Letts are more akin to the Russians than their northern neighbours with whom so much of their history is linked. German colonisation made their country an integral part of Livonia which, with Estonia, became the domain of the Teutonic Knights.[1] Union with Poland might destroy these crusaders' military power, but they were the principal landowners when the country was annexed by Russia in the eighteenth century. So the Letts had no chance to cohere as a people with their own national characteristics and aspirations, until the Tsars took progressive steps to reduce the influential position enjoyed by the Barons. The industrial revolution in Russia in the second half of the nineteenth century had a greater impact on the people of Courland and Livonia, into which Latvia had by that time been divided, than it had upon the Estonians. The ice-free ports of Windau and Libau gave Russia access to the Baltic for a growing volume of imports and exports when Riga and St. Petersburg were closed by winter ice; moreover, Alexander III developed Libau as an all-season base for his Baltic Fleet. By 1900 the Letts were more than smallholders and middle-class traders;

[1] Who, as a matter of interest to the English reader, included Englishmen. *Vide* Chaucer's *Knight's Tale:* " In Lettowe hadde he reysed (*campaigned*) and in Ruce."

they included an intelligentsia and an industrial proletariat in whom Russian repression encouraged the growth of Communism. Riots in 1905 might be suppressed, but their purpose remained; the more moderate Letts wanted political autonomy and an easing of Russian domination; the extremists sought to overthrow Tsarist rule.

By July 1914 the Letts numbered more than two million to whom, as to the Finns and Estonians, the Reformation had brought the Lutheran faith. Lithuania, on the other hand, was a stronghold of Roman Catholicism; also unlike its northern neighbours, this otherwise similar land to the south of Latvia had no coastline; the port of Memel was in Prussia. The people, of Asian stock, kith of both Prussians and Poles and sharing their love of war, were able to resist the early German colonisation which subjugated the other Baltic States. By the fourteenth century the Grand Dukedom of Lithuania extended from the Baltic to the city of Kiev. Union with Poland in 1401 enabled both states to defeat the Teutonic Knights, but their independence was then menaced from the east, Tsar Ivan III claiming the major part of Lithuania. Muscovy did not, however, achieve so much until the partition of Poland at the end of the eighteenth century. The Liths, who had by now lost their Byelorussian empire, were then forced to accept Russian rule. But this did not quench their obstinate spirit; they rebelled in 1812, in 1831 and again in 1863. On the third occasion Tsarist troops " swept up the bloody dust of rebellious Lithuania," [1] which was subjected to complete Russification, even so far as an attempt to suppress Roman Catholicism. But the Liths' faith proved as strong as their determination to retain their language and traditions: after the abolition of serfdom (1861) their intelligentsia added their voice to the clergy's against the Throne. The 1905 " revolution " had no violent impact on Lithuania, though the people called a Grand Assembly in Vilna which demanded territorial autonomy and an elected council. But this gained

[1] Bryusov's phrase in *Variations on the theme of " The Bronze Horsemen."*

them little more than the right to teach their own language in their schools: to the two million who occupied this predominantly agricultural province in July 1914, a measure of independence and a democratic form of government remained a dream.

*　　　*　　　*

Now to make the changes to the backcloth and the wings of the Baltic scene for the events which whipped these northern waters into a "sea of troubles." When Archduke Franz Ferdinand and his wife were assassinated at Sarajevo (28th June, 1914), Wilhelm II encouraged Austria-Hungary to present Serbia with a humiliating ultimatum. The Tsar ordered mobilisation to prevent Serbia from being crushed. Germany responded by declaring war on Russia (1st August), and on her ally, France, two days later. Twenty-four hours more and the German General Staff, by invading France through Belgium, drew Britain and her Empire into the conflict.

Among the Baltic countries, Denmark and Sweden remained neutral. But Russia's initial fervour matched the Kaiser's determination to achieve world domination; the people forgot their discontent and rallied to the Tsar. The Russian "steam roller" threatened disaster to East Prussia until Hindenburg and Ludendorf encircled Samsonov at Tannenberg (26th–29th August), and the Russian armies were driven back to their own frontier. There, except for a thrust into Galicia, the Eastern Front remained whilst Germany concentrated on victory in the West. Failing to achieve this by the middle of 1915, she turned again to the East, when Mackensen's offensive drove so far into Russia that all Lithuania and the southern part of Latvia along the Baltic coast suffered German occupation. Through Murmansk, Archangel and Vladivostok the Allies did what they could to remedy Russia's dire shortage of arms and ammunition, so that she could launch a counter-offensive in the spring of 1916. But though Brusilov's armies went through the Austro–Hungarian line like a knife through butter, Hindenburg was able to stem the rout. And " from the fall of Warsaw, in spite of momentary flashes of splendour and courage, the Russians were a blindfold, naked people, fighting a nation fully armed." [1] Their morale, sapped by decades of oppression and by the canker of sedition, was not proof against the loss of two million killed, wounded and taken prisoner. When Nicholas II misguidedly took personal command of his armies in the field, there was no one to moderate the obstinacy of the Tsaritsa even though she had been deprived of the evil counsel of Rasputin. She remained blind to the dangers of the growing shortage of food in Petrograd—the consequence of a railway system that was unable to meet both civil and military needs. The workers struck in March [2] 1917 when the garrison mutinied and joined in establishing a *Soviet* of Workers and Soldiers Deputies, Moscow and other towns following their example.

Too late the Duma defied the Tsar's prorogation order, demanded his abdication, and attempted to establish a new system of rule. But though their Provisional Government had the support of the Petrograd Soviet, it was an unstable partnership. The former's intention to continue the war was undermined by the latter's declaration that Russia wished to conclude a peace on the basis of " no annexations, no indemnities." In July it was nullified by the disastrous failure of a premature offensive against the Austrian front, and by Lenin's return from exile. And Kerensky's unhappy dual position as Prime Minister and as Vice-President of the Soviet was threatened by Kornilov's September attempt at a military coup and Lenin's demand for " all power to the Soviets." A month later Russia was troubled by more than peasant revolts and bread riots in the towns which neither police nor military were willing to suppress: parts of the Empire were seceding as quasi-indepen-

---

[1] Hugh Walpole.   [2] February by the calendar then used in Russia.

dent republics, and the armies in the field were so near to dissolution that the Germans could advance on Petrograd. This threat provided the spark for Lenin's dream: the Bolsheviks inspired the Congress of Soviets to organise a military force, ostensibly for the defence of the capital, which Trotsky used at the beginning of November [1] to seize the telephone exchange, the telegraph centre and all government offices. And whilst Kerensky hurried to the front in a futile attempt to bring troops back to quell the revolt, a threatened bombardment by the cruiser *Avrora* persuaded the other members of the Provisional Government to surrender the Winter Palace. The Menshevik majority in the Congress of Soviets protested against the Bolsheviks' unconstitutional methods, but Lenin's oratory swept them aside. In " ten days that shook the world," a mere handful of men who did not suffer from the laziness and indifference which are the curse of the Russian temperament, ruthlessly exploited the most critical phase in their country's history. Lenin and his supporters did not, however, establish a " dictatorship of the proletariat " easily: though Bolshevism spread across the country, its adherents were but a tithe of the population. Many were determined to oppose the new régime, and within a week of the Revolution Krasnov's troops threatened the capital. " We hoped to establish a compromise without bloodshed, but when blood has been shed, there is only one way left, a ruthless fight," declared Trotsky as he mobilised his Red Guards against this first attack by White forces, which heralded a civil war that was to rack Russia for three terrible years.

Lenin's aim was universal Communism, which he erroneously supposed would soon spread throughout Europe. But he knew that his own country was in chaos, the people overwhelmingly war weary and the army disintegrating so fast that it could no longer fight. If Russia was to be the centre of a new world order, the Soviet's first move must be to end

[1] The last week in October by the old Russian calendar, hence the usual references to the October Revolution.

the war: on 22nd November Trotsky invited the belligerent powers to conclude an armistice. The Allies made a brief but fruitless attempt to persuade the Russians to continue fighting; Germany and Austria-Hungary, who wanted to transfer their armies to the West, accepted the proposal on 15th December. A week later German and Russian delegates began peace negotiations at Brest-Litovsk, which were greatly complicated by the move towards independence which Finland and the Baltic States had made after Nicholas II's abdication.

Among these states, Lithuania had suffered the full fury of the war: in 1915 the retreating Russians had pursued a scorched earth policy, and thereafter the Germans had squeezed almost all that remained from this little state. But though the German generals wished to annex Lithuania and join it to Prussia, their statesmen recognised the Liths' obstinate desire for liberty. A congress of 200 delegates was allowed to gather in Vilna to elect a *Taryba* of twenty members; and they reacted to the October Revolution with a demand for independence.

The Letts showed as much patriotic fervour as the Russians in 1914, many joining the Tsar's Army—notwithstanding the pro-German influence of the Barons (who had never become Letts—or Estonians or Liths—as the Normans became Englishmen) and the German merchants who had settled in Riga. And such was their gallantry that, when the German Army invaded Latvia in 1915, the Duma authorised the establishment of eight battalions of Lettish Rifles who successfully defended Riga and Livonia for more than two years. The Letts reacted to the February Revolution by calling a National Congress which met in July and defined its aim as political autonomy. But before the Provisional Government could grant this, the defences of Riga crumbled, which prevented the workers of all three Latvian ports from declaring for Bolshevism in November. The rest of the people, peasants for the most part, were so opposed to the new régime—and in this they had the support of the Balts [1]—that they established a National Council which proclaimed Latvia's independence.

Estonia escaped the evils of German occupation until December 1917. Moreover, one of the Russian Provisional Government's early acts was to pass a decree which unified all districts with an Estonian majority into a single province with autonomous self-government. A National Council assumed power in July under the leadership of Konstantin Pats; and within a fortnight of the October Revolution Estonia seceded from Russia. But Pats's intention to establish a liberal democracy hung in the balance when the workers of Reval seized control of the capital and set up a *Soviet* shortly before Trotsky opened negotiations at Brest-Litovsk.

To ensure Finland's support for the war, the Tsar allowed the Duma to relax its control, but few Finns believed that a victorious Russia would do less than reimpose its oppressive rule so that, though many fought in the Russian ranks, 2000 joined the German Army. The Provisional Government restored representative government in Helsingfors, when the Diet resolved that it alone could make laws dealing with their country's internal affairs, and passed *en bloc* all bills held up by Nicholas II. It could not, however, relieve the distress and discontent caused by the food shortage, which was aggravated by the influx of some 40,000 Russian refugees, of whom many brought the seeds of unrest with them from Petrograd. But such difficulties could not subdue the Finns' sturdy belief in democratic rule: when the Bolsheviks seized power, the Diet declared Finland's independence (6th December, 1917).

*   *   *

In the light of this upsurge of aggressive nationalism amongst four of the subject peoples of a disintegrating empire, it is not surprising that one of the Germans' first demands at

---

[1] A convenient collective name for the Barons and the subsequent German settlers in Latvia (and the other Baltic States).

Brest-Litovsk was for Finland and the Baltic States, together with Poland (already occupied by the German Army) and the Ukraine (whose corn Germany desperately needed) to be allowed to secede. Trotsky raised no objections over Finland and Poland: the Bolsheviks recognised the former's independence on 4th January, 1918, and the latter's on the 10th. But realising that the other provinces would be effectively tied to Germany, either because they were already occupied or through the influence of the Balts, Trotsky evoked the Bolsheviks' avowed aim, " no annexations, no indemnities." The Germans retorted that unless Russia accepted their terms, hostilities would be renewed (except against the Ukraine which had embarrassed the Bolsheviks by signing a separate peace on 9th February). " We do not agree to shed any longer the blood of our soldiers in defence of one side against the other," answered Trotsky. " We are giving the order for a general demobilisation of all our armies in the strong hope that other peoples will soon follow our example. We are going out of the war. But we will not sign the peace treaty." The German General Staff responded to this theatrical gesture by ordering an advance on Petrograd. Recognising the desperate position in which this placed the Bolshevik Government, Lenin argued that they must accept the German terms as a temporary compromise until the expected revolution of the war-exhausted peoples of all Europe. But he had to threaten resignation before his colleagues allowed a new delegation to sign the German terms on 3rd March, 1918, when Russia agreed to withdraw her troops from Finland and the Baltic States.

The Allies, to whom the collapse of the Eastern Front presaged a near-mortal blow in the West, refused to recognise this treaty. They sent naval and military forces to Murmansk, Archangel and Vladivostok to prevent the large stocks of war stores that had accumulated in these ports from passing into German hands, to prevent a German advance on Murmansk and to enable a Czech army which had been fighting on the Eastern Front to withdraw across Siberia and embark for transhipment to France. These initial interventions by the Allies were not, however, on a sufficient scale to trouble Lenin who had more serious preoccupations. An elected constituent assembly, which he had promised should govern the country, had to be dismissed within twenty-four hours of its first meeting (19th January, 1918). Russia's administrative and economic machinery had to be patched up if a Bolshevik government was to endure. Of more immediate importance, the Soviet Republic had to fight for survival: Lenin had to contend with acts of sabotage, including a near successful attempt at his assassination, by authorising the Cheka to terrorise his opponents into allowing him to transform the country into a Communist state, whilst Trotsky had to create a Red army to defend the Revolution against the Whites. Savinkov's army, which assembled only 180 miles north of Moscow in the summer of 1918, was dispersed without great difficulty. But Kolchak, who had the help of the withdrawing Czech army, succeeded in securing all Siberia, and only met serious opposition when he tried to advance west of the Urals in September 1918. In the same month the Red Guards stemmed the advance of a third White army from the Cossack provinces on the Don. But the threat to Moscow was still serious when the Germans asked the Allies for an armistice in November. And this released the latter's troops to swell their Intervention forces; by the end of 1918, there were 15,000 British and American troops in the north, and 70,000 Japanese, 7000 American and 7000 British troops in Eastern Siberia, all supported by naval forces, whilst the French fleet moved into the Black Sea and occupied Odessa.

Meantime, Finland had been seriously disturbed by marauding bands of Finnish workers with Bolshevik sympathies. The fifty-two-year-old Baron Carl Gustav Mannerheim, a Finn of Swedish descent who had led the Tsar's cavalry until 1917, tried to raise a White force to suppress them but failed. Sweden declined help; the Allies were in no position to provide it. So the Finnish Government turned to Germany who responded by sending 12,000 troops under the command of a fifty-seven-year-old major-general of East Prussian birth, Count Rudigen von der Goltz. Together Goltz and Mannerheim drove the Reds from the country, the former securing Helsingfors on 14th April, 1918, the latter gaining a decisive victory at Viborg on the 29th. The Finns were then asked to co-operate in a German drive to cut the Murmansk railway which was held by the Reds and the Allies. But Mannerheim resisted this demand until the Allies' summer offensive in the West obliged Goltz to withdraw his troops from Finland in October.

Developments in Lithuania from the signing of the Treaty of Brest-Litovsk up to the Armistice were overshadowed by the country's continued occupation by a rapacious German army. On 16th February, 1918, the Wilhelmstrasse allowed the Taryba to proclaim Lithuania's independence, subject to a treaty of " perpetual alliance." The Taryba decided that their country's future form of government should await the election of a constituent assembly. Until then the supreme power was vested in a triumvirate who designated Augustinas Voldmaris as Premier. He formed a government in Vilna on 11th November, 1918, which was as anti-Russian (Tsarist or Bolshevik) as it was determined to be rid of its German conquerors.

For Latvia and Estonia, the Wilhelmstrasse planned a German controlled *Landesrat* which was set up in Riga to form a Baltic grand-duchy. Up to the Armistice, Latvia was in no position to resist this; much of the country was occupied by the German Army, whilst the Letts were divided between the peasants represented by the National Council at Valka, who wanted nothing short of independence, and the soviets in Riga, Windau and Libau who aimed to establish a Communist régime subservient to Moscow. Estonia, though not occupied by German troops, was similarly divided between the Communists in Reval and the rest of the country which supported Pats's National Council at Dorpat. Since a single Estonian regiment was insufficient to wrest control of the capital, Pats sent an emissary to Stockholm to ask for British help. For practical reasons this could not be given so the Barons appealed to Berlin. The Communists promptly fled, allowing the National Council to proclaim Estonia's independence on 24th February, 1918. But this was too late to forestall the German Eighth Army which occupied Reval on the 25th, arrested Pats, and drove the other members of the National Council abroad or underground. Thereafter, up to 11th November, Estonia was in danger of becoming a Prussian grand-duchy. Indeed, if Germany had triumphed in the First World War, all the Baltic States, though granted nominal independence, would have become Prussian provinces, whilst Finland, having gained a greater measure of freedom, would have entered into an alliance with the Reich.

*　　　*　　　*

But Germany did not triumph: her successes on the Eastern Front were not paralleled in the West. Though Brest-Litovsk freed German divisions for transfer to the West in time for major offensives in the spring and early summer of 1918, the Allies' counter-offensive which began in mid-July was more successful than the most sanguine hoped: 8th August was " the black day of the German Army "; by the end of September it was in full retreat. It was not pursued into Germany because the people behind the line succumbed to war-exhaustion and hunger: with the workers near to revolution, the German Government asked the Allies for an armistice which ended hostilities on 11th November.

In Estonia the German troops promptly mutinied, formed soviets, abandoned their arms and demanded to return home, so that they had to be withdrawn from the country. Pats was thus released from internment to resume his post as Prime Minister of a Provisional Government, which had met in Reval to reaffirm Estonian independence on the very day the Armistice was signed. The Finns reacted to the disastrous change in Germany's fortunes by electing Mannerheim as Regent. In Latvia the National Council proclaimed their country's independence on 18th November, though the Germans did not display the same eagerness to withdraw from Riga as they had from Reval. Only in Lithuania, which had been under German occupation for more than three years, was there no immediate demonstration of a national desire for freedom.

The Armistice terms were chiefly designed to ensure that Germany could not renew hostilities until a peace had been negotiated and signed; but they contained other clauses. Article XII laid down that " the Germans were to withdraw from the territory that was formerly part of the Russian Empire as soon as the Allies should consider the moment suitable having regard to the interior conditions of those territories." This was to ensure that the German Army kept the Bolsheviks out of the Baltic States, to all of which the Allies had accorded *de facto* recognition. Article XXIII required the internment of the greater part of Germany's Fleet in Allied ports, whilst Article XXV gave " freedom of access to and from the Baltic to the naval and mercantile marines of the Allies," which formally opened the door that had been shut by the High Seas Fleet for more than five years. The British Navy was free to enter a sea from which it had been denied access since 1914 [1] in order to enforce Article XXVI which declared that " the existing blockade conditions set up by the Allied Powers are to remain unchanged." More important to this story, the British Government could use the Royal Navy to help Finland maintain its independence and the Baltic States to resist a Bolshevik invasion.

[1] Except for a flotilla of submarines which operated with the Russian Fleet from 1915–17.

Chapter Two

RED WATERS

In the name of the Estonian nation we express our thanks to the British Government for sending the fleet and arms to Estonia which help us to fight and conquer Russian Bolshevism and anarchism.

The Estonian Provisional Government
to Rear-Admiral Alexander-Sinclair

THE PEOPLE of Britain were still suffering from the orgy of hysteria in which they had indulged as soon as the maroons were fired at 11.0 a.m. on 11th November, 1918, when the Foreign Office asked the Admiralty to send ships into the Baltic. They wished to implement Article XXV of the Armistice terms as soon as possible in order to enforce Article XXVI and to improve relations with the Baltic countries which had kow-towed to Germany for too long, " showing the flag " being a recognised way. The First Sea Lord, "Rosy" Wemyss,[1] had no doubts about these justifications for an incursion into the Baltic because he had represented the Allied Navies in the Forest of Compiègne. But there were other reasons which involved more difficult issues for diplomat and mariner.

In Petrograd the Council of People's Commissars had proclaimed the right of national self-determination, including secession, because this had for some time been an effective slogan for agitation amongst those parts of Russia that had been held within the Tsar's empire by force. But to Lenin the right of self-determination was not identical with a demand for secession: having established a Communist state he and

[1] Admiral of the Fleet Lord Wester Wemyss.

29

his colleagues wanted all nationalities to remain in it. " The downfall of the German occupation placed before Soviet Russia the task of liberating the Baltic territories." [1] " Soviet Russia must gain access to the Baltic coast and replant the Red Flag of the Proletarian Revolution there. Soviet troops must occupy Lithuania, Latvia and Estonia. The Baltic must become a Soviet sea." [2] So the titular freedom granted at Brest-Litovsk to the three Baltic States was now menaced by Bolshevik forces determined to fill the void when the German troops withdrew, these embryo countries having had no chance to do more than improvise puny defences of their own. Both Latvian and Estonian missions had made this abundantly clear to London, but the British attitude towards Intervention had been profoundly altered by the Allied victory over Germany. In the words of a memorandum by the Foreign Secretary :[3]

One result has been to modify the principal motive which prompted our expeditions to Murmansk, Archangel and Vladivostok. So long as a life and death struggle was proceeding on the Western Front it was of the first importance to prevent the withdrawal of German forces from Russia to France; but with the conclusion of a German Armistice this motive has no further force. For what then are we still maintaining troops in various parts of what was once the Russian Empire? It seems commonly supposed that these expeditions are partial and imperfect efforts to carry out a campaign against Bolshevism, and to secure the restoration of decent order and a stable government. This view indicates a complete misapprehension of what His Majesty's Government are able to do, or desire to do. This country would refuse to see its forces, after more than four years of strenuous fighting, dissipated over the huge expanse of Russia in order to carry out political reforms in a state which is no longer a belligerent ally. We have constantly asserted that it is for the Russians to choose their own form of government; that we have no desire to intervene in their domestic affairs. But it does not follow that we can disinterest ourselves wholly from Russian affairs. The Czecho-Slovaks are our allies and we must do what we can to help them. In the south-west corner of Russia in Europe, in Siberia, in Trans-Caucasia and

---

[1] *Pravda.*   [2] *Izvestia.*   [3] A. J. (later Lord) Balfour.

Trans-Caspia, in the territories adjacent to the White Sea and the Arctic, new anti-Bolshevist administrations have grown up under the shelter of Allied forces. We are responsible for their existence and must endeavour to support them. How far we can do this and how such a policy will ultimately develop, we cannot say. It must depend on the course taken by the Associated Powers who have far larger resources at their disposal than ourselves. For us no alternative is open at present than to use such troops as we possess to the best advantage; *where we have no troops, to supply arms and money; and in the case of the Baltic provinces, to protect, as far as we can, the nascent nationalities with our fleet*.[1]

When, therefore, a delegation from the Estonian National Council arrived in London a week after the Armistice to urge the immediate dispatch of warships and troops to protect their country,[2] the Foreign Office answered that troops were out of the question, but that warships might be sent, together with arms and equipment to enable the Estonians to defend themselves. The Admiralty was not so encouraging: the Deputy Chief of Naval Staff, Vice-Admiral Fremantle,[3] stressed the practical difficulties, especially the numerous mines with which the Baltic had been sown, many of which had had the safety device required by the Hague Convention removed, so that they remained dangerous even when separated from their moorings.

This was not the first time he had emphasised this objection. Mannerheim, on becoming Regent of Finland, had formulated a dual policy; to maintain his country's independence against Bolshevik aggression and to establish good relations with the Allies. For the last purpose he had organised an army of three divisions, but he was hindered by a food shortage which laid the people open to the poison of Bolshevik propaganda. Furthermore, while he could defend Finland's frontier because it was only threatened south of Lake Onega —the Allies based on Murmansk and Archangel, who were

[1] Author's italics.
[2] The German Commander in Reval also had the effrontery to ask for British warships to be sent to deal with his mutinous troops.
[3] Later Admiral Sir Sydney Fremantle.

co-operating with the Reds in that region, were to the north of this—he feared an assault on Helsingfors which the Finns had no navy to oppose. So he had asked for British naval assistance. But the Admiralty had answered that warships could only be sent into the Gulf of Finland if minesweepers first cleared the way, and that these were not available; there were more urgent calls for mines to be swept around Britain's shores. When the Bolshevik minelayer *Narova*, escorted by two destroyers, attempted to lay a field close to the Finnish coast on 19th November and had to be driven off by a shore battery, Mannerheim strengthened his request with an alarmist report that a Red fleet, comprising six battleships, plus destroyers and submarines, was about to leave Kronstadt escorting transports carrying Finnish renegades, Estonian units with Bolshevik sympathies, and the similar minded First Lettish Regiment, to attack Helsingfors, Reval and Libau. The Admiralty's realistic response was that this was in the highest degree unlikely; the Reds were not capable of sending such a fleet to sea, specially so late in the year. Mannerheim would have to be content with his own army and with food supplied through Sweden.

The Finns were, however, to have the British Navy's indirect support. On 20th November, the question of sending ships and arms to the Baltic States in response to the Estonian request came before Lloyd George's Imperial War Cabinet. A show of force in the Baltic was needed " to help strengthen the populations of that part of the world against Bolshevism and to assist British interests there." Fremantle suggested sending a light cruiser squadron to the Sound, accompanied by nine destroyers, which would " move on, possibly to Libau but eventually to Reval where the Admiral will get into touch with the *de facto* Estonian Government, appreciate the political conditions, and issue arms or not at his discretion." There were three difficulties. Information would have to be obtained locally about a safe route through the minefields; Reval was usually blocked by ice at the end of December; and, though it was "scarcely credible that the Russian ships could be in working order after having been for a year in Bolshevik possession, we have had some surprises from the Bolshevik Army and must be on our guard against unexpected efficiency in some, at any rate, of the Russian ships. Petrograd is only 180 miles from Reval and ships lying there would have to be on their guard against surprise. Should any probability of opposition from the Russian Fleet develop, the force would require to be reinforced by a division of battleships, at least a flotilla of destroyers and some submarines." Wemyss approved these proposals, adding that the initial force should be sent to Copenhagen immediately.

*   *   *

On 21st November the light cruiser *Cardiff*[1] led the German High Seas Fleet into the Forth for internment in accordance with the terms of the Armistice. Next day she sailed again, her destination the Baltic, to the chagrin of her officers and men who had been enjoying a respite from the strain of war sorties and patrols, and who had been looking forward to ten days' post-war leave to visit the homes and families of which they had seen so little during the past four and a half years, or to early demobilisation in the case of those who had joined for the duration of hostilities. These last were particularly disgruntled. Sharing their feelings were the crews of the other four ships of the Sixth Light Cruiser Squadron, the *Cassandra, Caradoc, Ceres* and *Calypso*, nine " V & W " class destroyers from the Thirteenth Flotilla, and seven ships of the Third Fleet Sweeping Flotilla. All were under the command of a young rear-admiral, Alexander-Sinclair,[2] who flew his flag in the *Cardiff*.

Sinclair had orders to proceed to Libau and Reval. His

---

[1] Details of the principal warships with which this book is concerned are given in Appendix B.

[2] Later Admiral Sir Edwyn Alexander-Sinclair.

primary aim was " to show the British flag and support British policy as circumstances dictate." A secondary object was to land arms which were being sent in the minelayers *Princess Margaret* and *Angora*. He was also to inform the Estonian and Latvian Governments that with these they must be responsible for the defence of their own countries. The Admiralty's orders added that he could count on the support of a squadron of battleships which would be sent to Copenhagen if there was any sign that they might be needed. More important, however, was the clause concerning Bolshevik warships; to quote Fremantle:

> It was extremely difficult to get the Foreign Office to understand that, to frame orders for a naval force, the officer in command must be told whether he is at war or not. It may be possible under some circumstances to tell a land force, " We do not want war if we can help it, and therefore you must let the other man fire first before you fire on him." But with a naval force you cannot do that. The first time the other man fires it may be a torpedo, and then you may not have very much more to say, if the torpedo hits. So you must be told whether when you see a suspect you are entitled to open fire on him at once.[1]

So, though Britain was not in a state of war with the Soviet Republic, the Foreign Office was persuaded that Sinclair should be told that " a Bolshevik man-of-war operating off the coast of the Baltic Provinces [2] must be assumed to be doing so with hostile intent and should be treated accordingly."

To comply with these instructions the Admiral ordered his force to fuel as soon as it reached the Danish capital. The cruisers and destroyers did so from their accompanying oilers, but the minesweepers, coal-burners of the " Town " class, could not obey. The collier *Tregarth* had failed to arrive, having run ashore, and no coal was to be had in Copenhagen. Any doubts Sinclair may have had about waiting for another

---

[1] During the discussion following a lecture at the Royal United Service Institution on 15th February, 1928.

[2] The Baltic Provinces of Imperial Russia did not cover the same area as the Baltic States, but in 1918–19 the former expression was often used in the latter sense outside Russia.

collier were quickly resolved for him.[1] The British Ambassador gave him an urgent appeal from Pats. The Bolsheviks were advancing into Estonia: " it is urgently necessary that a fleet of the Allied Powers should appear in Reval at the earliest possible moment to prevent anarchy and the inevitable massacre." So, forty-eight hours after arriving at the Danish capital, Sinclair's force sailed again, trusting to the protection afforded by the cruisers' paravanes as they followed the reputedly safe route through the minefields. One of the *Caradoc*'s officers noted that they first

proceeded to Libau in very cold weather and without reliable charts. It was almost 9 degrees F., with a strong, bitterly cold wind blowing from the land which was frozen and snow-covered, causing condensation over the water, and fog farther out to sea. On the shore, which was still under German control, it looked dreary, too. The town was some little distance from the harbour, and as there was no leave we could not visit it. All the ships used searchlights at night and kept alert watch, as it was still regarded as a hostile port. Vague wireless messages were received asking for British ships' assistance. These originated from Reval where the Red troops were in close proximity and a general massacre of the civil population was feared.

Next day Sinclair set course to the north. His ships steamed in line ahead, the cruisers leading with the *Cardiff* in the van, the nine destroyers following. The weather was misty with a long swell and a cold wind. Suddenly, around midnight, when the lights of Osel were abeam, the *Cassandra*, Captain E. G. Kennedy,[2] second in the line, was lifted bodily by a powerful explosion beneath her engine-room. Kennedy's ship had struck a mine in an uncharted German field. Her back was broken in two places, and she lost way so quickly

---

[1] Which was just as well since the first collier sent to replace the *Tregarth* struck a mine in the North Sea and sank, and the next one did not arrive until January. The Third Fleet Sweeping Flotilla was then employed off Copenhagen for a week before returning to Britain, since by this time ice prevented British ships from operating north of Windau, and experience had shown that there was no immediate need to sweep to the south of this port.

[2] Later to lose his life in command of the *Rawalpindi* when she was sunk by German battlecruisers in November 1939.

that only swift action by an alert officer of the watch in the next astern averted a collision. With the *Cassandra* deprived of all steam and power and lying low in the water, a dark, inert hull, her Captain faced the problem of whether she could be saved from sinking and taken in tow. The *Caradoc* sent her Engineer Officer across to offer help whilst the rest of the force stood by, illuminating the sombre scene with their searchlights. The answer was clear enough when, within twenty minutes, the stricken vessel's upper deck was awash; she would have to be abandoned.

Sinclair was then confronted with another problem. Only ten men had been killed by the explosion; how could the bulk of the cruiser's crew of more than 450 be saved? The boats of the force had a very limited capacity; in the dark they would have great difficulty in going alongside the water-logged hull. Two destroyers supplied the solution. Lieutenant-Commander F. G. Glossop manœuvred the *Westminster* against the *Cassandra*'s weather bow; but he had only taken off fourteen ratings before the movement of his ship against the cruiser's heavier plating in the prevailing swell threatened crippling damage to the destroyer's light scantlings, and he was obliged to withdraw. Commander C. G. Ramsey [1] then manœuvred the *Vendetta* with equal skill against the lee side of the *Cassandra*'s forecastle twice, and was well rewarded. Except for one man who slipped and was lost overboard between the two ships, all the remainder of the cruiser's crew of 440 officers and men managed to board the *Vendetta* dryshod, including a number who had wounds or broken limbs from the shock of the explosion. All this was accomplished within an hour of the cruiser striking the mine; at the end of that time the derelict sank by the bow, to touch bottom with her stern in the air before she broke in two and disappeared.

The *Cassandra*'s loss, almost at the outset of the Baltic campaign, was a serious blow, though it was softened by the

[1] Later Admiral Sir Gordon Ramsey, Commander-in-Chief Rosyth in the Second World War.

small loss of life. Sinclair also had to reduce his force temporarily by a second cruiser and two destroyers; the *Calypso*, which had struck a submerged wreck in the entrance to Libau and needed docking, carried the *Cassandra*'s survivors back to England. The *Westminster* and *Verulam*, which had been damaged in collision, went with her. But the Admiral was not to be deterred from continuing his voyage; a couple of days later the balance of his force reached Reval without further incident. The British ships were immediately welcomed as the saviours of Estonia where Pats's Government was inspiring the people to maintain their new-found freedom under the most adverse conditions. There had been no time to establish any proper organisation for running the country since the departure of the Germans. There was a serious shortage of food, no coal though the temperature was near freezing point, no raw materials with consequent unemployment and practically no money. For all the Estonians' pride of race, there was enough mistrust and dissension for many to fear a Communist rising in their midst. And, as if these troubles were not enough, there was a more immediate and greater danger which had brought some people near to despair; the Red Seventh Army, commanded by the Latvian-born Colonel Vacietis—assisted by their Baltic Fleet which carried out an amphibious operation against Narva on 28th–30th November, just before Sinclair's arrival—had captured this town, and also Walk and Dorpat, hundreds of whose inhabitants had been treated with great brutality. And they were now less than forty miles to the east of the Estonian capital.

Pats asked that his country should become a British protectorate; for a military mission to train an Estonian army; for two British destroyers to augment Estonia's tiny navy; and for a British battalion to garrison the capital, with a British fleet remaining in Estonian waters to make demonstrations behind the Bolshevik front. The White North-West Russian Army, which had been forced to retreat from Pskov, wanted money to enable it to obtain equipment from German sources, a considerable monthly sum for its maintenance, and a British liaison staff ; but since its Commander was suspected of plotting to overthrow Pats's democratic government and to supplant it with an autocratic one of his own, Sinclair gave him no encouragement. To Pats he stressed that the help which could be given was limited: British ships would remain in Estonian waters until the Gulf of Finland was icebound; rifles, ammunition and field-guns were on their way; officers and ratings from the British ships would instruct Estonian volunteers: otherwise the people would have to act on the proverb, " Heaven helps those who help themselves." To that end the many contending parties in the National Council must show a united front; the Baltic Barons, who were so scornful and unco-operative as to form an alternative government, could expect no British encouragement.

Sinclair also took positive steps to relieve the Red threat to Reval. Realising that the whole defence of Estonia would collapse if the capital fell, he turned a blind eye to orders which limited him to a coastal reconnaissance. On 13th December he took the *Cardiff*, *Caradoc* and five destroyers along the coast near Narva, where they spent the day shelling the Bolsheviks' rear. British naval gunfire against shore targets has seldom been more effective; it destroyed the only bridge across the river on the Estonian frontier, cutting the Bolsheviks' lines of supply from Petrograd. This had the immediate result of stemming their progress westwards. And on 24th December General Laidoner, the capable and energetic Estonian Commander-in-Chief, followed up this success by landing a force of 200 volunteers at Kunda to harass the Bolsheviks in the rear.

Before this, Sinclair had to weigh the need to succour Latvia against the likelihood of a reaction by the Red Navy to his aggressive moves. He knew that the greater part of the Baltic Fleet was immobilised in Petrograd for want of fuel, ammunition, guns and crews, which had been landed to strengthen the garrison of the city. But the dreadnought battleship *Petropavlovsk*, the smaller pre-dreadnought *Andrei Pervozvanni* and the cruiser *Oleg* were at Kronstadt with a number of destroyers, submarines and minesweepers which could put to sea. Four British light cruisers and nine destroyers, with no material advantage except greater speed, would in most circumstances treat such a force with healthy respect. Sinclair could balance other factors against paper strength; the supine attitude with which the Tsar's fleet had confronted Napier and Dundas during the Crimean War, and more recently the German Navy, and the inefficiency of ships whose officers had been butchered and which were now manned by soviet-controlled Bolshevik crews. For these reasons the Admiral accepted the risk involved in returning to Libau in the *Cardiff*, accompanied by the *Ceres* and half his destroyers, leaving no more than the rejoined *Calypso*, the *Caradoc* and the rest of the flotilla at Reval, where the *Princess Margaret* and *Angora* had arrived with 5000 rifles and other equipment for the Estonian Army. Sinclair would have taken this decision the more readily had he known that the Bolshevik Baltic Fleet was not only (to quote a Soviet source) " conspicuously weaker than its adversaries, both in the training of its personnel and in the state of their equipment," but so deficient of reliable intelligence that it believed the British force to comprise two battlecruisers, six pre-dreadnoughts, two monitors, up to eight light cruisers and twenty destroyers, " altogether in the region of 50 to 60 vessels." Brief visits by the submarines *Tur*, *Tigr* and *Pantera* to Reval on 28th November, 3rd and 24th December respectively, did nothing towards confirming this wildly inaccurate estimate—on the second occasion because of " severe weather and damage sustained," on the third because of " defective compasses, freezing up of periscope and trouble with other equipment including rudders, trimming tanks, batteries and radio," a tale of woe which clearly reveals the state of the Bolshevik Navy at this time. Patrols by the destroyers *Avtroil*, *Azard* and *Spartak*, sometimes supported by the *Oleg*, in the vicinity of

Hogland and Kunda Bay during the same period achieved no more. But observers ashore helped to sustain the Bolsheviks' belief in the presence of such a large British fleet by reporting that the already-mentioned Estonian landing at Kunda was covered by two British *battleships*.

Captain B. S. Thesiger [1] of the *Calypso*, the senior officer remaining at Reval, did not have to wait long to justify his Admiral's decision. According to a Soviet source:

From information received about the bombardment of Kunda by enemy ships, and of a landing there on 24th December; also as a result of reports from the Seventh Army of the appearance of enemy ships burning searchlights on the nights of 23rd and 24th December and, lastly, consequent on requests by the Army Command for the Navy's assistance, an order was issued to the Baltic Fleet on the night of 25th December to annihilate the enemy ships based on Reval. For this operation a special task force comprising the battleship *Andrei Pervozvanni*, the cruiser *Oleg* and the destroyers *Spartak*, *Avtroil* and *Azard* was formed. Member of the Revolutionary War Soviet of the Baltic Fleet, F. F. Raskolnikov, was appointed in command.

The destroyers, under the direct command of Raskolnikov in the *Spartak*, had the task of entering Reval Roads and bombarding the port, thus bringing to action any enemy ships which might be there. If the latter should be superior in strength, the destroyers were to retire on the *Oleg* which would remain in the vicinity of Hogland. The *Andrei Pervozvanni* would be in support. On the day the ships were to sail, 25th December, only the *Spartak* and *Andrei Pervozvanni* left Kronstadt, the *Avtroil* being at Petrograd, and the *Azard* and *Oleg* on reconnaissance in Kunda Bay. The *Azard* returned that evening with hardly any fuel left, so was unable to join the force. The *Avtroil* was delayed by an engine breakdown and heavy ice, and could not sail until the evening of 26th December.

The Commander of the Special Task Force, therefore, informed the Baltic Fleet Command that the operation was being postponed for 24 hours; but at 0700 on 26th December, on approaching the *Oleg* near Hogland, Raskolnikov signalled: " I am going to bombard Reval." [2]

---

[1] Later Admiral Sir Bertram Thesiger.   [2] *Piat Let Krasnogo Flota.*

One of the *Caradoc*'s officers recalls that on 26th December, by way of gratitude to the British ships,

the Estonian authorities invited their officers and crews to a banquet to take place onshore at noon. The sailors would be given a dance afterwards, at which women could be " hired," which caused much embarrassment. It appeared, however, that they would be no more than dancing partners, and all went well. In the morning the captains and many officers were ashore assisting in the organisation and training of the Estonian Army, now fairly well equipped and about 20,000 strong, when, suddenly and without warning the sound of gunfire was heard and shells commenced to drop both ashore and in the harbour. As these were coming from a strange craft on the horizon steaming fast, a signal was made to raise steam at once and proceed to sea.

The *Wakeful* was first out, in about fifteen minutes; the *Caradoc* soon followed, then the *Calypso*. The hostile craft turned away at great speed as the *Wakeful* opened fire, then turned again sixteen points, stopped and hoisted the white flag. She was brought into harbour by a prize crew, and turned out to be the Bolshevik destroyer *Spartak*. She had run on (Divel) shoal and stripped her rudder and propellers. She had a bad leak and was making a good deal of water when she was (towed by the *Vendetta*) into harbour and anchored. So a signal was made to her to raise steam to (work her pumps). Thereupon the Bolshevik crew called a soviet meeting to decide upon raising steam, a proceeding which was at once met with a peremptory order to raise steam at once. Whilst this seemed a most amusing episode, it gave us some insight into Bolshevik ideas.

The crew themselves, very dirty and in a dreadfully dirty ship, appeared pleased at being captured. Many of them had articles of various sorts, such as cameras and furs, obviously looted from shops and houses, which they sold to our crew at ridiculous prices, some even offering the things gratis, possibly fearing to be caught by Russians with them in their possession. Much valuable information was found in the ship; also an amusing signal which had been dispatched: " All is lost. I am chased by English." The proposed banquet took place in the evening instead of in the forenoon. The dinner was a long one and there was much speech-making: one felt ashamed at eating the food when there was so little in the town. We returned early to our ships, which had raised steam again.

Thesiger tells the reason for this:

When I got back from the banquet I sent for the interpreter to hear what information he had got from the papers in the *Spartak*. He had got a great deal, including what appeared to be a written record of telephone conversations with Trotsky: " Tell Raskolnikov that (the British) ships must be sunk, come what may. When our force appears the British, using their superior speed, will run away! " Four closely typed foolscap pages (told me) that Raskolnikov was himself at sea in a destroyer and that the *Oleg* was at anchor off Hogland and was to bombard Reval. It appeared obvious that I should go to Hogland and sink the *Oleg*. I admit I had orders not to attack any Russian ship unless first attacked, but this quite definite threat from Trotsky was a good enough reason for action. I therefore went to sea at once, with the *Caradoc* and the destroyer *Wakeful*. The (other) destroyers were left behind in case they were needed for anything.

My intention was to attack the *Oleg* at early dawn. At 0200 we passed a vessel with no lights burning. It was too dark to say definitely what she was but I was almost certain she was a destroyer. Both (the *Calypso*'s) officer of the watch and the *Caradoc* wanted to open fire, but I said " No." I felt that if they did so they would probably not have put her out of action before she had fired her torpedoes, and, as she had six tubes, one at least might have hit us.

When we got to Hogland, to our great regret we found no *Oleg*. Presumably the *Spartak* had told her of our presence. (But) when we passed the destroyer in the night I sent a (signal) to the *Vendetta* and *Vortigern* at Reval to put to sea and patrol the entrance to the Gulf of Finland. My object was to capture the destroyer. The *Caradoc* was sent north, I went south (in the *Calypso*), and the *Wakeful* between us. No ship could pass through this line without being seen. All worked out as I wished. The destroyer we passed in the night met the *Vendetta*, ran away from her and saw the *Vortigern*, so she turned east, trying to get back (to Kronstadt). She then met the *Wakeful*, went north into the *Caradoc*, and lastly south to me. She was now surrounded by five ships and so hauled down her colours and hoisted a white flag. We had fired very few rounds, not wishing to sink her and knowing that she would give in. The *Vortigern* put a party on board the *Avtroil*, which was the destroyer we had captured. This ended an interesting twenty-four hours which included two battles and a banquet between them.[1]

[1] *Naval Memories.*

A Soviet version of these " battles " has its own interest:

On 26th December, in clear, still weather the *Spartak*, proceeding at 16 knots, reached a position 5 miles from Wulf Island and opened fire on it with the intention of ascertaining whether there was a battery there. Since there was no reaction from the island, the *Spartak* altered course and shifted target to Nargen Island, with the (same) purpose. A small Finnish steamer was then sighted to the north, heading for Reval. She was stopped, an armed party was put aboard her and she was sent off to Kronstadt. Nearly three hours were thus wasted (before) the *Spartak* set course for Reval. The smoke of several warships leaving at very high speed, was then sighted.

To get away from them, the *Spartak* increased to full speed and altered course to NE., intending to break through to Kronstadt or to seek refuge among the Finnish skerries. The enemy's range quickly decreased to 6 miles, and it became possible to distinguish three to four destroyers and one or two light cruisers which opened fire. The *Spartak* replied, using her after gun. The range continued to decrease rapidly, the pursuing British destroyers attaining a speed of 35 knots, while the *Spartak* was unable to develop full speed because the crew operated the machinery incorrectly and had to stop first one turbine, then the other, so that no more than 23 to 25 knots was achieved.

About 1330 the blast from the *Spartak*'s forward gun, trained too far aft, knocked down the charthouse, scattered and tore the charts, damaged the bridge, and concussed the helmsman, so that the ship's position could not be determined. Ten minutes later it was realised from her wash that the *Spartak* was in shallow water. Course was altered too late; at about 1340 she stranded on Divel Shoal, losing her screws. The enemy ships were then about 3 miles from the *Spartak* which ceased fire and struck her ensign. Closing to five cables the British ships stopped engines, lowered boats, and sent a boarding party across. The *Spartak* was then towed into Reval.[1]

The same source explains why Thesiger failed to find the *Oleg*:

Having stood to the east of Hogland all day without receiving any reply by wireless from the *Spartak*, the *Oleg* transmitted a signal at 1800 to the Commander of Naval Forces: " At 0700 the

[1] p. 40 n., op. cit.

Spartak left Hogland to bombard Reval. She does not answer by radio. Am anchored off Hogland. Request instructions." The *Oleg* again spent that night at anchor, at first off Hogland, and then off Tyters Island.[1] On the morning of 27th December, not having received any answer from the *Spartak* for 24 hours, the *Oleg* decided that the destroyer was sunk, weighed anchor and, for lack of coal and provisions, requested permission to return to Kronstadt.

At 1225 the *Oleg* received a wireless message, from the *Avtroil*: " The enemy is firing at us "; ten minutes later, another one: " I can see enemy ships "; and finally at 1240: " I can see a three-funnelled enemy cruiser." After this the *Avtroil* ceased to transmit or answer calls. On receiving the first signal, the *Oleg*, then 13 miles to the east of Hogland, turned towards its northern extremity, brought all her boilers into use, and increased speed to 12 knots. At 1415 she passed Hogland and continued in a westerly direction. Half an hour later, however, (*having received the* Avtroil's *other signals*) she turned back and set course for Kronstadt. On 28th December the *Andrei Pervozvanni* and the *Oleg* reached Kronstadt (*to learn that both the* Spartak *and the* Avtroil *had been captured*).

About 1100 on 27th December the *Avtroil* was approaching the Revelstone Light and sighted enemy ships coming out to meet her. Turning east, and setting course along the south shore to break through to Kronstadt, she increased speed to 32 knots so that the range between her and the three pursuing enemy destroyers did not decrease. About 1230 the *Avtroil* sighted one light cruiser and two destroyers apparently leaving Kunda Bay. These closed the *Avtroil* rapidly and opened fire on her. The *Avtroil*'s topmast was knocked down by one of the first shots, when she surrendered and was taken into Reval.

According to Thesiger:

The *Spartak* had 7 officers and 95 men and the *Avtroil* 7 officers and 138 men. These we took prisoner. Both destroyers were new and up-to-date in every respect. I am not pretending this was war, but these were the first two ships (apart from the Great Surrender) that had been captured since the beginning of the war; all others had been sunk. As already mentioned, it appeared

---

[1] It seems likely that the *Oleg* shifted her anchorage as the result of receiving a warning signal from the *Avtroil* when she passed Thesiger's force during the night.

that the Political Head of the Bolshevik Admiralty, Raskolnikov, was on board one of these ships; he was said to be responsible for the murder of all their naval officers, even possibly murdering some of them himself. In any case I wished to identify him. I therefore had all the prisoners fallen in, and asked if they knew Raskolnikov. Several said " yes," but when I asked where he was they said he was not there. I happened to meet a Russian naval officer, who had escaped, and told him my difficulty. By great good luck he said, " I know Raskolnikov; I was at school with him." So I arranged for this officer to come on board, and fell the prisoners in again. He went down the line and said, " He is not here." I began to wonder if I had made a fool of myself. Then I had a brain-wave and said, " Search the ship." They did, and hidden under twelve bags of potatoes we found the Russian First Lord of the Admiralty! [1]

Notwithstanding the disastrous failure of the operation he had planned and led, ascribed by a Soviet historian to " the weak organisation and the carelessness of the ships in the region," F. F. Raskolnikov, who had been a sub-lieutenant in the Tsarist Navy, was valued so highly by the Bolsheviks that they negotiated an exchange of eighteen British officer prisoners for him in June 1919. He was more fortunate than the crews of his two destroyers: handed over to the Estonians they were kept on Nargen Island, where in February 1919 some forty were executed. Thesiger made Juhan Pitka, the energetic Estonian naval commander, a present of the *Spartak*, which was renamed *Wambola*, and the *Avtroil*, which became the *Lennuk*; they were welcome additions to a navy whose only other significant unit was the gunboat *Lembit*.

After this crowded week of events (*recalls the* Caradoc's *officer*) we visited Libau and transferred some of the prisoners of war to another ship, then returned to Reval where the Estonians were pulling together and making great efforts. The Red advance had been checked and they were being forced back. A number of Baltic German refugees were given passage from Reval to Helsingfors as it had been announced that the British ships were shortly being withdrawn on account of ice. We heard that Kronstadt

[1] p. 42 n., op. cit.

was already iced in, although only a thin film appeared at Reval and there was not sufficient at Helsingfors to prevent us entering and going alongside the quay as late as 1st January, 1919. We left again for Reval the following morning, carrying about 500 Finnish volunteers to assist the Estonian Army, and a tough lot they were.

On 4th January the *Caradoc*, *Calypso* and *Wakeful* left Reval and proceeded east to a position near Narva, where the Red and White armies' lines extended, and took up positions for bombardment. The *Wakeful* was in a small bay opposite the front line trenches, the *Calypso* was in an inlet eastward of that position opposite the rear of the Red positions, and the *Caradoc* in a long creek further east again in a position to attack the Red reserves and headquarters and a battery position. The Estonian Army was to make a simultaneous frontal attack. The ships kept under way and fired at close range. We could see the shells from the *Calypso* bursting over the snow-covered hills, though she was out of sight in the next bay. We approached cautiously to about 2000 yards off the coast and opened fire on the reserve positions of the Red Army, and very soon saw many black dots and clumps of moving figures running out across the white snow, seeking to escape. We then searched out the battery positions but could get no reply. The Bolshevik headquarters was hit several times and destroyed by fire, and was still burning with a red glow in the dusk as we left.

The ships then proceeded to rejoin the rest of the squadron. Before leaving we embarked a few British refugees at Reval, men, women and children, including Mr. C——, Russian born of British extraction, who told us of the life in Petrograd; tales of murder, starvation, disease, incompetency. He had escaped along the Finnish coast in a boat, passing the Kronstadt forts at night. He lay hidden in a small village on the coast until able to reach Viborg. While hiding he witnessed many hundreds of officers murdered on the beach and thrown into the sea. Some were taken in boats, ostensibly to prison at Kronstadt, and after hands and feet had been amputated were thrown into the water.

So much for the Royal Navy's activities in support of Estonia up to the first week of January 1919, when many officers supposed that the British force was to be withdrawn from the Baltic until the April thaw made it possible for the Red Fleet to resume hostilities.

Meantime, Sinclair in the *Cardiff*, with the *Ceres* and his other destroyers, had been attending to Latvia where the people suffered conditions more wretched than those in Estonia. The Letts were divided in their loyalties: whereas the majority, whose stronghold was Livonia, supported Ulmanis's Government which aimed to establish an independent state with a democratic constitution, a substantial minority centred on Courland espoused Communism.[1] There were also, as in Estonia, the Baltic Barons,[2] who hoped to regain their old ascendancy over the country. And when the occupying German Eighth Army followed up its departure from Estonia by withdrawing from Livonia, Ulmanis's troops—for whom geography prevented the British warships giving the support which had been so effective on the Estonian coast—were unable to stem the advance of an estimated force of 20,000 Reds. There was a serious danger that, with the aid of a fifth column in Courland, the whole of Latvia would be overrun. Realising this, Sinclair dispatched the *Ceres* and two of his destroyers to Riga, together with the *Princess Margaret*, Captain H. H. Smyth, which carried Mr. Bosanquet, who had been sent by the Foreign Office to act as British Political Representative on the Admiral's staff.

When the minelayer arrived in the Dvina[3] on 19th December, Smyth, who was the senior officer, found himself required to do much more than land arms. From Ulmanis, whose Government had been obliged to withdraw to Riga, he learned that the 40,000 Germans who still occupied the city intended to evacuate all Latvia as soon as possible, allowing their guns and stores to fall into Bolshevik hands. There was consequently nothing but the *Baltische Landeswehr*,[4] numbering some 700 Balts, whose formation the German

---

[1] Under the leadership of Peteris Stucke who had also headed the Communist rising in Reval in 1905.

[2] Led by von Manteuffel.

[3] Not to be confused with the other river of the same name which flows into the White Sea at Archangel.

[4] i.e. Baltic Militia.

Commander had authorised after the Armistice, to stiffen the retreating Lettish infantry as they fell back before the advance of 12,000 Bolsheviks. So, whilst the *Ceres's* Captain of Marines did what he could to organise and train companies of Lettish volunteers, Smyth, supported by Bosanquet, pressed the German High Commissioner [1] and Military Commander [2] to observe Article XII of the Armistice terms. Smyth tabled ten requirements, the first two being the most important: " the Germans are to retain sufficient force in the district to hold the Bolshevik forces in check, and are not to permit them to advance beyond their present positions; the forces not required for the above are to retire with all dispatch in accordance with the Armistice conditions now in force." The German leaders replied that they had not realised that the first of these points was the Allies' interpretation of Article XII: they would, however, agree to it because " the defence of the Baltic countries lies near our hearts. We are not only here to defend a German race, but consider ourselves morally bound to protect a country which we have freed from the former governmental organisation." This piece of hypocrisy—the German aim remained what it had been before the Armistice, to establish a Baltic grand-duchy—was followed by an excuse for doing nothing of the sort: " the defence was rendered difficult to us by the demoralisation of the German troops " for which they gave the specious excuse that " we were hindered by the attitude taken up by the Estonian and Lettish Governments, because they represented that we were the oppressors of the population (whereby) our soldiers were forced to look upon themselves as agents of an unpopular policy: the desire for fighting was thus absolutely destroyed. We have been endeavouring since the end of November to get fresh (volunteer) troops from Germany " who would be used to defend Latvia provided that the Letts co-operated with them. To ensure this, the German General stipulated that he should command all forces opposing the Bolsheviks, *including* Letts,

---

[1] August Winnig.　　[2] General von Esdorff.

to which effrontery he added the demand that, " for the German volunteers, who are fighting here, full rights of citizenship should be accorded after the fighting has stopped." Bosanquet had no hesitation in rejecting this impudent attempt to increase the pro-German population of Latvia: the Germans, he said, were bound to defend Riga unconditionally. Their General responded, with a metaphorical shrug of his shoulders, that there was little he could do in present circumstances to persuade more than a very small proportion of his Eighth Army to fight Vacietis's Bolsheviks; he would, however, again represent to Berlin the urgent need to send fresh troops. In the face of this attitude, Smyth and Bosanquet could only reinforce their requirement that the German General should rally his men to fight the Bolsheviks, with the threat that if he was " not able to carry out the terms of the Armistice here, the *general* peace terms might be affected."

The Germans had, however, done nothing five days after this conference, by which time Red troops had advanced to within twenty-five miles of Riga. So, with a Communist rising hourly expected, Smyth ordered the embarkation of refugees, when some 350 British, Allied and neutral subjects sought sanctuary on board the *Princess Margaret*. Next evening, 29th December, 1918, he learned that two Lettish regiments, which had fallen back on the city, had mutinied and were planning to join forces with the Bolsheviks. After a night disturbed by desultory sniping in the glare of the British ships' searchlights, Ulmanis gave these mutineers half an hour to surrender. Then, notwithstanding the letter of Sinclair's orders which forbade intervention in the internal affairs of the Baltic States, Smyth decided that he was justified in ordering the *Ceres* to open fire on the mutineers' barracks. This had such an excellent effect that Ulmanis was encouraged to say that no further revolt was expected in Riga " so long as the presence of British ships continued." But Smyth was unable to view the future so favourably: he knew that his ships could no more stem the Red advance on the port than the Letts themselves, especially when he learned that the whole of the *Landeswehr*, together with the half-trained companies of Lettish volunteers, had been ordered to the front. He could only make preparations to hold the jetty, and land patrols to maintain some semblance of order, until the arrival of German reinforcements which their High Commissioner promised within forty-eight hours. " These, however, did not materialise," is the laconic comment in Smyth's report.

During the next night, the British patrols, though unable to stop a considerable amount of firing in various parts of the town, prevented serious disturbances. But by the morning of 1st January it was clear that Riga must fall very soon. So Sinclair ordered his force to prepare to leave at daylight on the 3rd. Before this, Smyth's ships embarked more refugees, including members of the Provisional Government and its more prominent supporters whose lives would be in danger if they fell into Bolshevik hands. And on the evening of the 2nd, Sinclair himself arrived in the destroyer *Valkyrie* to confirm the seriousness of the situation and to give orders for the British shore patrols to be withdrawn at 8.0 p.m. There followed an anxious night—the return of the *Landeswehr*, after hard fighting and serious losses, so disturbed the populace that they began looting and setting fire to parts of the town—until dawn allowed the *Valkyrie* to lead the British force down the partially frozen Dvina towards the sea. Sinclair had no alternative but to leave the port to fall to the Bolsheviks since it was clear that the German Army would offer no resistance.

Ulmanis and his colleagues moved to Libau to continue their struggle to establish a free and independent Latvia. But Sinclair was under orders to return to England. As soon as the *Ceres*, *Princess Margaret* and destroyers joined the *Cardiff*, they headed for Copenhagen, where Smyth landed his refugees. There, too, they met the *Caradoc*, *Calypso* and the rest of the British force from Reval. All sailed in company to reach Rosyth on 10th January. The Admiral and his officers and men might regret that they had left most of Latvia under the

Red mantle of a puppet Soviet, but they had the satisfaction of knowing that they had set Estonia on the road to freedom, had created a sense of security in Finland which Mannerheim publicly acknowledged, and had taken the measure of the Bolshevik Fleet.

*   *   *

Their withdrawal did not, however, leave the Baltic void of British ships, as Lloyd George had first intended. On 23rd December, Wemyss wrote:

The situation as regards the operations now being carried out by the Navy in the Baltic Provinces is one that calls for consideration with a view to determining our future policy. It appears that the original objects of the operations have been attained (but) the situation is now developing in a manner which promises to involve us in heavy commitments. Demands for assistance of all kinds are being made. Rear-Admiral Sinclair has hitherto refrained from holding out a hope that any of these can be acceded to. As regards the possibility of the Estonian and Latvian Governments being able to maintain themselves against the Bolshevik forces, the situation is complicated by the presence of German forces and by the Bolshevik element in the local population. The Germans have been evacuating their army and the evacuation is almost, if not quite, complete. They have indirectly assisted the Bolshevik cause by the destruction of railways and bridges, and their departure has undoubtedly produced a feeling of insecurity in the towns and facilitated the Bolshevik operations. In Estonia the Bolshevik element is small, (but) in Latvia, especially at Riga, there is a considerable Bolshevik element, and it is clear that British assistance, if it is afforded, will be as much concerned with suppressing this as with defending the country against the Bolshevik Army.

The time has come for a decision as to our future policy. We have lost one new and efficient light cruiser and 11 lives. The existence of the Bolshevik Navy, though it is believed to have little efficiency, cannot be ignored. Ice conditions may at any time necessitate the withdrawal of our squadron. If we are to support and assure the independence of the Baltic Provinces, we should put in hand the immediate preparation of a land expedition of considerable strength.

The Naval Staff pursued the matter on the basis of this minute, but as Fremantle recalled some years later:

The circumstances were extraordinarily difficult. In the first place we had to get the attention of the Foreign Office (which) was occupied with the preparations for the Treaty of Versailles which was a big undertaking, and they looked upon everything that was going on in the Baltic as a matter of minor importance. Then, when we had got the attention of the Foreign Office, the next thing was to get the attention of the Cabinet which not only had the Treaty of Versailles on its hands, but also had the appalling state of affairs in our own country, the violent unrest which accompanied the process of demobilisation, the Councils of Action being formed all over the country and the shouts of " Hands off Russia." [1]

Nonetheless the War Cabinet discussed the Baltic problem on 31st December, 1918, three days after the " Coupon " Election had returned Lloyd George to power, by which time the Admiralty had reinforced Wemyss's warning about the need to prepare " a land expedition of considerable strength," with a letter to the Foreign Office which concluded:

To adopt any middle course would have the effect of raising hopes which we have no intention of fulfilling, and would jeopardise any prospect there may be of the Governments (*of the Baltic States*) being forced to co-ordinate their efforts to combine with the (White North-West) Russian Army and to use all the forces they can raise against their common enemy. We would also run the risk of being obliged, should the Bolsheviks occupy the towns of Riga and Reval, to withdraw our ships and would incur the onus of abandoning our protégés at the most critical moment.

But the War Cabinet remained opposed to the dispatch of a military force. They agreed only on the " middle course " against which the Admiralty advised: two light cruisers, accompanied by five destroyers, should be sent to relieve Sinclair's squadron.

Since Beatty had been forewarned to detail the requisite ships from the Grand Fleet, they were able to sail in time to

---

[1] p. 34 n1., op. cit.

meet Sinclair's returning force at Copenhagen on 6th January, 1919. Much more important, however, to the whole future of the British campaign in the Baltic, Beatty nominated in command Rear-Admiral Walter Cowan, for no man was better equipped to ensure that the Cabinet's decision did not have the unfortunate outcome which Wemyss and his colleagues feared.

Chapter Three

WALTER COWAN

I hope you will not have the Litany in my flagship; but if
you insist will you please omit the petition where we ask to
be delivered from battle, murder and sudden death. Hang
it! I've never been trained for anything else.

> *Rear-Admiral Sir Walter Cowan to*
> *the Chaplain of H.M.S. Hood*

" Mere ships do not make a fleet, nor do they form the right
arm of an empire; for the strength of a nation does not lie
in armour, guns and torpedoes, but in the souls of the men
behind these things." [1] But men are nothing without leaders;
their strength is in their admirals and their captains, of whom
the Royal Navy has produced so great a company. " If all the
outward and visible signs of our greatness should pass away,
we would still leave behind us a durable monument of
what we were in the sayings and doings of the English
admirals." [2]

Walter Cowan may not be among those on the higher
pinnacles of fame, but the pages of British history would
be the poorer if his name was not inscribed upon them.
Unique may be an overworked adjective, but one is justified
in applying it to him. From the time he was a young lieutenant until he was past his seventieth year, this outstanding
man-at-arms marched to the sound of the guns wherever and
whenever their voices were raised in opposition to his Sov-

---

[1] General Kuropatkin, Commander-in-Chief of the Russian Army in the
Russo-Japanese war.

[2] Robert Louis Stevenson in *Virginibus Puerisque*.

ereign's enemies. At twenty-seven he gained the Distinguished Service Order; forty-five years later, aged seventy-two, he was awarded a bar to this decoration. Yet fortune never favoured him with the chance to win a famous victory: his greatest success required more than the qualities of a fighter, the skill of a seaman, and the resolution of a leader. It needed outstanding initiative and moral courage, for mines were not the worst hazard with which he had to contend in the Baltic in 1919. One false move in his dealings with the Baltic States, and they might have succumbed to Bolshevik or German domination as easily as an error of judgment in interpreting the Allies' ambivalent policy could have led to his recall.

Nothing in Cowan's hereditary background, or the environment of his early years, suggested that he would develop into such a remarkable flag officer. He was born in 1871. His father was " a soldier—Royal Welch Fusiliers—but never a very earnest one." [1] His mother's forebears included no more recent warrior than a knight who gained his spurs at Agincourt. He never went to a school, only to a crammer, but he was broken to hunting with the Calpe Hounds at the age of five. The Navy was not his choice of career; it was only by the chance that his father was in the Plymouth garrison when Cowan was twelve, and came to admire the *Britannia* so much from occasional visits to Dartmouth that he determined to send his son there.

A year later Cowan was appointed a naval cadet. Two years more and he was in the Mediterranean where the ships, though steam-driven, still practised competitive sail drill and precise manœuvres more appropriate to the parade ground than to the realities of battle. Instead of gaining the taste for war which prompted Keyes [2] to say of Walter in 1940: " He only wants to die for his country," he was invalided home suffering from " sun-stroke." When it seemed that he had recovered, he joined a training brig in home waters; but in

[1] Cowan's own description.   [2] Admiral of the Fleet Lord Keyes.

a few months he was again on the sick list, and this time invalided from the Service. Fortunately for Cowan and the Navy, this decision was subject to review after six months, when the Admiralty authorised his return to the Mediterranean as a midshipman. Thence he went to the West Indies until promoted sub-lieutenant when he transferred to the East Indies' flagship. But he disliked having charge of a gunroom; he was happier as first lieutenant of a gunboat until he was again invalided home, this time with dysentery.

It would have been understandable if Cowan had then accepted that his health was not sound enough for a sea career. His resolute decision, when a medical board passed him as fit, gives the first glimpse of the personality he was to become: he volunteered for the Cape Station because this included West Africa, scorning its notorious climate for the chance of active service. He took part in the Brass River [1] punitive expedition in 1895; in the next year he was a member of the expedition sent to Mwele [2] where he gained the African Medal; and in 1897 he added the Benin clasp for his part in the capture of that " horror city " by a landing party of 1200 men. Cowan acquired an appetite for battle from these experiences which fifty subsequent years failed to satisfy. As a lieutenant of twenty-seven his one desire was to join Kitchener's force advancing up the Nile. Evading an appointment to the Royal Yacht, he accepted command of the destroyer *Boxer* in the Mediterranean from where he could importune the Commander-in-Chief for a transfer to Egypt. In six months he was successful, joining the *Sultan*, one of several shallow-draught gunboats operating in the upper reaches of the Nile, in which he helped the Sirdar's army to rout the Khalifa's Dervishes at Omdurman. After Kitchener had entered Khartoum, Cowan's little ship was sent up the White Nile to forestall Marchant's misguided attempt to annex the Sudan. Before the Fashoda crisis was settled by

[1] In Nigeria.   [2] In East Africa.

negotiation in December, the mountains of Abyssinia were in sight from the *Sultan*'s bridge and her captain had been mentioned in dispatches and awarded the D.S.O.

After Wingate's expedition, which compassed the Khalifa's death in September 1899, Cowan wrote: " It seemed now that the fighting was over in the Sudan, that South Africa was the place for me. After the fight at Benin, I had said to an old friend that the next thing to try for was to fight the Khalifa, and now I remarked to Jimmy Watson that we must go for Kruger." He had little difficulty in persuading Kitchener, who had been ordered to South Africa as Roberts's Chief of Staff, to take a naval A.D.C. before the Admiralty could object to this unauthorised addition to the Army's staff. As much at home on a horse as on a ship's bridge, he survived the rigours of an arduous military campaign on the veld,[1] for which he was mentioned in dispatches, escaping the enteric fever which decimated the British troops, as well as avoiding enemy bullets, until Roberts was ordered home. Having heard rumours that the Admiralty had struck him off the Navy List for his unauthorised absence from the Service, Lieutenant Cowan then decided that he would be well advised to return and face Their Lordships if he was not to jeopardise his career.

He had completed more than five years of almost continuous active service, but half of this had been with the Army without Admiralty authority, so the Second Sea Lord decreed that it could not count for promotion. Any resentment which Cowan may have felt at this decision was soon forgotten in courting Miss Catherine Cayley, and a long hunting honeymoon in Galway, which lasted until he received an appointment to H.M.S. *Prince George.* " Despite his seniority and his medals," recalls a brother officer, " which we felt might be an embarrassment to us, we rather resented the arrival of this war hero in our ship. We need not have worried; he was an asset to

---

[1] He was at Klip Drift, Paadeberg and Cronje's surrender, then at Popham Cross and in the march on Bloemfontein before pursuing de Wet into Pretoria.

the smartest battleship in the Channel Fleet." At the end of June the prodigal was promoted commander at the early age of thirty.

For the next thirteen years the guns were silent for Cowan whilst he served as Executive Officer of the battleship *Resolution* and in command of the destroyer *Falcon*, where he fired Fisher's wrath during exercises by his unorthodox action against an attacking submarine when he lassoed its periscope! Nonetheless, he was next appointed in command of the light cruiser *Skirmisher*, and whilst there in 1907 he was again selected for promotion. A captain at thirty-five, he next commanded the Channel Fleet's destroyers, the armoured cruiser *Cressy* and the newly completed light cruiser *Gloucester*, " the best disciplined and best tuned-up ship I ever commanded." Then, for the first and only time, he had an administrative appointment as Chief of Staff to the Admiral of Patrols, before going to the pre-dreadnought battleship *Zealandia* where, in circumstances to be related, he fell foul of the Admiral commanding his squadron, Sir Lewis Bayly. This might have prejudiced his future prospects had peace prevailed; but in August 1914 his ship was ordered to join the Grand Fleet at Scapa Flow. And from there, on 10th September, he swung his ship out of the line to ram and sink *U13*. But this was small compensation for the excitements of the chase which Beatty and Tyrwhitt enjoyed in the Heligoland Bight action: " my heart ached that I had not been with them all."

Fortunately Beatty's battlecruisers were soon moved from Scapa to Rosyth, the *Zealandia's* squadron going with them; and when command of the *Princess Royal* fell vacant at the beginning of 1915, Cowan transferred to her. He was in this dreadnought battlecruiser at the Dogger Bank action and at Jutland, when his fighting spirit rejoiced at the determined way in which Beatty led his ships in pursuit of Hipper's. Cowan was awarded the C.B. for this action,[1] but a decoration

---

[1] In which his ship suffered more than 100 casualties and required six weeks to effect repairs.

was small satisfaction when the " hope of an annihilating victory died. For us in the battlecruisers it was a bitter disappointment. The lessons of the fight, written into my soul, were that if you do not seize your chances when they offer and strike, you will never get them again." Beatty, and Pakenham who commanded the Battlecruiser Force from December 1916, so much appreciated Cowan's work that in June 1917 he was ordered to hoist his broad pendant in the *Caledon* as Commodore First Light Cruiser Squadron. Five months later his ships accompanied the Battlecruiser Force in a high-speed dash into the Bight in an attempt to cut off a part of the High Seas Fleet from its base. Cowan pressed the pursuit until the *Caledon* was punched amidships by a large-calibre shell from a German battleship; then it was " time to go home. They gave a posthumous V.C. to one of my men."

Commodore Cowan's reputation may be judged from a letter he received from Keyes in May 1918: " I want you to know that, if you had only been free, no one but you should have commanded the *Vindictive*.[1] Dear gallant Walter! I cannot tell you how I wish you could have shared in this—but you will have your day, too, and soon." Cowan's day was, indeed, not far off, but it was not the kind that Keyes envisaged. He was promoted rear-admiral in September; two months later the Armistice brought the High Seas Fleet to Rosyth. At dinner that night everyone was understandably cheerful, except for Cowan. " Why are you looking so sad? " asked his host. The reply was wholly in character with the man: " Nothing left to live for." " He was, I think," recalls one who was there, " the only officer in the Grand Fleet who was sorry that the war was over." [2] Since the task of guarding the interned German ships, at which his squadron took its turn in December, was an especially melancholy one for Cowan, it was fortunate that he was summoned to London

---

[1] For the assault on the mole at Zeebrugge.
[2] Admiral Sir Bertram Thesiger in *Naval Memories*.

in December to be told that he was to take his squadron into the Baltic in the New Year.[1]

*   *   *

This sketch being designed to show the man he was, it will be best to outline Cowan's subsequent career before telling the story of his year in the Baltic. He was not long home from this mission when he was ordered back for a different purpose: his flagship went to Danzig to support the plebiscite troops whilst a referendum decided the city's future. This quasi-diplomatic task ended Cowan's time in command of a cruiser squadron. Almost immediately he was offered the finest sea appointment available to an officer of his seniority: in March 1921 he hoisted his flag in the *Hood* in command of the Battlecruiser Squadron.

Units of the Atlantic Fleet seldom went farther afield than Gibraltar or Scandinavia. Rear-Admiral Sir Walter Cowan was more fortunate; in 1922 his squadron was ordered to Rio de Janeiro for an international exhibition. " Few things gave me greater pleasure and satisfaction whilst First Lord," wrote Lord Lee of Fareham, " than the brilliant success of your mission to Brazil. I should like to send you my warmest congratulations on the remarkable achievement of your squadron." Cowan next cruised to the West Indies, to hear in September that ships were being sent to restrain the wilder excesses of Mustapha Kemal's campaign to expel the Greeks from Asia Minor. " We were doing nothing of military value, but merely having a pleasant time, so I took it upon myself to wire to David Beatty, then First Sea Lord, that we were ready to start for the Mediterranean at any moment should he consider allowing us to go there. But nothing came of it." Tyrwhitt [2] wrote from the Mediterranean: " I gave up all idea of a scrap on hearing that the *Hood* had been ordered home.

---

[1] When he was created a K.C.B. for his war service.
[2] Later Admiral of the Fleet Sir Reginald Tyrwhitt.

I knew that if there was going to be a row, you would be in it."

Cowan continued in the *Hood* for the customary two years, being promoted vice-admiral soon after he struck his flag in 1923. Then he had to suffer the intense competition produced by the swollen Navy of the war years for the limited number of jobs available when the Fleet had been drastically reduced by the Washington Naval Treaty. He was two years on half-pay before he was appointed Commanding Officer Coast of Scotland at Rosyth. Realising that he could not expect command of the Atlantic or Mediterranean Fleets when men like Keyes were available, he next accepted the lesser appointment of Commander-in-Chief North America and West Indies, " about the most pleasant command of any, with the war behind me." He was required to do little more than show the flag in the Western Hemisphere, to deal with an occasional hurricane and to salvage the cruiser *Dauntless* from a shoal off Halifax.

Promoted admiral in 1926, Cowan finished his career as First and Principal A.D.C. to King George V. In 1929 he was placed on the retired list at the age of fifty-nine. Since it seemed unlikely that he would hear his beloved guns again, he was content " to have finished for good with official life and to live my own life without let or hindrance, and without being a bother to anyone else." Separated from his wife—she bore him a daughter but no heir and died in 1934—Cowan was indeed free to live his own life, much of it out with the Warwickshire Hounds; but he had not " finished for good with official life " any more than he was right in supposing he would never again hear the music of the guns.

The Second World War came when Cowan was nearly seventy; nonetheless, he immediately importuned the Admiralty for employment, offering to serve in the rank of commander. The Second Sea Lord,[1] an old friend from his Baltic days, sent him to join the staff of the Naval Control

[1] Admiral Sir Charles Little.

Service Officer at Grimsby. This office job only whetted his appetite for active service and, when Keyes became Director of Combined Operations, he appealed to him. In November 1940 he was appointed Naval Liaison Officer to No. 11 Commando, when age did not deter him from taking full part in their rigorous training. He embarked with them at the beginning of 1941, to sail in a full gale: " I have seldom gone to bed happier than that night." They landed at the Cape for a twelve-mile route march in full equipment; the Admiral was the first man back on board. At Alexandria his first call was on the Commander-in-Chief, A.B. Cunningham,[1] who had been his Flag Captain in the West Indies. With him he was soon at sea in the *Warspite*, to hear the sound of his beloved guns in action against Italian aircraft.

Cowan was so stirred by the Commando Brigade's raid on Bardia and similar attacks on points behind the Axis lines, that when this force was disbanded he attached himself to the 18th King Edward's Own Cavalry in the Indian Armoured Corps. With this regiment, to quote the official history of the Indian Division in North Africa, he " was always in (the) line, showing the most complete contempt for shell fire. It was his great grief that (his colonel) could not allow him to accompany the Indians on their raiding parties." But on 26th March, 1941, the 18th Cavalry was in action with the Afrika Corps at Bir Hakim, which Cowan afterwards described in a letter to Keyes:

We were holding an unprepared position with 500 men. They attacked us with many tanks and a whole division, and the first wave went clean through, and everyone near me was either knocked over or captured. I got behind an empty Bren-gun carrier and they missed me. After a lull the second wave came on. I'd got into the carrier. An armoured car stopped about 40 yards off, and four men got out and came at me. I let drive at them with my revolver and one dropped in front. The others ran back behind their A.C. Then the captain of it shouted and gesticulated that I should put my hands up, but this I could not do, so he fired a

[1] Later Admiral of the Fleet Lord Cunningham of Hyndhope.

burst at me and missed. He again hailed me and got no response, so fired another burst and again missed. I didn't think he could, as I wasn't trying to take cover—just stood with my revolver hanging down empty, so he had every chance and was welcome to it. But I felt after missing me twice that was enough, and I got out of the carrier and pointed to my empty pistol, and walked up and asked what he wanted. He motioned me to get up on to his car, and that was the end, and I grieve that it's all over.

The Admiral was again wrong about his future. After nine months he was repatriated because of his age, and back with commandos under training before returning to the Mediterranean and joining Tito on the island of Vis. But in the middle of 1944 he was forced to accept that he could no longer live such an active life, and returned to England. He was, nonetheless, a happy warrior; on 1st September the *London Gazette* announced that he had been awarded a bar to his D.S.O. " for gallantry, determination and undaunted devotion to duty as Liaison Officer with commandos in the capture of Mount Ornito, Italy, and during attacks on the islands of Solta, Mljet and Braz in the Adriatic, all of which operations were carried out under very heavy fire from the enemy."

In the final year of the war he visited the 4th S.S. Brigade in Holland after the capture of Walcheren, spent some days in the cruiser *Norfolk*, and crossed the Rhine in the wake of the Allied armies. When he reverted to the retired list after VE-Day, the Admiralty wrote: " You have upheld the highest traditions of the Royal Navy, and your fame is universal and undying." His last honour, unique for a sailor, came in November; he was gazetted Honorary Colonel of the 18th Cavalry at the regiment's own request: " Of the several distinctions which have come my way in my sixty odd years of service, I think that none has given me greater happiness and pride." He visited them at Risalpurh on the North-West Frontier in 1948. Thereafter he lived alone at Kineton in Warwickshire until he died in 1956 at the age of eighty-five, a sailor home from the sea, and a hunter home from the hill.

*　　　　　*　　　　　*

Such are the facts of Cowan's life. What of the man whose only love was war, whose horizon when away from the sea was bounded by horse and hound? The salvage of the cruiser *Dauntless* showed that he was a seaman of uncommon skill. His early promotion to commander, and to captain, testify to exceptional talent for command which he proved during the First World War. His achievements as a junior rear-admiral earned him the Battlecruiser Squadron when commands were few. He went on to become a full admiral and a commander-in-chief. His work with the commandos when he was more than seventy emphasises that, despite poor health in his early years, he was a man of exceptionally tough physique. From West Africa at the end of the nineteenth century to Italy near the middle of the twentieth he displayed a contempt for danger such as most men would wish to emulate. His unauthorised attachment to Kitchener's staff in defiance of Admiralty authority shows his moral courage: he never hesitated to put forward views in which he believed. In the Grand Fleet his gospel of war differed from that of his Commander-in-Chief : " the decisive range is that at which you cannot miss, and the sooner you get into it if you are fortunate enough to have the speed, and determined enough to chance your own loss, the better for you and the worse for the enemy." As for " the bogey of the torpedo menace, under battle conditions I think it could safely be assumed that only one out of every twenty-two torpedoes fired would hit." This is not the place to argue whether Cowan was right or wrong; Jutland might have been a more decisive British victory had Jellicoe adopted different tactics, but Cowan's doctrine might have resulted in disaster. He did not persist in thrusting these views on his Commander-in-Chief, which might have led to his relegation to an appointment away from the Grand Fleet and subsequent failure to fly his flag. By the chance that his ship was transferred to Rosyth, he came under Beatty, an old friend of gunroom and Nile days, and of the hunting field, and an officer who shared his fighting spirit. Through him he was given command of the *Princess Royal*, in which he achieved such distinction as to gain the prize of commodore of the Light Cruiser Squadron in which he went to the Baltic.

Cunningham, who first met Cowan in South Africa, has written:

When we started in the *Calcutta* (*for the West Indies*), and having known him in the Baltic and at Rosyth, my feelings towards him were those of respectful admiration. But having served with him for more than two years in the much more intimate appointment of Flag Captain and Chief Staff Officer, I (came) to regard him also with real affection. I do not think that in the whole of that period we ever had a serious disagreement. He taught me a lot. His ideals of duty and honour were of the highest, and never sparing himself he expected others to do the same. We all knew his reputation as a fighting sailor, and of his unbounded courage. Nothing ever daunted him. His views on men and things in general were always refreshing, though sometimes unorthodox. To say that he inspired us is no exaggeration. Hasty he undoubtedly was; but if in any haste he unjustly hurt people's feelings or wounded their susceptibilities he was at pains to make amends at the earliest possible moment.[1]

Cunningham was far from being alone in liking Cowan as well as admiring him. Keyes wrote: " I don't think I have ever been quite so taken with anyone as I am with Cowan. He is the gallantest little sportsman I ever met." One of his flag lieutenants remembers that " he was awfully kind to me and my wife in Bermuda. My two years' commission on that station was one of my happiest." His navigator in the *Calcutta* recalls another human touch, finding him in his cabin engrossed in rearranging his medal ribbons into the most attractive pattern instead of the regulation order. He

[1] *A Sailor's Odyssey.*

had an old-world courtesy; despite the failure of his own marriage, he would allow no one to speak unkindly of a woman. He had, too, a felicitous knack of getting on with foreigners, who were as impressed by the unusual personality of a man who measured only five feet six inches, as they were charmed by his speeches. These were especially pleasing when delivered impromptu, in contrast to his normal shy, reserved nature which made it difficult for him to express himself, though he could write delightful letters.

Nonetheless, Cunningham qualifies his praise; he uses the word " hasty." Another writes: " he had moments when he was pretty difficult and irritable." Having the highest ideals and never sparing himself, Cowan was too inclined to expect as much of others. In his seventies he remarked to one who met him during the Second World War: " When I commanded a squadron I made the mistake of expecting too high a standard of discipline." To this must be added his highly strung nerves; he was plagued by too quick a temper. He reacted to a signal reporting that a tanker had been mined in the Baltic by placing the Navigating Officer of his flagship, who had routed her, under arrest. This defect, allied to his determination to enforce his own standards of efficiency, duty and discipline, made him a difficult man to serve. All went well with a subordinate who was stolid enough to absorb his tantrums. The *Gloucester* was an example. As an admiral he was equally happy with two of his Flag Captains; with Charles Little during a part of his year in the Baltic, and with Cunningham in the West Indies. But it was not always so. To mention one minor and, for that reason, significant example of his methods, on seeing a whaler inexpertly handled by its coxswain, he would, without attempting to conceal his anger, direct that the man should be severely punished. Little or Cunningham would reply, " Aye, aye, sir," and confine themselves to giving the petty officer a verbal reprimand, knowing that by next day Cowan would have forgotten the incident; their ships were happy ones. But for a captain who was as highly strung as Cowan, who accepted his judgment and reduced the luckless man to leading seaman, the result was, at best, an unhappy ship, at worst, mutiny.

The legend that Cowan was responsible for more mutinies than any other officer who has served in the Royal Navy is, nonetheless, unjust. He suffered one in the *Zealandia* in 1913, but this occurred when he had only been in her for a month. An equally new Executive Officer ordered stokers to perform work that had been done by seamen during the previous two years of the battleship's commission. The stokers' resentment culminated in a refusal to clean upperdeck brightwork and to scrub their coaling suits one evening after coaling ship at Gibraltar, on the grounds that they should first have been given time to wash themselves. Discipline was restored by a guard of Marines, and Admiral Bayly ascribed the incident to the foolish behaviour of the Executive Officer who was removed from the ship. Unfortunately, though acquitted of responsibility, Cowan was at fault for a different reason: he decided to punish the men concerned by stopping their leave and giving them extra drill. Bayly would not accept this summary punishment for so serious an offence; he ordered twelve of the stokers to be court-martialled, eight being found guilty and awarded two years' imprisonment. But the Admiralty had to annul this sentence on the legal ground that the accused had already been dealt with, an error of judgment for which Cowan received Their Lordships' displeasure.

Cowan experienced a second mutiny whilst he was in the Baltic, of which the details will be related later. For the moment it will suffice to note that his flagship, the light cruiser *Delhi*, was not the only ship of the Baltic Force to suffer disaffection amongst her crew, and that since this malaise extended to vessels which never came within the orbit of Cowan's command, responsibility can hardly be ascribed to him.

Lastly, there was trouble in the Battlecruiser Squadron. Cowan's early association with the Army had imbued him with the too long a-dying tradition, exemplified by Lucan's failure to remove Cardigan from his command after Balaclava, that incompetence should be overlooked in an officer of good family who rode a good horse. So he invited Mackworth, his Flag Captain in the *Delhi*, to accompany him to the *Hood*. The combination of the two had survived with the stimulus of active operations, but it had the most unfortunate results when there was little for either to do except strive for the standards of discipline and efficiency which they shared. Mackworth, being as highly strung as Cowan, was not the man to cushion his Admiral's more intemperate demands. Consequently the *Hood* was a very unhappy ship, and a few members of her company showed their discontent by displaying red bunting on their mess tables. This incident was magnified out of all proportion to its significance so that, when the present writer joined his first ship five years later, the Cowan-Mackworth combination was still an evil legend in the Atlantic Fleet. But though Cowan might be at fault for not recognising his Flag Captain's limitations from his experience of him in the Baltic, there can be no doubt that the major blame was Mackworth's: Little and Cunningham had no undue difficulty in running flagships for Cowan that were as happy as they were efficient. And if his Commander-in-Chief [1] had held Cowan responsible he would not have given him this verdict: " The Battlecruiser Squadron under your command has earned by hard work and high ideals a reputation for smartness, cleanliness and efficiency which will long remain an example."

Cowan's record is not therefore to be sullied by his unfortunate association with mutiny, least of all during his year in the Baltic. " I am sorry," wrote Madden, " that your return occurs when the Fleet is dispersed (*for Christmas leave*). It would have given every officer and man, and me in particular, much gratification to have put to sea and welcomed you in the old naval style as a mark of your comrades' appreciation

[1] Admiral Sir Charles Madden.

of the fine work performed by you and those under your command." The Commander-in-Chief could pay his subordinate no higher tribute: there was, as Cowan noted on the letter, no precedent for such a ceremony since Nelson's day. "I hope," Madden continued, "that those who are greater than I will realise how all-important and successful your work has been." They did: Cowan was created Baronet of the Baltic.

Chapter Four

LIBAU

It would appear desirable that the gallant Admiral who was responsible for the success of the various operations and who shouldered the responsibility should receive some award adequate to his services.

Minute by Admiral of the Fleet Lord Beatty [1]
on Cowan's Baltic Despatch

BEFORE sailing for the Baltic, Cowan was briefed by Fremantle. " It seemed to me that there was never such a tangle, and my brain reeled with it. An unbeaten German army, two kinds of belligerent Russians, Letts, Finns, Estonians, Lithuanians; ice, mines—60,000 of them! Russian submarines, German small craft, Russian battleships, cruisers and destroyers all only waiting for the ice to melt to ravage the Baltic. I felt that I had better get out there as soon as possible to get wise before the Gulf of Finland thawed out. . . ." What then of the orders under which Cowan left Rosyth in the cruiser *Caledon*, together with the *Royalist* and five " V & W " class destroyers?

The primary object of your visit is to show the British Flag and support British policy. The Estonian and Latvian Governments have been supplied with 10,000 rifles, together with machineguns and ammunition, by Rear-Admiral Sinclair. Any further supply should only be granted should you be reasonably convinced that the Estonian or other Government is of a stable nature and can control the Army, and that (it) will not be used in a manner opposed to British interests which may be summed up as follows: to prevent the destruction of Estonia and Latvia by external

[1] Who succeeded Wemyss as First Sea Lord on 1st November, 1919.

aggression, which is only threatened at present by Bolshevik invaders. The Germans are bound under the terms of the Armistice to withdraw from the ex-Russian Baltic Provinces, and in no case should you have any dealings with (them). Whenever we are in a position to resist Bolshevik attacks by force of arms from the sea we should unhesitatingly do so. A Bolshevik man-of-war or armed auxiliary operating off the coast of the Baltic Provinces must be assumed to be doing so with hostile intent and treated accordingly. It is essential that you should not interfere with local politics, nor give colour for the assumption that Great Britain is favouring one party or another. You should be careful to raise no hope of any military assistance other than the supply of arms. No men are to be landed from your squadron unless under some very exceptional circumstances.

On arrival at Copenhagen, you should, if Rear-Admiral Sinclair has left a light cruiser and destroyers at Libau, relieve these ships from the force under your command. Riga and Reval are not to be visited without Admiralty authority, except that a destroyer may be sent for purposes of communication, and to acquire intelligence.

Further paragraphs warned Cowan of the mine danger, and that his ships should avoid being iced in. Finally, he was instructed to enforce the blockade of Germany.

This last aspect of Cowan's orders might be reasonably clear. For the rest, such phrases as " to show the British Flag," and " to support British policy," were generalities. Specifically, he was " to prevent the destruction of Estonia and Latvia by external aggression," but to achieve this he was to do no more than supply their forces with arms, and " resist Bolshevik attacks . . . from the sea." Had the Admiral supposed that he was meant to interpret such instructions literally, he must have represented that he had been given an impossible task. Fortunately he knew the difficulties which the Admiralty was experiencing with the Foreign Office and that he was, in fact, expected to act as he thought best in the light of the conditions which he found when he arrived in the Baltic. And he was not the man to shy at the responsibility which this placed on his shoulders.

Cowan's immediate reaction to his meeting with Sinclair at Copenhagen on 6th January, 1919, was, nonetheless, too impetuous. The Sixth Light Cruiser Squadron's activities off Reval—the prospect of hearing " the sound of the guns "— led him to wireless the Admiralty for permission to proceed forthwith to the Estonian capital and to carry out occasional bombardments of the Bolshevik front. This evoked more than a formal " not approved "; Their Lordships drew his attention to the paragraph of his instructions which said: " Riga or Reval are not to be visited." So he dispatched the *Royalist*, Captain the Hon. Matthew Best, together with two destroyers, to pay a short visit to Libau, whilst he raised the need for reinforcements to counter Russian naval operations " should Libau and Reval both be in the hands of the Bolsheviks by the spring."

Best returned with much useful, albeit disturbing, information. There might be 2000 German troops in Libau, but only 800 could be expected to obey their Commander's orders. The Germans had, moreover, thrown into the sea the 500 rifles and ammunition recently landed by H.M.S. *Angora* for use by Lettish volunteers. Ulmanis and his colleagues therefore thought it would be impossible to hold Libau against the Bolsheviks, who were seventy–eighty miles away, unless the Allies landed a division of 10,000 men. The Lettish Prime Minister also feared a Communist rising; 3000 refugees had left by sea to avoid this terror. A dozen merchant ships which were in the port could be used to evacuate the Lettish volunteers, 1000 White troops whom Prince Lieven had recruited from Russian ex-prisoners of war, and so many of the population as could not escape across the German frontier fifty miles to the south. But the German High Commissioner claimed that these were under his control, so the Allies were asked to provide the necessary vessels. " The Lettish Government cannot or will not do anything for itself," was Cowan's comment.

On 17th January the Admiral paid his first visit to Libau

in the *Caledon*, accompanied by three destroyers, when he learned that all was reasonably well in Estonia. Laidoner's troops were advancing south-east: by the 20th they were to be in Dorpat and Narva; by the end of the month they would reach Lake Peipus and Walk so that the country would be nearly clear of Bolsheviks. But the situation in Latvia was, if anything, worse than Best had found it. The Bolsheviks were expected to reach Libau by the end of the month when the Germans would have evacuated the country. Latvia's only hope of survival appeared to lie in a force of Swedish volunteers which a Colonel Edlund was trying to recruit. " The Letts would quickly join (them) in large numbers (which) might well lead to a Bolshevik repulse," Cowan was assured. " It might be that Riga may be retaken. There is little weight behind (the) Bolshevik thrust and a resolute and well-directed resistance by a force of 10,000 or 15,000 men would break it up." But Bosanquet, who was now acting as Cowan's Political Adviser, learned that the Swedes would need one million kroner a month to provide troops in such numbers: " I would, therefore, submit for the serious consideration of H.M. Government the question of furnishing financial aid. Action should be taken at once while Libau is still intact."

However, when Best returned to Latvia on 25th January, he found that Vacietis's troops had not advanced so quickly as expected. The Government's nerves had also steadied following the arrival of a couple of French destroyers which suggested greater Allied support, " and there were signs of a change in the German attitude, of a more effective occupation and a more vigorous command." Cowan confirmed this when he paid his second visit on the 31st. Lettish troops had checked the Bolsheviks short of Windau, so that Libau was quiet. The Germans were, however, hindering the dispatch of Swedish volunteers by offering to provide the needed loan, subject to unacceptable conditions designed to strengthen their hold on Latvia. Britain responded to these developments by dispatching 5000 more rifles together with fifty machine-guns and five million rounds of ammunition which were brought to Libau by Cowan's ships on 9th February. These arms were transferred to the Lettish transport *Saratov*, so as to be safe from the treacherous treatment the Germans had accorded the *Angora's* cargo until the Lettish Government could recruit the troops to use them.

On the same day the Admiral heard that Windau had fallen to a force of 500 Bolsheviks which brought them within forty miles of Libau, and that a Lettish attempt to recapture the port had been repulsed. Cowan was delighted when Ulmanis asked for a British ship to shell the Bolshevik gun positions. As soon as he had received Admiralty sanction— quickly given because, as Fremantle minuted, "it would be deplorable that the fine port of Libau should fall into the hands of the Bolsheviks"—the Admiral took his flagship north and anchored her off Windau. And when the *Caledon's* 6-inch guns opened fire they did more than destroy the batteries protecting the harbour entrance: the Bolsheviks left the town with greater speed than they had entered it.

This stopped the panic flight of refugees from Libau, whilst Cowan noted other encouraging signs. The Lettish National Force under Colonel Kolpak's command had grown to 3500 officers and men. Ulmanis had agreed with Pats that, as soon as possible, they would establish a common front against the Red invaders. And the chances that the Germans would comply with Article XII of the Armistice terms seemed to have been improved by the arrival of Major-General von der Goltz, who had done so much to drive the Bolsheviks from Finland.[1] The Admiral, therefore, reported that the Letts "appear to me to be far more worthy of support than hitherto." He added that their most pressing needs were food, especially grain, clothing, boots and an Allied loan to pay their own troops, if not the Swedish volunteers.

---

[1] The laconic brevity with which Cowan and Bosanquet separately reported this news to London shows that neither had an inkling of the trouble Goltz was soon to cause them and the Allies.

An incident during Cowan's return voyage to Copenhagen shows how the comings and goings of the British warships between the Danish capital and Libau served to maintain the Allied blockade. The *Royalist* intercepted the German S.S. *Wojan*, found she was carrying an unlicensed cargo from Lubeck to Memel, and sent her to Rosyth with an armed guard aboard. Since the Admiral was aware that his force was insufficient to ensure that no such illicit traffic passed, he sought the help of the French Senior Naval Officer in the cruiser *Montcalm*, who arranged for his ships, albeit fewer than the British, to carry out periodic sweeps in search of blockade runners. Against this Cowan had to contend with an additional task: at the beginning of February the light cruisers *Concord* and *Curlew* were withdrawn from Danzig: henceforth the Admiral was required to provide ships to maintain a wireless link with the British Mission in Warsaw and to join with other Allied vessels in safeguarding the distribution of relief supplies for Poland.[1]

On 13th February two more ships of the First Light Cruiser Squadron, the *Phaeton* and *Inconstant*, together with five " V & W " class destroyers, reached Copenhagen as reliefs for Cowan's force, the Admiralty having decided that service in the Baltic was sufficiently arduous for the vessels employed there to be changed every six weeks or so. The Admiral, with the *Phaeton*, Captain J. E. Cameron, and three destroyers in company with his flagship, therefore paid another visit to Libau to give Cameron a first-hand picture of the situation before he became S.N.O. in the Baltic. No new threat to Windau or Libau had developed; on the contrary, German troops were arriving in such strength that Goltz was contemplating an advance on Riga in about ten days' time. But the Letts had no illusions about his intentions: Cowan reported that they needed:

---

[1] Cowan was not otherwise concerned with Poland's fierce struggle for independence, most of which lies chronologically outside the period covered by this book. He did not therefore find it necessary to visit Danzig himself (until 1920, *vide* p. 60).

(*a*) Guarantees against Latvia remaining permanently over-ridden by German influence, consequent on the German troops being called upon to rid the country from the Bolshevik danger. I am much in sympathy with (this) as the Balts are very pro-German in their sympathies and influence, the difference between this province and Estonia (being) very marked, Estonia's inhabitants showing a much more united front.

(*b*) That during the German operations against the Bolsheviks a check should be put on their overbearing, and often cruel, treatment of the civil population.

(*c*) Their oft reiterated and urgent requests for money, food and clothing. Their requirements are so modest and so very necessary, that I find it hard to understand why they do not receive consideration from His Majesty's Government. Had they a grant of money from the Allies they might well be able to clear their country of Bolsheviks without further assistance from the Germans, which I submit would have a lasting benefit to British prestige and influence.

The Admiral added that he was not hopeful of the arrival of Edlund's volunteers: " the Swedish Government is, if any-thing, antagonistic to this expedition, the German parties in Sweden and Latvia (having) an undue influence." In truth, German interests were doing all that they could to " sabotage " a force which would be detrimental to their plans.

Cowan's first period of service in the Baltic ended on 21st February, 1919, when the *Caledon*, *Royalist* and accompanying destroyers left Copenhagen for Rosyth. Except for the flag-ship's bombardment of Windau, there had been nothing to compensate officers and men for the peace-time pleasures which most of the Grand Fleet was enjoying in home waters. But the Admiral's thoughts were on the spring when the Bolshevik ships would emerge from Kronstadt and might be brought to action. He made his wishes clear to the Admiralty: " My general impression on leaving the Baltic is that these provinces should soon be clear of Bolsheviks, unless very strong reinforcements are sent, of which there is no indication. The doubtful element is what naval action will be attempted when the ice melts; and if Their Lordships would consider allowing me to go back there when this time comes it would be a matter of the greatest satisfaction to me."

*　　　　*　　　　*

In London Cowan was able to discuss with Fremantle the Government's policy which was so succinctly summed up in a minute by the Director of Operations, Captain Dudley Pound:[1] " We cannot expect to achieve much result in bolstering up the Baltic States until our policy becomes a really positive one. At the present time, with the exception of a few arms and a little coal, it is an entirely negative one." The Cabinet had reasons for its equivocal attitude, though the extent to which Fremantle was able to enlighten Cowan about them is debatable. Certainly they cannot have been as clear as they appear now.

At the end of 1917, Clemenceau, out of concern for the capital which France had invested in the Ukraine, initiated a political and military Convention dividing much of Russia into spheres of Allied interest, Britain accepting the White Sea area. More recently the French Premier had proposed an extension to this agreement designed to allow France a free hand in Poland—she wished to make her an ally strong enough to contain Germany to the east—when Britain had accepted responsibility for the Baltic States. His Majesty's Government thus became the agent of the Allied Powers; it was not free to settle the support it should give the Baltic States; the Supreme Allied War Council at Versailles had to be consulted. But the " Big Four," Clemenceau, Lloyd George, Orlando and Wilson, were too busy trying to reconcile their conflicting viewpoints on peace terms for Germany to have much time for the problems posed by Bolshevik Russia, whilst Foch, the Allied Generalissimo, was chiefly concerned

[1] Later Admiral of the Fleet Sir Dudley Pound, First Sea Lord during the Second World War.

to ensure that Germany complied with more clauses in the Armistice Terms than Article XII. As late as 24th February, more than three months after the Armistice, the Foreign Office was telegraphing Paris:

> Has any decision been come to upon proposal to afford assistance to Baltic States against Bolsheviks? Admiralty are pressing for instructions and point out that more effective assistance than they are at present authorised to afford to Estonia and Latvia is necessary if those territories are to be saved from menace which threatens them.

The Big Four's inability to reach a decision arose out of a number of irreconcilable attitudes. They needed to liquidate their Intervention forces for reasons ranging from the public cry of " bring the boys home," through one of Wilson's Fourteen Points which specified " co-operation with Russia in the establishment of her own national policy with institutions of her own choosing," to a need to placate the Red sympathies of organised Labour.[1] They had seized on Lenin's January offer to discuss peace, which the Bolsheviks needed to consolidate their position, to call a conference of Russian Governments on Prinkipo Island.[2] But this was still-born because the Whites declared themselves " the only lawful group making for national renovation " and refused to associate with Bolshevism. So the Allies' solution to their dislike of this creed, which few supposed could retain its hold on Russia for long, was to give all possible support, short of sending troops, to the White forces of Kolchak in Siberia and Denikin in the Crimea and Caucasus. Any other part of Russia which opposed Bolshevism was likewise to be encouraged. But though the

[1] " Large sums were contributed to the Comintern (*Zinoviev's organisation for furthering the Communist cause abroad*) by benighted workers the world over, whose money served to pay the clever and unscrupulous agitators by whom the subscribers themselves were duped. Strangely enough, it was not only the labouring classes that were hypnotised. ' Parlour ' Bolshevism became a craze among weak-minded intellectuals. The phrase ' the greatest Jew since Christ,' applied to Trotsky, was launched by a well-meaning but hysterical (American) Red Cross Leader (Raymond Robbins) and for a time accepted by many quite intelligent people." (*The Story of S.T.25.*)

[2] In the Sea of Marmora.

Baltic States' desire for independence conformed with one of the Allies' declared war aims—self-determination for subject peoples—the All Russian Council in Paris declared their country to be indivisible. Any Allied action which might lead to a free Estonia, Latvia or Lithuania would, therefore, dismay the Whites and compromise the Allies' future relations with the Tsarist Empire which they supposed would be restored.

There would, however, have been no pressing need to define the Allied attitude towards the Baltic States if Article XII had served the purpose for which it had been included in the Armistice Terms. The Germans might have a plausible excuse for not complying with it immediately: they could not maintain discipline in their Eighth Army. Nor could Berlin be expected to do much to rectify this when the Social Democrats' claim to govern Germany was so strongly contested by the Spartakists, a situation which was not resolved until the defeat of their January revolt,[1] and the subsequent meeting of a National Assembly at Weimar on 6th February. But the decision to send fresh troops to Latvia was taken before this by the remnants of the German General Staff; Goltz went to Libau as the instrument of a proud military clique that had never recognised any authority except the Emperor, not as the servant of a republican government which he scorned as unsoldierly.

The Weimar Government needed to mitigate the effects of the Armistice, notably the occupation of the Rhineland and the continuation of the blockade, whilst they tried to persuade the Big Four to modify the harshness of their peace terms by creating trouble for the Allies to the East. This suited the General Staff: they understood that their ambitions had been baulked in the West—for the time being; but on the Eastern Front the German Army had not been defeated; on the contrary it had compelled Russia to sign the Treaty of Brest-Litovsk. It was, therefore, all to Germany's advantage to forge the

[1] By Gustav Noske who shortly afterwards became German Minister of Defence.

alliance with Russia which had been the Kaiser's dream: it would enable them to rebuild an army with which to renew hostilities in the West. So the Bolsheviks were not to be antagonised by resisting their attempts to conquer states that had been Russian territory. Moreover, it would be much easier for a new German Army to assume the guise of liberators and oust the Reds from these states, where German influence was so strong that their independence had been demanded at Brest-Litovsk so that they could be united into a grand-duchy, than it would be to dominate them once they had achieved independence under Allied protection.

Goltz's memoirs testify to his qualifications to conduct such a Machiavellian policy. " Why not revive under a new form in agreement with the Whites, and under the flag of an anti-Bolshevik crusade, our old Eastern policy which was forgotten in August 1914," he wrote, and added the cynical alternative, " (or) why not work for an economic and political rapprochement with (Red) Russia which, having massacred its intellectuals, needs merchants, engineers and administrators and whose frontier provinces, devastated and depopulated, might offer a fertile land for hard-working German peasants? " With all the arrogance of the Prussian military caste he described himself as the last of Germany's generals. He had certainly proved himself an able one. But he was much more than this. Years of experience of the political and military mazes of the Baltic enabled him to play the meddlesome activities of the Allies, the stubbornness of the Latvians, the fanfaronade of the Baltic Barons and the ruthless ambitions of the Bolsheviks, all to Germany's advantage. He was a sharp thorn in the Allies' side from soon after he landed in Libau " as Germany's ambassador, once again to build up her Eastern policy." But he had an Achilles' heel, an intense ambition for personal power. " In Latvia, I alone have supreme command over all troops and military installations," he announced as soon as he arrived. " As the troops at the front, immaterial of what nationality, are solely under my command, so also are military persons behind the front of whatever nationality—German, Lettish, Baltic or Russian." He aimed to do more than establish a Baltic grand-duchy: he wanted to be its ruler. And he dreamed of extending his domain to Prussia whence militarism would be reborn and enable Germany to achieve her destiny in the front rank of world Powers. Since he was to cause Cowan more trouble than any other single individual whom he encountered in the Baltic, the Admiral's opinion is of special interest: "I had rather an admiration for von der Goltz, who was a good example of an unbending Prussian, but he rode the commonest horse that I ever saw a high-ranking soldier of any nation sit upon!"

This, however, is looking ahead: in England, in February, the Admiral had yet to meet Goltz. He only knew that the General's arrival in Libau had tightened German control over Latvia. Their High Commissioner transferred the Departments of Justice and Food to the Provisional Government but refused to give up the railways, ports and telegraphs. More important, Goltz claimed the sole right to recruit volunteers for which he would provide officers. Ulmanis had rejected this but "needed arms, ammunition, equipment, machine-guns, artillery, aeroplanes, armoured cars and every kind of war material," to build up his own army. "It is important to us to know to what extent and in what way H.M. Government are willing to come to our assistance."

*   *   *

Cowan's last action before leaving the Baltic had been to send the "little coal," to which Pound referred, to Reval in the holds of two colliers escorted by two destroyers. Commander E. C. O. Thomson went with them to gain intelligence. He found that the *Lennuk* and *Wambola* had been repaired and commissioned with Estonian crews. And from Leningrad he heard that at a meeting of commanders of the Baltic Fleet held on 17th January, the whole of the Baltic Fleet was stated to be unfit for active service. Trotsky stated that, to create a fighting fleet, it was necessary to abolish the ship soviets and that all authority should be transferred to the commanders, a commissar being attached to each to arbitrate on any dispute that may arise with the crew.[1] At the same meeting Trotsky said: " In the near future, the Revolution must, if it is to escape destruction, put the British and French fleets out of action; and it is therefore essential that Soviet Russia shall reorganise her fleet."

But the ships ready for sea in the spring under the command of A. P. Zelenoy would be limited to the battleships *Petropavlovsk* and *Andrei Pervozvanni*, the cruiser *Oleg*, the destroyers *Azard* and *Gavriil* and two submarines, for all of which there would be only a small amount of fuel.

A week later, 28th February, the *Phaeton* and two destroyers returned to Libau, where Cameron met the Commander of the Estonian Navy, Captain Juhan Pitka, who had brought the *Lennuk* from Reval with the belated intention of bombarding Windau, to find that he had been forestalled by Cowan, the port now being occupied by German, Lettish and White Russian troops, not Bolsheviks. The Estonian—who was soon to be promoted admiral—impressed Cameron as " a man of very considerable energy and character, although his technical experience is somewhat limited; he is a Director of a Salvage Company and not by training a naval officer." Pitka wanted the Supreme Allied Council to force the Germans to give up control of Russian vessels lying in Libau, so that they could be used for an attack on the Bolsheviks from the Gulf of Riga when Goltz began his advance, now scheduled for 5th March.

On 2nd March, Cameron learned that documents found on Colonel Edlund had revealed that the Balts [2] were planning

[1] i.e. the ships were to be commanded by Tsarist officers willing to serve under the Bolshevik Government, with trusted commissars to ensure their loyalty to the new régime, instead of by soviets of sailors. (By the same realistic compromise with Communist dogma Trotsky created a Red Army able to defeat the armies of Denikin, Kolchak and Wrangel.)

[2] Inspired this time by the influential von Stryck.

a *coup d'état.* Ulmanis had no conclusive evidence implicating Goltz in this, though the Germans had facilitated the Balts' leader's escape to Stettin to avoid arrest. The General had, however, made the conspiracy a barefaced excuse for an attempt to seize the arms and ammunition stored in the *Saratov,* though his troops had not pressed this to the point of bloodshed when the Letts resisted. News of these developments prompted Fremantle to minute:

I fear it is only too probable that the Balts may be planning a *coup d'état,* in which they count on the support of the Germans, now 8000 good troops, well commanded, and being reinforced. The obligation is on the Germans to ensure the security of the Baltic Provinces against the Bolsheviks, but they are sending many more troops than seem to be necessary for that. We have asked four times for a decision from the Supreme War Council as to whether we should stop further reinforcements from being landed, the last time being yesterday. The only reply received has been that the question was in the hands of Marshal Foch.

So the Secretary of the Admiralty wrote formally to the Foreign Office: "The work of the British naval officers in the Baltic would be much facilitated if they could be informed of the policy which they are required to support, and My Lords desire urgently to impress on the Secretary of State for Foreign Affairs the necessity for formulating such a policy." A letter from Wemyss to the British S.N.O. at Archangel is equally revealing: "Alas, what you say about the lack of instructions is absolutely true. You are not the only person who feels it. Every department that has to deal with Russia is complaining; and we find ourselves in some difficulty in contending with the situation in the Baltic for that reason. The fact of the matter is that the Government do not know what policy to put forward."

However, the Admiralty's letter obliged the Foreign Secretary to spur the Supreme Allied Council into taking a decision. The War Office had recently sent a small Military Mission to Latvia; Major A. H. Keenan, a Black Watch officer who knew the Baltic States, and a staff of two had been carried by the *Inconstant* to Libau where on 6th March her captain, F. A. Marten, was instructed to inform Goltz that:

> No further movements from the west to the east of German troops and supplies, or coal between German and east Baltic ports, will be permitted and the existing blockade of German Baltic ports will be strictly maintained. No German ship will be permitted to enter Libau or other ports in the eastern Baltic unless I receive instructions from the British Admiralty that they have permission to do so.

But the General's answer to this attempt to restrain him was an impudent challenge:

> In face of the shortage of provisions, munitions, equipment and reinforcements, no course remains open but to evacuate the occupied territory of Latvia, as the supply of German and Lettish troops cannot be maintained without sea transport. I am thus compelled to relinquish the repulse of the Bolshevik troops which had already been successfully commenced, to expose Latvia to Bolshevism, and to withdraw my troops towards the German frontier. At the same time, I would ask that communication from Libau to Windau may not be suspended so that provisions, equipment and military stores for the Windau garrison of 450 men may be sent. Otherwise the garrison of Windau is endangered.

The Supreme War Council's reaction to this must have made Marten wonder at how little the Baltic situation was understood in Versailles: he was required to report whether the moment was suitable for the withdrawal of all German troops from Latvia. He answered that there could be no question of this, unless they were replaced by Allied or neutral troops, if the Bolsheviks were to be prevented from overrunning the whole country. And pending more realistic instructions he intended to allow sea supplies to Windau to continue.

The War Cabinet considered a fresh Admiralty submission in the middle of March:

> British men-of-war were sent to the Baltic at the beginning of December last, but no definite policy was formulated. The

situation has (now) developed considerably. Estonia has cleared her territory of Bolsheviks. She may, nevertheless, be exposed to a serious invasion when the Bolsheviks choose to concentrate troops for that purpose, and to naval operations towards the end of April when the ice melts. Latvia has been overrun by the Bolsheviks who are now in possession of some three-quarters of the country. The demoralised German troops who permitted this have been replaced by 12,000 efficient and well organised troops under a capable general, and are now (advancing) against Riga. The Supreme War Council has decided that no further reinforcements, and no supplies for the troops at present in Latvia, are to be landed. This order is being enforced by the British squadron.

The Admiralty realise that it is not their function to lay down, but rather to execute the policy laid down by the War Cabinet. Seeing, however, that the great majority of the information relative to the Baltic Provinces comes from the naval officers who have been and are serving (there), and that it is upon them that it devolves to execute the policy, the Admiralty may be permitted to state their reasons for requesting a fuller statement for the future:

(a) If the present policy continues, naval operations on a considerable scale will be necessary in May when the Bolshevik Fleet will be free to move. It is necessary to commence preparations without delay.

(b) The present policy of assisting the Provinces to maintain their integrity is being carried out by the Navy, with (the) assistance of military supplies. A loan has been asked for by both countries, so also have foodstuffs and coal. No action has, as far as is known, been taken by the Government departments concerned, except for a supply of 2000 tons of coal to Estonia.

(c) We have no permanent representative in Estonia or Latvia, with the exception of a Military Mission of two junior officers and a gentleman connected with the supply of timber. The proper execution of any policy appears to necessitate the presence of permanent representatives at both capitals.

(d) We are in the inconsistent position that, while we are placing every obstacle in the way of German assistance towards defending Latvia against the Bolsheviks, we are giving no effective help to the Letts. If the Germans withdraw, on account of our denial of sea transport, the onus will be on us of having delivered the country to the mercy of the Bolsheviks. On the other hand the Germans behave as an army of occupation and place every obstacle in the way of the organisation of a Lettish National Force.

(e) Requests are constantly made to British naval officers on the spot for statements as to the Allied intentions and for assistance of every description. It is manifestly injurious to British national and naval prestige that such requests should go unanswered.

(f) If operations take place in May in the Gulf of (Finland), we must be prepared for losses, both of ships and men, against an enemy with whom we are not formally at war, and against whom we cannot at present exercise such fundamental belligerent rights as blockade and capture of merchant vessels. They would be incurred in pursuit of no definite British interest, and in defence of a cause which is not being supported by the resources of the State, other than a naval force. It is essential, if our naval force is required to undertake operations of war, that it should do so in pursuance of a definite and coherent policy.

This powerful document obliged Lloyd George to decide that the Supreme War Council must agree to Diplomatic and Military Missions being sent to the Baltic States whose reasonable demands for arms, equipment, money, food and other essential commodities should be met. He would not, however, accept any marked increase in the strength of the British naval force. Realising that events might force the Government's hand, Fremantle sought authority to warn Beatty that a considerable fleet, including four battleships, monitors, light cruisers, destroyer and submarine flotillas, an aircraft carrier, minelayers, twelve minesweepers and coastal motorboats (C.M.B.s), with the necessary auxiliaries might be required in May to exercise control of the Gulf of Finland. This force was to be based on Poldiski for which anti-submarine net defences, searchlights and guns would be provided, all commanded by the Vice-Admiral First Battle Squadron. Wemyss approved except for the last of Fremantle's points: " It is in my opinion unlikely that the operations will come off so that (this) omission won't mean much. If the operation comes off after 15th May the question of choice (of admiral) may then arise." The Deputy Chief of Naval Staff's foresight was to be justified but, by withholding approval at this stage, the First Sea Lord ensured that Cowan was never superseded. If a more senior officer had been sent to the Baltic it might have been Fremantle himself, since in April 1919 he was relieved at the Admiralty by Rear-Admiral J. A. Ferguson, and on 1st May hoisted his flag in command of the First Battle Squadron, following the abolition of the Grand Fleet and its replacement by an Atlantic Fleet in which Madden relieved Beatty as Commander-in-Chief.

Cowan's return to the Baltic stemmed from the Cabinet's decision to make no increase in the strength of the Baltic Force. If it had to be limited to two light cruisers and ten destroyers, it should be commanded by the man who was not only well acquainted with the difficult problems involved but had proved that he could handle them wisely. So the *Caledon*, now commanded by Captain Geoffrey Mackworth, again wore Cowan's flag when she led the relief force, which included the *Cleopatra*, Captain Charles Little, five " V & W " destroyers and five of the smaller " S " class. They went by way of Christiania to land a consignment of gold, and on to Libau with 20,000 rifles, six 6-inch howitzers, twelve 18-pounders and twenty lorries for the Lettish forces, which were transferred to the *Saratov* under Keenan's control.

*   *   *

Cameron, now advised by Mr. Grant Watson,[1] had been having a very difficult time with Goltz. Because the Allies had refused to allow further German troops to enter the country, the General had stopped his advance on Riga; by the end of March 1919 he had progressed no farther than Mitau. Having no intention that these tactics should be spoiled by Pitka's proposed flank attack, he had refused to comply with

---

[1] Whom the Foreign Office had sent as Political Adviser in Latvia on Bosanquet's appointment as Consul-General in Reval.

Admiralty instructions to hand over the Russian vessels in Libau to the Estonians. And in an attempt to force the Allies to lift their embargo on supplies coming in by sea, he had, in contravention of Article XIV of the Armistice terms ordered his troops to live off the country to the extent of confiscating the limited stocks of flour and other staple foodstuffs in the Libau area, so that the Letts were reduced near to starvation. The British ships, amongst them the *Wolfhound*, Lieutenant-Commander J. C. Tovey,[1] did what they could in the way of relief from their own small stocks as Cunningham (then a commander), who took the *Seafire* to Windau, remembers. " The appearance of the children was pitiable; lean, ragged little scarecrows with pale faces and sunken eyes who gathered abreast of the ship holding out their bony arms and crying plaintively ' Mister! Mister! Please bread! ' It took our kind-hearted sailors no time at all to improvise a soup kitchen on the jetty. Practically all of our rations went into it; but we had the satisfaction of knowing that for the three or four days we were there the small people were tolerably well fed." [2] Nonetheless, Cameron feared food riots and bloodshed if the Allies did not send supplies soon; they were more urgently needed than arms so long as Goltz would not allow Ulmanis to recruit the men to use them. Fortunately, by the time Cowan's force arrived on 3rd April, the Minister of Commerce was back from a visit to London with news that gave " the greatest comfort and satisfaction "; a first supply of flour was due to reach Libau in the middle of the month. Pound thought the *Phaeton*'s captain should have dealt more firmly with the Germans, going so far as to seize the disputed ships by force. Cameron deemed it wiser not to add fuel to the fire of Goltz's hostile attitude. From the distance of nearly half a century it is easy to suggest that Pound was right, but in March 1919 Cameron was not alone in failing to judge the depths of

[1] Later Admiral of the Fleet Lord Tovey, Commander-in-Chief, Home Fleet in the Second World War.
[2] *A Sailor's Odyssey.*

the General's chicanery. On 5th April, Lord Curzon [1] wrote to Balfour:

> The Senior Naval Officer Baltic, the British Military Mission, and the British Diplomatic Representative at Libau, have jointly telegraphed that the Allied Governments are incurring a grave responsibility in hampering the operations of the German troops when the Bolsheviks are in a position to bring up reinforcements. I need not discuss the merits or the reverse of compelling the Germans to maintain and increase their forces in Latvia to stem the Bolshevik invasion. In the absence of an adequate Latvian force, or of Allied troops, the measure may have been a necessary evil. But I cannot help thinking that, once this course had been decided on, it was illogical to withhold from the German force the means of rendering it effective: and the continued denial of supplies can only result in exposing it to grave risks, and so defeating the end which the Allies had in view.

The *Caledon*'s return was marked by a reminder that Goltz had his own troubles. He had recently uncovered a Spartakist movement in one of his regiments: the arrest of the ringleaders provoked a demonstration outside German headquarters, where mutinous troops demanded the release of their comrades and Goltz's arrest. Although this obliged the General to send the whole regiment back to Germany, he was astute enough to turn it to his own advantage when dealing with Cowan. Returning from a visit to Keenan, the Admiral was stopped outside German headquarters by a sentry and asked whether he had a pass. Since one can readily picture Cowan's anger at being subjected to such an indignity by a soldier of the nation which the Allies had so recently defeated, his note of protest was very moderately worded: " Sir Walter Cowan would be glad if orders could be given whereby he remains free of interference by those under Generalmajor Graf von der Goltz's orders when he is on shore in uniform." Goltz apologised, but had the audacity to add: " A mutiny was the reason guards were placed which was occasioned by the lack of equip-

---

[1] Minister of State who was acting as Foreign Secretary in London in Balfour's absence at the Peace Conference.

ment for the men resulting from the (Allies') sea blockade," and: " A pass is enclosed herewith for use in case of need." This provoked Pound to minute: " It is scarcely consistent with the dignity of the British S.N.O. at Libau that he should carry a pass furnished by the Germans." Ferguson castigated it as " an insult."

Cowan was more concerned with the news that came from Riga of the appalling privations the people were suffering as a result of the German failure to recapture the city. " In the event of my Government authorising me to raise the blockade can you give me a forecast of the date by which you could retake Riga? " he asked Goltz. To this pointed question the General gave the most evasive of answers; he wasn't sure whether his Government intended that he should retake Riga; even if it did, he wasn't certain that he had enough loyal troops to do so. When he added a question of his own, whether the blockade would be raised only if he agreed to retake Riga, Cowan's reply was brief; the Allies were ready to revictual the city as soon as it was retaken. A couple of days later the Admiral was dismayed to learn that the onset of the spring thaw had compelled the Germans to suspend serious operations. Three weeks was the normal period for what the Russians were accustomed to call this "state of roadlessness"; but Goltz did not hesitate to say that " an attack on Riga so desirable to me on humanitarian grounds is (now) on military grounds unfortunately impossible within any time limit that I can foresee." And to ensure that the Allies did not use this as an excuse for continuing the blockade, he told Cowan he could not be sure of holding Mitau unless it was raised. So, on 14th April the Admiral was authorised to inform Goltz: " British Government are prepared provisionally and until further notice to allow supplies to go by sea to the German army in Latvia provided that Germans undertake to do nothing to impede recruitment and organisation of Letts." Goltz rejected this offer as soon as it was made; his plans might be hindered by lack of supplies, but they would be wrecked by a sizeable Lettish army. Besides, he knew much more than Cowan of what was about to happen in Libau—though the Admiral was sufficiently aware of trouble brewing to remain there with most of his force.[1]

It was fortunate that he did. Learning that a German patrol had disarmed and arrested several Lettish guards stationed by the Naval Harbour,[2] Cowan anticipated an attempt to seize the *Saratov* by sending the *Seafire* to berth alongside her whilst she raised steam to move to an anchorage in the Outer Harbour. Having been idle for so long, this took twenty-four hours: the *Seafire* was still alongside on the morning of 16th April when the Lettish Government ordered 700 rifles to be landed and sent to their G.H.Q. Though the Germans did not hinder this, their subsequent reaction was swift, as Cunningham recalls:

A large, unkempt, wild-looking, fierce-eyed customer with a bushy black beard was ushered into my cabin. After much animated conversation, part Latvian, part my almost wholly-forgotten German, with a few scraps of almost incomprehensible English, we gathered that the Latvian G.H.Q. a mile or so away in the forest, had been attacked and captured by the Germans. Something had to be done, and that quickly, so I decided to go and see for myself. As the black-bearded one and myself walked through the forest we came upon German soldiers staggering back with beds, pots and pans, chickens and loot of every sort. We hurried on and presently came to a large house in a clearing. It was burning fiercely, and beside it a battalion of German troops were forming up to march off. Several Latvian officers, who had been roughly handled and their coats torn off, rushed up and began to explain what had happened. After much excited and voluble conversation I gathered that the headquarters had been set ablaze after all the senior officers had been arrested and the records

---

[1] In addition to providing a guardship at Danzig, Cowan was always obliged to leave one ship at Copenhagen to act as a wireless link with the United Kingdom.

[2] The port of Libau comprised an Outer Harbour, enclosed by breakwaters, and two good inner harbours. Of these, the Naval Harbour, to the north, consisted of several basins approached by a narrow channel spanned by a swing bridge. The other, the Commercial Harbour, was a long narrow stretch of the river with wharves on the town side.

removed. By the time I had learnt this, the troops had already marched off to the strains of a blaring brass band. There was nothing that I could do at the moment; but it was obviously no time for a ship full of arms to be lying alongside the jetty.[1]

Returning hot-foot to his ship, determined to tow the *Saratov* to safety, Cunningham found that she had steam and was ready to cast off. With doubts as to whether the swing bridge would open to the call of the *Seafire*'s siren, with visions of having to land an armed party to do the job, prepared to shoot any Germans who resisted them, he led the transport out of the Naval Harbour. Fortunately all went well: the *Saratov* was safely anchored in the Outer Harbour near the British cruisers without incident.

By this time Cowan had realised that the Germans were not to be content with arresting the Lettish military leaders. So he ordered the *Seafire* and the *Scotsman*, Lieutenant-Commander D. J. D. Noble, into the Commercial Harbour, where they were berthed by the time that armed Balts surrounded the Lettish Government offices. Fortunately only two Ministers were there. Ulmanis and his Finance Minister chanced to be near the British Legation and were able to seek refuge with Keenan. How two other Latvian Ministers escaped is told by Cunningham:

The *Seafire* and *Scotsman* secured alongside the wharf abreast the Custom House, and around it we saw considerable German activity which quickly died away when the destroyers appeared. Then started a series of farcical incidents. The first thing was to dislodge the machine-gun parties at the ends of the wharf. Our guns were already manned, and a polite message was sent to the Germans to say that if they did not remove their machine-guns immediately they would be blown away. They went. A little later a German officer in need of medical attention was brought on board. It seemed that he had been ordered to seize the Custom House, a mission that was defeated by our sudden arrival. So mortified was he at his failure that he decided to commit suicide by shooting himself with his revolver. He had made an extremely bad job of it, and had merely chipped a bit of skin from the side

[1] p. 88 n 2., op. cit.

of his head. He was treated with a few inches of plaster from the *Scotsman's* medical chest and sent ashore again. Then a couple of the deposed Latvian Ministers succeeded in getting on board. We accommodated (one) in our small chart-house, where he promptly seized upon my typewriter and busied himself in producing inflammatory pamphlets.

All that day and well on into the night the situation remained tense. Soon after dark two Latvian trawlers, secured close under our bows, attempted to remount their guns which had been removed under the terms of the Armistice. We were not aware of what this portended; but seeing no reason why the Baltic Barons should exercise sea power under our very noses we ordered the trawlers to cease their operations forthwith or be sunk. They made little objection. During the evening meal I was informed that a German officer wished to see me, a truculent young Baltic Baron armed to the teeth and in German uniform. His instructions were to ask my permission to search the Custom House. We had no orders to take any part in events on shore, so permission was given subject to our visitor being accompanied by a British officer. At the same time he was warned there was to be no fighting on pain of the destroyers' guns opening fire. I sent Noble to take part in the search, and he took with him a petty officer armed with a loaded revolver. Accompanied by a party of German soldiers, they made an exhaustive peregrination of the extensive cellars and storerooms tunnelled under the huge building. In one dark passage, where the search party evidently expected to find something, Noble told the petty officer to be on the alert. The petty officer drew his pistol and promptly let it off by mistake, fortunately without hitting anyone. This naturally caused a commotion. The Germans seemed anxious to shoot or bayonet someone; but Noble passed it off airily by waving his hands and repeating the only word of German he knew—" *Nichts* ! *Nichts* ! " The search continued. Meanwhile, as Noble had not returned after two hours, I began to feel anxious, so went to the Custom House to see what had happened. The German sentries outside made half-hearted efforts to stop me; but telling them to go somewhere else in the best German at my command I pushed my way past them and tracked down the search party. I found them in an upstairs room, having rounded up five men and one old woman, who were about to be interrogated. The young ruffian in charge had opened the proceedings by sitting down at a table and putting two loaded pistols in front of him. However, the search party discovered nothing. The prisoners were liberated, and we went back on board and to bed. They had been searching for the missing members of the Latvian Government.[1]

Cunningham received two other visitors during the evening whom he sent out to the *Caledon*. According to Cowan,

they proved to be officers in the *Baltische Landeswehr* who reported the overthrow of the Lettish Government and the institution of a temporary military dictatorship and " Committee of Safety," the apparent head of which was Baron von Manteuffel, commanding the unit of Baltic German troops which had effected the arrest of the Government. They asked me if they could hope for the support of my Government to this administration and against any possible interference by the Germans. As they were unable to satisfy me that they represented anybody but the body of troops they belonged to, which had caused these disturbances, and were not able to convince me that they had not acted in collusion with the Germans, and also stated their intention was to arrest Ulmanis and the other Ministers in the event of their leaving British protection, I sent them on shore and said that any further communication from them must be in writing, and I have not seen them since.

This same day, 17th April, the American Military Mission, which had recently arrived in Libau, returned from a visit to the Front, accompanied by a Lett officer. " At the station," wrote Cowan,

they were met by an armed guard of the *Baltische Landeswehr*, who attempted to arrest the Lett officer. The American officers (Colonel Warwick Greene and Colonel Dawley) acted with great resolution and, though the station was packed with troops and German lookers-on, refused to permit the arrest, informing the *Baltische* officers that if the Government had fallen, military control of the town was in the hands of General von der Goltz, and at his direction alone would they consent to the arrest of anyone in company with, and attached temporarily to, their Mission. On this the Baltic officers fell back, the Lett officer was placed between Colonel Greene and Colonel Dawley and they passed out of the station and back to their house without interference.

On the 18th the Admiral visited both British and American

[1] p. 88 n 2., op. cit.

Missions from whom he gathered that he had been instrumental in ensuring that the *coup d'état* had not been as successful as its instigators had envisaged.

The original plan seems to have been that simultaneous action was to be taken by the Baltic Germans to overthrow the Governments at Libau and Reval, probably on 23rd or 24th April, but it appears that sending a destroyer in to bring the *Saratov* out of the Naval Harbour on the 16th precipitated their action. Now there is uneasiness amongst the so-called " Committee of Safety," which has made several attempts to gain interviews with Keenan and myself, and are evidently most anxious to obtain advice and recognition from us. I saw for a few minutes Ulmanis, whose behaviour and bearing is most correct and resolute. He, as well as Keenan, have sent messages far and wide to the Lettish troops and people to keep quiet, offer no resistance for the present, and to have patience. Ulmanis has great hopes that the Allies will intervene to reinstate him. In the meantime all distribution of food supplies has been suspended and the " Committee of Safety " informed that they are now responsible for the starvation of their own country.

In response to an urgent telegram from Cowan, Grant Watson, who had been visiting Lithuania, returned to Libau on the 19th and accepted the Admiral's suggestion that, for his own safety, he should live on board the *Seafire*. The French torpedoboat *Dunois* and sloop *Meuse* also reached Libau on the 19th, commanded by Captain Brisson whose determined leadership was matched by his willingness to co-operate with the British force: though under orders to proceed to Reval, Helsingfors and Stockholm, he readily responded to Cowan's suggestion that his ships [1] should remain at Libau, and sent the *Meuse* to join Cunningham's destroyers in the Commercial Harbour. The Admiral and Brisson then agreed with the British and American Missions that an officer from the latter

[1] The force at Brisson's disposal in the Baltic was limited to three torpedoboats in addition to the *Dunois*, and three sloops in addition to the *Meuse*. The only other Allied ships in the Baltic were a flotilla of U.S. destroyers but these were restricted to safeguarding American food shipments organised by the Hoover Relief Administration. When Hoover asked for a larger American force, President Wilson's strong aversion to becoming embroiled in this part of the world compelled him to tell Hoover that he must rely on the British Fleet.

should see Goltz and ask for an explanation for recent developments. " This was effected on 21st April, the gist of Goltz's remarks being that the actions of the Baltic troops in arresting the Government, and in raiding and disarming the Lett Headquarters and troops, were unauthorised by him; but he considered the arrest of the Government a necessary evil." So next day Cowan presided at an Allied meeting at which it was resolved that Goltz should be required to effect " the removal of the officer commanding the Baltic troops which arrested the Government, and the officer commanding the detachment which raided the Lett Headquarters, and that these two units should be removed from Libau, and the Lettish officers and troops, whom they had disarmed, should be re-established in every particular." These demands were delivered with a time limit and a reminder that the Allied representatives were not in Libau to discuss terms but to dictate them. At first it seemed that Goltz would refuse. On the 21st Cowan sent him a brief note whose wording is an admirable example of the restraint with which he handled the Prussian: " I beg to bring to your notice that Lettish troops in the Naval Harbour are apprehensive of further interference by German troops to-night or to-morrow." This, and the warship's searchlights playing all night on the threatened area, proved sufficient to deter Goltz from further aggression. His subsequent compliance with the Allies' demands is an impressive testimony to Cowan's diplomacy, backed by the strength represented by the small British and French naval forces in Libau.

One further extract from Cunningham's memoirs shows how this strength was exerted by two destroyers, each manned by reduced complements (a result of demobilisation) of fewer than a hundred officers and men:

We had established a line of naval sentries on the jetty about twenty-five yards out from the *Seafire* and *Scotsman*. Ten yards farther afield was a line of Germans, who tried to restrain the crowd of people flocking down to the jetty to see what was going on.

Now and then small boys or girls dodged through the line of Germans and came to one or other of the destroyers. Invariably they were given a large slice of bread and jam or anything else we had. One day during the dinner hour a small girl was making her way back through the German sentries when one of them knocked her flying with a box on the ear. I heard a roar of anger and sounds of commotion on deck, and arrived there just in time to find the ship's companies of both destroyers swarming over the rails fully determined to do battle with the German sentry and to heave him into the river. They would have done it, steel helmet, rifle and all, if we had not been able to reduce them to order and discipline. An incident of that sort might well have provoked fighting and bloodshed.

One morning I went on deck to see a large force of carpenters erecting a high wooden barricade on the jetty abreast of the destroyers. I sent for the German officer in charge and demanded to know the reason, and he, most politely, told me that the General had heard we were being troubled by the populace and the palisade was being built to ensure our privacy. He informed me that there would be a door in it with a sentry on duty. The Germans were obviously annoyed by our fraternisation with the people. It took them about two days to finish their barricade complete with an armed sentry to control entrance and exit. I went out and asked the officer if the job was quite finished. He assured me that it was, and now we should have no further trouble with the crowd. The jetty was a long one, so the *Seafire* and *Scotsman* immediately shifted berth to other billets outside the confines of the barricade where, as before, we were soon being visited by the people with their children. We waited with interest for the explosion which came within the hour. An enormous red staff car drove at full speed on to the jetty. It contained Goltz himself, who stood up in the car berserk with rage and started shouting and waving his arms in the air. He addressed no remarks to us. What he roared to his staff was anybody's guess.[1]

We, however, have no need to guess what Cowan thought of this incident: " Commander Cunningham," he informed the Admiralty, " has on one occasion after another acted with unfailing promptitude and has proved himself an officer of

[1] p. 88 n 2., op. cit. On another occasion Goltz and his staff were rash enough to ride down to the jetty, when an enterprising sailor sounded the *Seafire*'s siren. Its piercing shriek emptied every saddle inside ten seconds, the horses bolting—to British delight and Prussian fury.

exceptional value and unerring decision." The Italian Navy was to learn as much in the Mediterranean in 1940–43.

The Admiral paid an equally generous tribute to Keenan: " I have received (from him) every help and advice. His firm and correct dealing with the Germans and the moral influence he has exercised over them, and also the successful and untiring efforts he has made to keep the Lettish troops calm, thereby avoiding unnecessary bloodshed, has maintained and increased the prestige of our country scarcely to be hoped for under the circumstances." But neither he nor Cowan could persuade Goltz to release Ulmanis's Ministers and allow them to resume office. The General maintained that they had Bolshevik sympathies and were a danger to the district for which he was responsible to the Allies. Prince Lieven suggested that he might resolve the situation by forming a coalition government of Letts and Balts, since Colonel Balodis, who had succeeded to the command of the Lettish troops at the front after Kolpak's untimely death from a stray German bullet, had promised his support. Cowan favoured this solution to Latvia's political problems, but did not believe the moment ripe; and Lieven accepted his advice that he would best serve the country's interests by using his influence to prevent friction between the Lettish and Balt troops opposing the Bolsheviks, it being highly undesirable that this task should be left to the Germans. Cowan's discretion was justified twenty-four hours later: the Supreme Allied Council instructed him to require the instant reinstatement of Ulmanis's Government and the removal of all German restrictions on the recruitment of a Lettish Army.

He was not, however, destined to remain at Libau to ensure that Goltz complied. Pitka had arrived the previous day in the *Lennuk* with news that Kronstadt was free of ice, and very early on 25th April came a wireless report that the Red Fleet was out. This threat, which was of much greater consequence to the British Baltic Force than German machinations in Latvia, was like a magnet to a man with Cowan's love for battle. Leaving Ulmanis and his colleagues on board the *Saratov* and in the care of Grant Watson and Keenan, the *Caledon* left harbour, accompanied by the *Seafire* and *Sepoy*, within the hour's notice at which the British ships normally kept steam. And as they headed north at high speed, the flagship's wireless sent out an urgent call for the *Cleopatra* and the destroyers which had recently been detached to Copenhagen, to join their Admiral with all dispatch.

*   *   *

From now on so much of our story is concerned with operations in the Gulf of Finland that this chapter is best concluded by taking stock of the *coup d'état* in Libau and pursuing subsequent events in Latvia so far as the beginning of June. The German plan to allow the Bolsheviks to overrun the Baltic States, whence they could subsequently be expelled, rather than allow these countries to achieve freedom under Allied protection, did not suit Goltz's own ambitions. For all that he might deny it to the Allied representatives, he had instigated the revolt to prevent the Lettish troops from having the satisfaction of taking part in the capture of Riga: holding his own troops facing the Latvian capital on the leash he had authorised Baron von Manteuffel to effect this *coup*. He then thought it tactically wise to accede to Cowan's demand that this *deus ex machina* should be expelled from Libau, but he had no other intention of listening to the Allies' scolding: the *coup* had to be consolidated. Finding an obscure Latvian attorney with German-Balt sympathies who was willing to declare the German forces to be a *bona fide* army of occupation and Latvian mobilisation illegal, he chose an equally obscure Germanophile Latvian pastor, Andrieus Niedra, to act as Prime Minister of a puppet Balt Government which took office on 10th May, 1919. Before this, however, the Supreme Council had taken the situation sufficiently seriously to set up a Baltic Commission to grasp the nettle of Goltz's ambitions. And on 4th May they required Berlin to replace him in command and to declare that theirs was not an army of occupation, only an " auxiliary force."

Berlin prevaricated whilst Goltz prepared to move on Riga. At the crucial moment a group of Lettish officers hindered his plans by kidnapping Niedra, but not for long: a substitute was quickly found who ordered the liberation of the capital on 15th May. Then, however, Berlin intervened: Goltz was forbidden to use his troops for an assault on Riga. Since he could not cancel the attack without serious harm to his personal prestige, he was obliged to allow the *Baltische Landeswehr* and Balodis's Lettish troops to effect this on 22nd May. But this was not to be a set-back to his ambitions: having allowed the *Landeswehr* a few days of unbridled terror against Letts with Bolshevik sympathies in Riga, whither Niedra (who had escaped his captors) and his Government had moved, Goltz ordered a further advance, which was not directed against the Bolsheviks to the south-east of the capital, but into northern Latvia. With the apparent purpose of helping Balodis to link up with a Lettish force fighting on the Estonian southern front, the General aimed to occupy Livonia so that the *Landeswehr* could launch an attack on Estonia.

At the same time he instructed his troops to adopt a hostile attitude towards the British. " It is plainly evident," he wrote, " that the English are aiming to prevent any access of strength for Germany and to prevent the coming alliance of Germany and Russia by any and every means. With the help of the Estonians and Letts, England is going to create a vassal state here which is to be thrust as a wedge between Germany and Russia. It is not a question of whether we will fight or not. We *must* fight if we are not to go under. We must act now or be strangled by England's diplomatic negotiations." A couple of destroyers recently arrived at Libau were the first to experience this hostility. Five junior officers from the *Velox* were arrested by a German patrol and detained for three hours on the pretext that they had entered a military area. Cowan's irritation at Goltz's flat refusal to accede to the demand of the Captain of the *Velox* for an apology, with the consequence that the matter had to be settled at the Paris-Berlin level, was exceeded by his regret that the officers should have been allowed to land with sporting guns at a time when the smallest incident was likely to provoke German truculence. The Admiralty endorsed this by conveying their displeasure to the *Velox*'s Captain; but one wonders whether this was Cowan's intention since he had qualified his own strictures with the sardonic comment: " It is a matter of surprise to me that British officers should seek to kill game in the breeding season."

On 29th May the cruiser *Royalist* reached Libau when Commodore A. A. M. Duff (to quote Cowan), " took charge of affairs in the Western Baltic; and thereafter, by his quick and accurate grasp of the whole German situation, freed me from a very considerable proportion of my preoccupations. He at once established a dominating influence over the other Allied officers and Missions, and controlled them all with the utmost decision and harmony "—except in so far as Greene and Dawley favoured the Balts. The consequent tendency of these two Americans to support the German point of view in their reports did nothing to resolve the disparate opinions held in Versailles. Balfour had not only to reject the American Secretary of State's suggestion that Cowan and Duff ought to collaborate with Goltz against the Bolsheviks, but also to repudiate his assumption that, by the Armistice terms, the Allies had become allies of Germany in the Baltic States. The Foreign Secretary held that the Allies were neither pro-Russian nor pro-German: their purpose was to restore peace in a much harassed part of Europe.

Duff awoke a few mornings after his arrival to find that German troops had occupied the Naval Harbour and were moving batteries of field-guns into positions from which they could make it untenable. This situation was one that could not be allowed. " If we are not in a position to issue orders to the Germans," he wrote, " they will very soon issue orders to us." Cowan had his own characteristically strong views:

Since the Germans have been allowed openly to defy and disregard the orders of the Allies given them three weeks ago, the situation in Latvia could not be more involved. Had the suggestions of those on the spot, constantly reiterated from January last, been acted upon, i.e. a British General sent out to amalgamate and equip the forces of Letts, Balts and Russians so as to sweep the Bolshevik invasion away, and to render the presence of the Germans no longer necessary outside the Prussian front, all would now have been very well in these Baltic Provinces. But I am afraid the results of not doing so will very soon become apparent, and be a most difficult and disagreeable hindrance and obstacle to the peace of the world and the success of the League of Nations.

The Admiralty reacted quickly; authorising Duff to withdraw from Libau at his discretion, if necessary embarking the Diplomatic and Military Missions, they telegraphed to Paris on 31st May:

The harbour of Libau is being put in a state of defence by the Germans, and the guns which have been mounted on shore are a direct menace to our ships. The Germans in Latvia appear to be only slightly, if at all, under the control of the German Government, and should Goltz either permit fire to be opened on our ships, or threaten to do so unless they withdraw, our ships would have to evacuate Libau. (We should then) be deprived of the only base in the Baltic from which the blockade could be carried out.

The Admiralty—and Cowan—then learned that on 28th May, 1919, the Supreme War Council, disturbed by the possibility that the Germans might refuse to accept the terms of the recently published Peace Treaty, with the consequent need to renew hostilities, had pusillanimously agreed to Goltz remaining in Latvia, subject to four conditions:

(a) The General will receive instructions to prepare the way for the establishment of a Coalition government;

(*b*) He will return their arms to the Lettish troops that have been disarmed;

(*c*) No hindrance may be placed in the way of the mobilisation and instruction of Lettish troops;

(*d*) The new Lettish Government will be left free to carry out its functions without any hindrance from the German authorities.

A period of 15 days, starting on 1st June, is allowed for carrying out these conditions. At the end of this period, the Allies will examine the attitude they will maintain towards Goltz.

To Duff's news they responded by instructing Foch to demand the immediate removal of the offending guns, coupled with a formal apology, adding that until these conditions were met no German ship of any kind would be permitted to enter or leave the port. On 8th June the German Government had the effrontery to reply that:

(*a*) Evacuation was taking place:

(*b*) Goltz had not kept back arms from the Letts:

(*c*) Mobilisation would endanger the lines of communication of the German troops:

(*d*) It was impossible for Goltz to interfere in Latvian affairs, as he had been ordered to abstain from doing so.

*   *   *

Goltz's open defiance of the Allies, with the clear connivance of Berlin, must be left at this point so that we may go back to 25th April and record events in the Gulf of Finland after Cowan's arrival at Reval. But before doing so, we may with advantage take a brief glance to the south. The Bolsheviks began their advance into Lithuania in January: a month later they captured Vilna, obliging the Provisional Government to withdraw to Kovno. There, as already mentioned, Grant Watson established contact with Voldmaris and his colleagues; but for want of access from the sea he could offer them no immediate prospect of Allied help. Since the Lithuanian Army numbered only 6000 men who lacked modern equipment, there was little besides the German army of occupation, some 30,000 strong, to prevent the country being overrun. This unhappy position was further complicated in April; ignoring the Liths' claim to liberate Vilna, Polish troops [1] captured the old capital. Thus, by May, the greater part of Lithuania, though claiming independence, was dominated by and dependent on a German army; the north-east territory was occupied by Bolsheviks who wanted the whole province for Red Russia; and the south-east was dominated by Poles who, mindful of history, wished to gain a much larger area notwithstanding contrary denials issued by the Warsaw Diet.

[1] Commanded by the Lithuanian-born General Pilsudski.

Chapter Five

BIORKO SOUND

Others may use the ocean as their road,
Only the English make it their abode.

Edmund Waller in 1659

A BRITISH Relief Mission visited Reval early in April 1919,
headed by Lieutenant-Colonel S. G. Tallents [1] who reported
that relations between the Estonian Army, the Finnish volunteers and the Lettish detachments which were holding the
Bolsheviks to the north and south of Lake Peipus were satisfactory—on the whole: " the Estonians make an exception in
favour of Letts (to) their general rule of killing all Bolshevik
prisoners, hoping to seduce Letts from the Red Army. But
the impression which they have thus attempted to create had
been damaged shortly before my visit, when 400 men of a
Bolshevik Lettish Regiment, upon advancing to surrender,
had been shot down by the Estonians owing to a mistaken
reading of their intentions." So much could not be said of
the White Russian Army, now 6000 strong, directed from headquarters in Helsingfors by General Yudenitch. In command of
the Tsar's armies in the Caucasus he had shown considerable
ability, decisively defeating the Turks. But in exile at the age
of fifty-seven he had allowed his judgment to be undermined
by the insatiable appetite for intrigue which inspired his chief
supporters. " There is no Estonia," he declared, with singular
ignorance of the realities of his position. " It is a piece of
Russian soil, a Russian province. The Estonian Government
is a gang of criminals." So he wanted his army to be supplied

[1] Later Sir Stephen Tallents, the distinguished Civil Servant.

direct by the Allies instead of through the Estonians whom, he claimed, took more than their share. The Estonian authorities retorted that Yudenitch's troops had been equipped at the expense of their own men. " They further say that the Russians are unwilling to fight in Estonia. It was plain from the conversation at a supper party of Russian officers, which I (Tallents) attended, that their whole interest is concentrated on plans for an attack on Petrograd." Yudenitch also feared that a successful Estonian drive against Vacietis's army would enable them to arrange an armistice whose terms would include disarmament of the Whites; but Pats insisted that there was " no chance of a settlement with the Bolsheviks until they had been driven from Estonian territory by force of arms, and Petrograd had been captured." Tallents's report concluded with these prescient paragraphs:

In Lithuania and Latvia I found German troops in complete occupation, and these cannot be withdrawn without effective substitution unless both countries are to be resigned to the Bolsheviks. Estonia is free of Germans and shows a much stronger national spirit, but she is more hardly pressed by the Bolsheviks. The presence of many Russian refugees, coupled with the nearness of Kronstadt and Petrograd, leads the Bolsheviks to regard an independent government in Estonia as a special menace. The military activity of the Germans in Latvia and Lithuania tends to strengthen the Bolshevik threat to Estonia, as it prevents the Red armies from advancing towards East Prussia. The three countries themselves desire to join forces for defence against the Bolsheviks, but they are hampered by mutual jealousies. The Lithuanians resent Polish claims to the Vilna district; and the Letts are jealous of the greater activity and independence of Estonia.[1] All three countries feel themselves to be utterly dependent on Allied support, moral as well as material. The position of Finland is not comparable. Her economic life is already restarted. Her White Guards are

[1] Although a Baltic Confederation, to include Poland and Finland as well as the Baltic States, had been mooted at the beginning of the year, no progress had been made, because of the Polish-Lithuanian dispute. Indeed, for this reason no full meeting of the five countries was held until January 1920, when considerations outside the scope of this book helped to ensure that the concept would never come to fruition.

well armed and patrol the frontier by day and night, and she seems least in danger of Bolshevism within her own borders.

If the Allies desire (independence for the Baltic States) they must pursue it promptly. The first need is for a commission on the spot (to) assist the various Governments in their desire for combined action. (Since) Britain, through her sea power, holds the key to these countries, a strong British Commission should be appointed. Its best headquarters would probably be at Reval, which can be kept open during the winter by icebreakers. The Estonian Government is more ripe to receive help than either the Lithuanian or the Lettish. Russian officers are continually arriving in Reval with first hand information of internal affairs in Kronstadt, Petrograd and other parts of Russia, and Reval would form a useful starting point for an extension into Russia, if at any time political conditions made this possible and desirable.

From this one thing will be clear: when Cowan reached Reval in the *Caledon* on 25th April the situation was more satisfactory there than at Libau. It was nonetheless disquieting. Laidoner had so far been successful in defending his country, but he realised that, with the coming of spring, the northern end of his front could be turned by an amphibious landing. Of what avail Pitka's two destroyers and a gunboat, notwithstanding the strong fighting spirit of their crews, against Zelenoy's fleet when intelligence reports suggested that it had been increased to the *Petropavlovsk* and *Andrei Pervozvanni* " in the capacity of floating batteries " (as a Soviet historian puts it), the cruiser *Oleg* (and perhaps the *Rurik* and *Variag*), the destroyers *Azard, Gavriil, Konstantin* and *Svoboda*, eight more of older classes, the minelayer *Narova*, up to seven submarines and some twenty patrol craft, minesweepers and other miscellaneous vessels. Hence Pitka's visit to Libau, when Cowan had pledged his support, though the disparity between the force at his immediate disposal—two cruisers and half a dozen destroyers—and the Bolshevik Fleet, was sufficiently marked to be (in his own moderate words) " somewhat of an anxiety."[1]

---

[1] Cowan could not call on the few French warships in the Baltic because Brisson had tempered his desire to help with one reservation: " Admiral, I will

Indeed, he would have been foolhardy to have faced such odds if his ships had not possessed the advantage of some ten knots over all but the enemy destroyers; if he had not also realised the enemy's other weaknesses, in part traditional, in part the consequence of the Revolution, though these did not now include the excessive estimate of the strength of the British force that had marred their intelligence in December. All this discounted their paper strength and, for a fighter of Cowan's temperament, was enough for him to accept the risks involved, though he could expect reinforcements. The 6-inch gunned cruiser *Dragon* had arrived at Danzig to act as guardship, whence she could reach Reval in twenty-four hours, whilst six " V & W " class destroyers of the First Flotilla were on their way from Britain to relieve the smaller " S " boats. For the Admiralty had " reached the limit of its functions in pressing that more definite action on the part of our naval forces would be less irksome to carry out than the sort of tepid friendship we display by means of our Navy at present "; and the Cabinet had yielded to the need to increase the Baltic Force. This was not, however, to include heavy ships; the days had passed when Cowan could expect a battle squadron. Notwithstanding a strong plea from Madden, his Commander-in-Chief, the Admiralty decided that the danger from mines and submarine attack did not justify hazarding such valuable ships. It is difficult to recall another instance (prior to the Second World War when air power so greatly changed maritime operations) of a flag officer being required to contain enemy battleships with a force which did not include similar vessels.

*   *   *

do anything for you, but you must not ask me to fight the Russians." He knew that the sympathies of his crews for Bolshevik Russia were too strong: for this reason the French fleet sent to the Black Sea mutinied and had to be withdrawn, to the embarrassment of the French Government, whose policy was more anti-Red than the British.

First news of a possible Bolshevik move came on 30th April; Vacietis was expected to land troops in Papon Bay on 1st May. This was so far to the west of the front line as to be highly unlikely; nonetheless, Cowan took his force to sea. Finding nothing in the bay he steamed farther east but was deterred from approaching Kronstadt by the risk of floating ice damaging his cruisers' paravanes. A couple of days later the *Curacoa* arrived from England to relieve the *Caledon*, and on 7th May Cowan transferred his flag to her, taking Mackworth with him. On the 9th he went over to Helsingfors to congratulate Mannerheim on his country's formal declaration of independence. The Admiral was greatly impressed by " the handsomest foreigner I have ever met, very tall, gracefully built with beautifully made clothes," who was " confident that his country is purified of Bolshevism." Assured that Finland was not to be amongst his problems, Cowan left for a quick visit to Libau—Duff had not yet arrived—with fateful consequences. On the morning of 13th May, the *Curacoa* struck a mine some seventy miles west of Reval whilst steaming at twenty knots. The Admiral chanced to be in his bath at the time—characteristically a cold one. Leaping out, he hurried forward to the bridge wearing only an overcoat—until his coxswain could bring him a pair of trousers—to learn that the damage to his new flagship was confined to right aft where a number of compartments had been flooded. The casualties, moreover, amounted to no more than one rating killed and half a dozen officers injured. Since she could still steam at nine knots the *Curacoa*, unlike the luckless *Cassandra*, reached Reval some eight hours later.

Nonetheless, the incident had a serious implication; with only two cruisers at his immediate disposal, Cowan could ill afford to have one out of action. But he had no alternative to shifting his flag to the *Cleopatra* and, as soon as temporary repairs had been effected, to sail Mackworth's damaged ship to England. Nor did he wait for the *Dragon* to come north before giving the protection he had promised Laidoner for an

Estonian landing in Kaporia Bight designed to relieve Bolshevik pressure on the Narva front. On 13th May he took the *Cleopatra* and three destroyers to Seskar Island, from where he " maintained a constant watch on the bay whilst the Estonians were in contact with the Bolshevik troops, bombarding and pushing forward here and there and landing more men, under the direction of Admiral Pitka who has always shown a most correct instinct for war, both on land and sea." [1] The British ships were only thirty to forty miles from Kronstadt, sometimes at anchor, at others under way, but there was no activity by the Bolshevik Fleet until 17th May, when a great deal of smoke was observed over the harbour. This heralded a sortie by four minesweepers escorted by the destroyer *Gavriil*, commanded by an ex-Tsarist officer, V. Sevastyanov, who was under the watchful eye of a commissar, towards Kaporia Bight.

The *Gavriil* was sighted by the *Cleopatra* shortly after 0900 on the 18th when Cowan immediately ordered his flagship, together with the *Shakespeare*, *Scout* and *Walker*, to weigh. Within ten minutes these four ships were heading for the enemy, and half an hour later they opened fire at a range of 16,000 yards. Meanwhile Sevastyanov had ordered his minesweepers to return to Kronstadt at their best speed of ten knots whilst his own ship drew the British fire. The range was so great that the *Gavriil's* shots fell short of their target, but she sustained seventeen splinter hits before Cowan's ships came within half a mile of the Russian minefields protecting

---

[1] A less formal portrait of Pitka (also Cowan's) must be quoted: " He had only two speeds, full ahead and stop, and wasted a lot of (fuel) in the process. His two destroyers rather went to his head. Always clad in a thick greatcoat (Lord knows what he had on underneath), despite the fact that it is sometimes almost as hot in the Gulf of Finland as I have been in the Sudan, with a pistol strapped round his middle and generally clutching a loaf of our bread, he was quite a figure, and a very clever and fearless fighter. His tactics were to get as near to the enemy as he could and then fling his very mixed bag against their flank. He often got away with it, more especially if we were able to back it with some shelling." The prowess of this versatile warrior was subsequently recognised, on Cowan's recommendation, by the award of the K.C.M.G., a British honour which Laidoner also received.

Kronstadt, and under fire from the 6-inch guns of Grey Horse Battery. Since the Admiral could also see the *Petropavlovsk* and the *Oleg* under way outside Kronstadt, he did not feel justified in further pressing the pursuit. He manœuvred his force to seaward of the mined area whilst continuing to fire at the *Gavriil* until she drew out of range at 1030—or as a Soviet historian has it, " the courage of the crew and the skill of the commander of the *Gavriil* ensured success for the Soviet destroyer in this battle with superior enemy numbers." [1] There can be no doubt that in opening fire Cowan was complying with his orders: " a Bolshevik man-of-war operating off the coast of the Baltic Provinces must be assumed to be doing so with hostile intent and treated accordingly." Yet when the Parliamentary Secretary to the Admiralty [2] made a brief statement about the engagement in the House of Commons, he refused to reply to a Labour Member's question " whether the British ships had orders to fire on the Bolshevik ships." The Navy's reaction to this was expressed by the *Cleopatra*'s Navigating Officer: " I'd like to know what *he'd* have done if half a dozen craft flying enormous red flags fired on him! " In truth, the Government was too conscious of growing British opposition to Intervention, notably from the Labour Party, to do public justice to Cowan and those serving under him. " The Government's ' hush-hush ' policy with respect to the movements of our forces in Russia is causing no little irritation," wrote the *Naval and Military Record*, a journal by no means prone to support the Left—though persistent rumours that British troops were to be sent to Petrograd were emphatically denied. Nor was this to be the last occasion when the truth about the operations of the Baltic Force was sacrificed on the altar of political expediency. One of His Majesty's Ministers stated that the ships were only engaged on a normal " summer cruise " which, as will be seen, proved too much for the British sailors' sense of humour.

On the day following the *Gavriil*'s escape the *Dragon* joined

[1] *Baltiisky Flot.*   [2] Dr. Macnamara.

the watching British force which remained in the vicinity of
Seskar, except for one destroyer on patrol close to the Russian
minefields where she occasionally came under fire from Grey
Horse and Krasnaya Gorka.[1] This enabled Cowan to withdraw his flagship to Reval on the 23rd to meet reinforcements.
First to come was a submarine flotilla of " E," " H," and " L"
class boats with their depot ship, H.M.S. *Lucia*, under the
command of Captain Nasmith,[2] a submariner who had been
awarded the V.C. for his exploits in the Sea of Marmora.
Judging that submarines were the most effective weapon for
his purpose, Cowan immediately sent two to watch the
entrance to the swept channel into Petrograd Bay, so that he
could withdraw his ships from Seskar. Next to arrive were
the rest of the First Destroyer Flotilla headed by the *Wallace*,
Captain G. W. M. Campbell. Equally welcome were three
minesweepers, the *Banbury*, *Lanark* and *Hexham*, more especially
when the large fleet oiler *War Export* struggled into harbour
after striking a mine in the same field as that which had taken
toll of the *Cassandra*. These small vessels were quickly set to
work to clear the Red Route, the name by which the safe
track between Reval, Libau and Copenhagen was known
because it was so coloured on the ships' charts. The 24th
also brought another cruiser, the *Galatea*, whose passengers
included Lieutenant-General Sir Hubert Gough.

*　　　*　　　*

Cowan, who was convinced that the various forces fighting
against the Bolsheviks in the Baltic would only co-operate
effectively if they were placed under the unified command of
a British general, had done more than represent this to the
Admiralty. Early in April he wrote to the Chief of the
Imperial General Staff[3] who answered: " You want me to

---

[1] Whose guns were of 11-inch calibre (12-inch according to some authorities).

[2] Later Admiral Sir Martin Dunbar-Nasmith, Commander-in-Chief Western
Approaches early in the Second World War.

[3] Field-Marshal Sir Henry Wilson.

send a general to help in the Baltic States. ' Yes,' on one
condition—and that is that the Big Four lay down a broad
policy, otherwise ' No.' And since 22nd November of last
year I have been trying to get a policy—trying, trying, trying,
and with not a shadow of success." It was another month
before the Baltic Commission in Paris made up its mind. It
would not agree to a British general assuming command,
but it accepted Tallents's recommendation that strong Diplomatic and Military Missions should be sent, Gough being
appointed head of the latter. An Irishman from Tipperary,
a cavalry officer with a strong personality and a gay, boyish
charm of manner, his moral courage as well as his physical
bravery matched Cowan's. His career, too, had been unusual.
In 1914 he had led the " mutiny " at the Curragh; yet, when
war came, his promotion was so rapid that he attained command of the Fifth Army at the age of forty-six, and greatly
distinguished himself in many Western Front operations. But
his tactics at the Third Battle of Ypres (Passchendaele) in 1917
aroused such controversy that in March 1918 Lloyd George
was in no mood to appreciate the skilful way in which he
extricated the decimated remains of his force in the face of
a three-fold German superiority. Requiring a scapegoat for
the British failure to hold this enemy push, the Prime Minister
ordered Gough's recall. Cowan welcomed him as an old
friend who had " been through the furnace of undeserved
defeat," whom he hoped would have a further chance to
prove his prowess as a fighter. This was not to be—Gough
never received another active command—but the Admiral's
generosity was in marked contrast to the Government's; not
until 1936 was it admitted that the General had been the
victim of an injustice which must have been especially humiliating to a man whose father, brother, uncle and cousin had
all gained the V.C. Belatedly Gough was then created a
G.C.B.

Before leaving for the Baltic Gough received written
instructions from the C.I.G.S. He was required to report

how best the Allies could assist the Baltic States to defend themselves against the Bolsheviks and against German domination, and to advise the Provisional Governments on the organisation, training and equipment of their own forces and how they should be used against the Bolsheviks. He was to study the relations between the Estonians, Finns and Russians with special reference to the extent to which the Russian North-West Army could continue operations against the Bolsheviks, and its requirements in the way of arms, equipment and other stores. In Latvia and Lithuania he was to promote Allied influence, neutralising that of Germany, and to control the movements of the latter's troops with an eye to their ultimate withdrawal. He was also required to work in close collaboration with Tallents who returned to Reval at the end of May as head of a Diplomatic Mission under orders from the Foreign Office " to report upon the political situation in each of the Baltic Provinces and to co-ordinate the general line of policy to be followed in regard to them." For all this the General was provided with strong staffs, both for his own headquarters which he established at Helsingfors, and for his branch Missions in the other capitals which he frequently visited in the *Galatea*, placed by Cowan at his disposal for this purpose.[1]

The War Office's orders to Gough might be clear enough but those who briefed him before he left London held disparate views. Churchill, as Secretary of State for War, urged the need to smash Bolshevism by military action, even if this involved Allied Intervention on a major scale. From the distance of half a century it is easy to argue that Churchill was as right then, if in the climate of the time unrealistic, as he has so often been since in his attitude to Soviet Communism. But in 1919 his was almost a lone voice; he was never able to persuade the Cabinet to agree with him. When Gough visited

---

[1] Gough's staff included Captain C. W. Bruton as naval adviser, Colonel du Parquet, who headed a number of French officers, and Major-General Alfred Burt who will long be remembered by the Letts for his work in Riga.

the Foreign Office, Curzon stressed that he must ensure that Britain was not committed to sending an army to the Baltic. The General was thus placed in the invidious position of having to decide whether he should follow the policy of H.M. Government or urge the very different one advocated by the Minister to whom he was responsible. From all that we know of Gough we may be sure that he would have supported Churchill had he believed him to be right; but experience and discussions with Cowan and Tallents soon led him to accept Curzon's view. It is therefore the more to be regretted that, whilst Churchill bore him no grudge—he was indeed among the first to acknowledge the injustice he suffered in 1918 (" the strongest critic has been unable to find ground for censoring his conduct at the battle of 21st March " [1])—the Prime Minister was soon to be unfair to Gough again.

In his relations with the Whites, Gough was unfortunate from the day following his arrival at Reval. On 25th May, 1919, Yudenitch came over from Helsingfors intending to assume command of the Russian North-West Army in the field. Acting on Cowan's advice that the Estonians would not accept this, Gough compelled him to return to Finland. Next morning the *Cleopatra* escorted the *Galatea* to Helsingfors where, after salutes had been exchanged, Gough was received by the Regent. Mannerheim did not disguise his disappointment, even indignation, when the General dispelled the illusion that he had come to encourage a Finnish advance on Petrograd, and said that the Finns could expect no support from the Allies if they essayed such a campaign. The possibility that Mannerheim might, nonetheless, march into Russia was removed six weeks later when he was defeated in the first election for the office of President by the more pacific Staehlberg.

*　　　　*　　　　*

---

[1] *The World Crisis, 1911–1918.*

I (Cowan) left that evening (28th May) for Reval, bringing with me Professor (*sic*) Goode who informs me he is working for Military Intelligence, and Professor Cotter whom I also gathered to be a Secret Service agent. The presence of both these appeared to be distasteful to the Government of Finland, and inconvenient to our Consul at Helsingfors, which was my reason for granting them this passage.[1]

Next day Cowan received a report that Vacietis was about to make another attempt at a landing in Kaporia Bight covered by his fleet. This intelligence was confirmed that evening by *L16* which sighted the *Azard* escorting six minesweepers, with the distant support of the *Petropavlovsk*. The submarine's attack on the Red destroyer was unsuccessful, but the minesweeper *Kluz* was damaged by a bomb from an Estonian plane. To counter this move Cowan left Reval in the *Cleopatra* at 0500 on the 30th, accompanied by the *Dragon*, *Galatea*, *Wallace* and five more of Campbell's flotilla, arriving off Seskar at noon. There the ships anchored except for the *Walker* which joined *E27* and *L16* on patrol near the Russian mine barrage. The Bolsheviks reacted to this bait next morning by sending out the *Petropavlovsk* and the *Azard* accompanied by minesweepers.

Approaching the Shepelevsky Light the *Petropavlovsk* stopped engines while the *Azard* went past Kaporia Bight. Proceeding at 19 knots she sighted an enemy submarine on the surface and turned towards her, but the submarine dived. The *Azard* then sighted a destroyer proceeding south-east at slow speed. Closing her, the *Azard* opened fire at a range of 6 miles, but at this moment she was herself attacked by the enemy submarine which fired three torpedoes which passed close to her. The enemy destroyer having opened fire, rapidly closed the *Azard*. Simultaneously two more groups of enemy destroyers appeared from the north-west, one coming at full speed towards the *Azard*, the other turning to the east. Pursued by the enemy, the *Azard* altered course to the east, firing with her after guns. She was then again attacked by the submarine and turned to the north, after which she began to retire towards the *Petropavlovsk*, which opened fire with her 12-inch guns

---

[1] The reader will soon realise that there are special reasons for quoting this evidence of " cloak and dagger " activity.

at a range of 7 to 8 miles. The enemy destroyers, after closing to within 4 miles of the *Petropavlovsk*, turned away. When the *Azard* and the minesweepers rejoined the battleship, she increased speed and set course for Tolboukin Light. On passing Krasnaya Gorka the squadron was attacked by an enemy aircraft which dropped a bomb on the minesweeper *Zapal*.

This Soviet account,[1] though containing exaggerated accounts of the part played by *E27* and *L16*, is otherwise reasonably accurate. Cowan was sufficiently impressed by the *Petropavlovsk*'s " heavy and well-disciplined fire " to argue the need to take the Bolshevik's naval efficiency more seriously than hitherto, but the *Cleopatra*'s navigator made the damning comment: " Imagine one of our battleships running from a handful of light cruisers and destroyers." The British force was at anchor again by lunch-time when the Admiral held a council of war to discuss the best means of enticing Zelenoy's ships far enough out to bring them to action. " The Admiral is only too keen to fight them in open waters, but says he's not going playing about among shoals and minefields and risking losing a ship on one or the other with no adequate return. It's the old North Sea tactics on a small scale." This reference to the First World War is understandable, but its accuracy questionable. The Kaiser required his admirals to present the threat of a " fleet in being " which accordingly avoided action with the Grand Fleet (except by miscalculation on 31st May, 1916). The Tsar's admirals held back their Baltic Fleet for the defence of Petrograd, a strategic concept which the Bolshevik Navy inherited—and which, incidentally, their successors followed in the Second World War.

The immediate result of this conference was a decision that, with the exception of the submarines and their depot ship, the British force should establish a base farther to the east from which it could more rapidly counter any Bolshevik sortie. Cowan chose Biorko Sound, a large anchorage on the Finnish coast, much too reminiscent of Scapa Flow to be

---

[1] From *Piat Let Krasnogo Flota*.

popular with officers and men, but admirably situated within twenty miles of the northern end of the mine barrage. As a prelude to implementing this, the Admiral took his force back to Reval on 1st June where he received news from Laidoner and Pitka which suggested that the Bolshevik Fleet would soon be more active than hitherto. Since Tallents's visit in April the Russian North-West Army had been increased to some 16,000 men, largely by Red desertions; a whole regiment complete with band had changed sides. Encouraged by this, General Rodzianko,[1] their commander in the field, was planning an early advance on Petrograd, notwithstanding the strength of Vacietis's army, some 50,000 men, one-third of them Lettish and Estonian sympathisers: he believed these to be inefficient and expected more desertions. The Estonians had agreed to give this move passive support such as the use of Reval and Narva as bases; but their army, together with the various volunteer units and the Lettish detachments working with them, would only be used to help Latvia to free herself from the Bolsheviks, and to thwart Goltz's aggressive intentions which now went further than conquest of Estonia; he hoped that he might link up with Rodzianko, thereby extending his future Baltic " empire " so far as Petrograd. Whilst understanding the Estonian attitude, Gough arranged Allied support for the Russian advance to the extent of providing liaison officers at Rodzianko's headquarters as well as supplying him with arms direct instead of through the Estonian authorities.

There was, though Cowan could not know it, a further reason why the Red Fleet was likely to be more active. The Bolsheviks were seriously concerned about the situation on the Narva front: according to a Soviet source:

Under enemy thrusts, the troops of the Seventh Army were streaming back to Petrograd. The supporters of Trotsky devised a plan for evacuating Petrograd and destroying the Baltic Fleet;

[1] Who at a later date was to be better known in Britain as a horseman and show jumper.

but the leadership of the defence of Petrograd was taken over by the Soviet of Workers and Peasants for Defence, under the direction of Lenin and, thanks to the measures which they adopted, Petrograd was soon prepared for defence. Reserve regiments were formed from the workers. Enemies and traitors at the H.Q. of the Seventh Army and in other military organisations were ruthlessly annihilated. In view of the importance of the defence of the sea approaches to Petrograd, the Soviet Command paid special attention to strengthening the Baltic Fleet. At the end of May the agent of the Council for the Defence of the Republic, Stalin, arrived at Kronstadt. The Commandant of the fortress and the Chief of the Naval Base were placed under the command of the Revolutionary War Soviet of the Baltic Fleet, and the maritime sector of the Front was placed under the Commandant of the fortress. The Fleet's responsibility for the defence of Petrograd was thus increased. At the same time political workers were assigned to the ships, their crews checked, and the hostile and corrupt elements expelled and replaced by fresh men.

Through Gough, Cowan quickly obtained the Finnish Government's agreement to his proposed use of Biorko; indeed, they placed their own torpedoboats and minesweepers based there at his disposal. And on 2nd June he sailed the *Vivacious* and *Voyager* to watch the approaches to Petrograd Bay in case the Bolsheviks should attempt to forestall his arrival by mining Biorko Sound. *En route* these two destroyers sighted the *Azard* and *Gavriil* and engaged them across the barrage. On the afternoon of the 4th the *Versatile, Vivacious* and *Walker* had a further brief engagement with these Bolshevik vessels which were afforded distant support by the *Petropavlovsk*—as always, from well behind the barrage. Though this action was as ineffective as before, it was followed by a disaster. Soon after the destroyers ceased fire, one of the two submarines on patrol, *L55*, Lieutenant-Commander C. M. S. Chapman, attempted a torpedo attack. This was not only unsuccessful but the boat broke surface and, before Chapman could submerge again, the *Gavriil* obtained a hit which holed the pressure hull. The *L55* then sank with the loss of all hands, though it was some days before Cowan and Nasmith accepted that she was

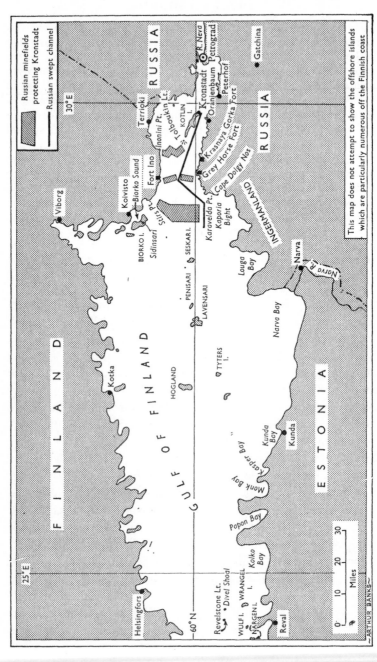

The Gulf of Finland in 1918-1920

missing, when they supposed she must have strayed into a minefield.[1]

Cowan reached Biorko on 5th June, 1919, where he established an observation post in Stirs Point Lighthouse to give immediate warning of any Russian movement out of Kronstadt. As a further precaution against surprise attack he anchored three destroyers to seaward with steam at five minutes' notice. Nonetheless, on the evening of 9th June, a "white night" in these waters, the *Azard* and *Gavriil* left Kronstadt without being observed and approached within gun range of the *Versatile*, *Vivacious* and *Walrus*, opening fire on them at 2200. These three British vessels immediately slipped their cables and returned the enemy fire, whilst Cowan brought his other ships out in support. But the Bolsheviks, after firing some eighty rounds without effect, retired behind their minefields. Cowan's reaction to this aggressive move, which might have done serious damage to one or more of his ships, was expressed in a letter to the Admiralty.

Owing to the minefields, and the fact that I have only light forces, (my) chances of offensive action are limited; and as I have no means of carrying the war into (enemy) country and harassing them at their anchorage, the initiative remains with them. My force has to remain at short notice (for steam) as we have no defended base to retire to; and if I did not keep a constant and close watch up to the edge of their minefields, the Estonian left flank would be uncovered; also there would be further mine-laying in the Gulf of Finland. The remedy for this is amongst the following: (a) Long range monitors, (b) Coastal motor boats, (c) Torpedo and bomb-carrying aeroplanes, (d) Minelaying. These would interfere with and confine the enemy's activities, and would not, as at present, leave him quite undisturbed to observe us and prepare plans for breaking out and possibly bombarding and devastating both shores of the Gulf, and thereby assisting the Prussian invasion of the Baltic which is now in full swing. Their Lordships' information regarding the state and efficiency of the Bolshevik ships may be better than mine, but owing to the disparity of gun power and range between us, we cannot afford to

[1] In 1928–31 the Soviet Navy salvaged and repaired the *L55* which was then added to their fleet.

assume they will be content to allow us to contain them all through the summer, unless their ardour is cooled and their plans interrupted by offensive action on our part, or an effective minefield is laid to keep them in.

The Admiralty replied:

The difficult position in which you are placed is thoroughly realised but cannot be avoided so long as the present policy of the Government remains in force. This precludes offensive action against Kronstadt by monitors, coastal motor boats or bombing aeroplanes. Torpedo carrying aeroplanes could not be used against ships at Kronstadt as the torpedoes cannot be dropped in less than 10 fathoms. It is hoped that the mines now being sent will render the situation more favourable. In the meantime it must be realised that any departure from the policy laid down may seriously embarrass the Government. The unsound nature of the situation is being again placed before the Cabinet.

The one crumb of consolation which this contained, Cowan already knew; that at the end of the month the *Princess Margaret* would return to the Baltic, this time to fulfil her minelaying role. And she would be accompanied by the Twentieth Destroyer Flotilla, equipped for the same purpose, led by the *Abdiel*, commanded by one of the Navy's more colourful characters, Captain Berwick Curtis,[1] who was to many something of a pirate. Fortunately for the Admiral's peace of mind, he was soon to learn that the Cabinet's reaction to " the unsound nature of the situation " would be more vigorous than his previous experience of Whitehall's attitude could lead him to expect.

*   *   *

Now to appease the reader whose interest has been titillated by a brief reference to the British Secret Service. Normally, public interest in this organisation has to be satisfied with the " startling revelations " of our Sunday newspapers and the

[1] Later Vice-Admiral Berwick Curtis.

exploits of fictional characters ranging from the reasonable—
Somerset Maugham's Ashenden is the classic example—to the
outrageous, notably Ian Fleming's James Bond. To this rule
there has, however, been one significant twentieth-century
exception. In the absence of all normal channels for information from Bolshevik Russia, British Agent S.T.25, otherwise
Paul Dukes, had been sent to Petrograd to acquire intelligence
and there, disguised as a workman, soldier or member of the
Cheka, he carried his life in his hands for eighteen months.[1]
For this he was subsequently knighted and allowed to publish
much about his experiences. Hence we know that, whilst for
a long time his couriers were able to leave by way of the
Finnish frontier, and sometimes to return to Petrograd, so
many were being captured by the spring of 1918 that Whitehall
decided to open a new route. Two of the smaller type of
C.M.B.—forty-foot motorboats of such shallow draught that
minefields presented no obstacle, and capable of a speed of
thirty-five knots—each with a crew of two officers and a chief
motor mechanic, commanded by Lieutenant Augustus Agar,[2]
were shipped to Hango. Disguised as Agent S.T.34, Agar
contacted Agents S.T.30 and S.T.31 at Helsingfors and
arranged to operate from Terrioki, a village near the Finnish
frontier some thirty miles east of Biorko and only about
twenty-five miles by sea from Petrograd. From this headquarters of the quondam Petersburg Imperial Yacht Club,
Agar intended:

to cross the line of forts in one of my boats shortly after midnight
at slow speed: once through, to push on at full speed to the mouth
of the Neva, when speed would be reduced again until we arrived
at a pre-arranged spot. We carried a small rowing " pram " on
board, which we launched and either brought off an agent or took
one ashore. The return journey was made early in the morning,
usually at daylight under the Red Flag and a special pendant only

[1] It was through Dukes that the Admiralty obtained, early in 1919, details
of the minefields protecting Kronstadt, which were of great value to Cowan.
[2] Later Captain Augustus Agar.

flown by commissars. After passing the forts, course was shaped towards Tolboukin Lighthouse to divert suspicion, and, when out of sight, again north and back to our base. In all, thirteen trips were made and only twice were we challenged and came under fire.[1]

With the details of most of these trips we are not concerned; they were not normal naval operations and Captain Agar has published his own story. He was, however, also to be of material assistance to Cowan. Having decided to use Terrioki he had to get his boats there from Hango. To attempt the inshore route might excite undesirable speculation amongst the Finns who saw the boats pass. A British destroyer in Helsingfors harbour suggested a better solution: Agar visited Cowan from whom he achieved more than the *Voyager* to tow both C.M.B.s round to Biorko. The Admiral's quick mind jumped at the possibility that the boats might serve a more lethal purpose than courier trips: he instructed Nasmith to send torpedoes from the *Lucia* to arm those tiny craft. With these shipped in their troughs, *C.M.B.s 4* and *7* made the short passage round to Terrioki under their own power, giving Fort Ino, the largest fortress on the northern shore of Petrograd Bay, a wide berth to avoid arousing the interest of its Finnish garrison.

On 13th June, 1919, the garrison of Krasnaya Gorka, the principal fortress on the southern side of the Bay, and its satellite, Grey Horse Battery, were encouraged by news of Rodzianko's advance to revolt against the Red régime.[2] Bolshevik troops succeeded in recapturing these strongholds next day, but were soon obliged to retire before an Estonian Ingermanland force. Laidoner could not hold back troops recruited from the Narva region when their help was so clearly

---

[1] From a lecture given by (then) Commander Agar at the Royal United Service Institution on 15th February, 1928.

[2] According to Paul Dukes, the commander of Krasnaya Gorka was obliged to initiate this premature revolt in order to forestall his arrest on suspicion that he was planning a rising intended to take place simultaneously with a revolt by the Kronstadt garrison.

needed by a garrison which included many men from the same area. To quote a Soviet source, they " created a serious situation on the right flank of the Petrograd front. Kronstadt with its forts, and all the rear points of the Soviet front fell under the fire of Krasnaya Gorka's guns. The rebellion had to be suppressed as quickly as possible," for fear that it would lead to the fall of Kronstadt which in the hands of the Allies would be a veritable " pistol pointed at the heart of Communism." On the 16th Zelenoy ordered his ships to bombard this recalcitrant fortress from behind the minefields where he supposed they could not be reached by Cowan's force.

He counted without Agar. Observing the activities of the *Petropavlovsk* and *Andrei Pervozvanni* [1] during his first two successful courier trips, " the temptation to steal out and attack (them) with our two torpedoes was hard to resist." A quick visit to Biorko resulted in an urgent signal to Whitehall. The reply gave a man of Cowan's fighting spirit and moral courage all the discretion that he required: " Boats to be used for Intelligence purposes only unless specially directed by Flag Officer." To Agar " the Admiral said he couldn't direct me to attack but if I did I could count on his support. I left at once! " And that same night, 16th June, *C.M.B.*s *4* and *7* sailed from Terrioki flying the White Ensign, their crews dressed in naval uniform instead of civilian guise. But ill-luck befell *No. 7* in the first half-hour: she struck a submerged obstruction and broke her propeller shaft, leaving Agar no alternative except to abandon his enterprise and tow her back to harbour. Next morning, to his chagrin, the two battleships he had hoped to attack returned to Kronstadt. They were, however, replaced by the *Oleg*, commanded by N. Milashevich, which resumed the bombardment of Krasnaya Gorka. Since

[1] This pre-dreadnought was commanded by the ex-Tsarist officer L. M. Galler who later rose to the rank of Admiral of the Fleet and served as Chief of Staff to the Commander-in-Chief of the Soviet Fleet in the Second World War, when he was sentenced to ten years' imprisonment for being too co-operative with the Soviet Union's Western Allies.

it would be several days before *C.M.B. 7* could be repaired at Helsingfors, Agar decided to attempt an attack on this cruiser himself that night in *No. 4*, manned by Sub-Lieutenant J. Hampsheir, R.N.R., and Chief Motor Mechanic M. Beeley, R.N.V.R. " Arriving off Tolboukin Lighthouse we could distinguish quite clearly the destroyer screen through which we had to pass before reaching a position from which to discharge our torpedo. I throttled down to slow and crept ahead as we passed close to two destroyers. I could see (their) black hulls and waited for the gun flashes. We were a ' dead sitter ' but, luckily for us, remained unseen," whilst Hampsheir and Beeley reloaded the torpedo's discharge cartridge which had been accidentally fired. " Finally the job was done though the waiting seemed endless and nerve-racking. Again I put on more speed and we were soon through the screen and in position. I fired our torpedo at the *Oleg* as if it were an ordinary practice run. (Then) I turned and made towards the Estonian coast hoping to mislead the enemy as to where we had come from. Within a minute there was a thick column of smoke from the *Oleg*. Flashes came from all directions, the forts, the destroyers, the ship itself, which were followed by splashes as the shells threw up columns of water soaking us to the skin. We were not far from Krasnaya Gorka when we turned north towards the Finnish shore at 35 knots," to reach Terrioki shortly after 0300. " The whole operation had occupied less than four hours." [1] The *Oleg* sank in twelve minutes, albeit with the surprisingly small loss of only five men, and a couple of days later Agar flew over the scene in a Finnish plane and had the satisfaction of spotting his victim lying on her side on the bottom. A delighted Cowan pressed the Admiralty to recognise this exploit as quickly as possible. The award of the Victoria Cross to Agar " for conspicuous gallantry, coolness and skill in penetrating a destroyer screen, remaining in close proximity to the enemy for twenty minutes

---

[1] The quotations in this paragraph are from Captain Agar's *Footprints in the Sea*.

126

whilst his torpedo was repaired and then successfully completing an exceptionally difficult operation in far from ideal weather conditions, finally escaping notwithstanding heavy fire from enemy warships and forts," was announced a month later. Hampsheir was awarded the D.S.O. and Beeley the C.G.M.

Unfortunately, the sinking of the *Oleg* was followed by news which deprived Agar of the opportunity of an attack on the other Bolshevik ships employed bombarding Krasnaya Gorka. The Russian North-West Army refused to advance to help the Estonian Ingermanland troops, who were too few to enable the garrison to resist a further Bolshevik assault upon a fortress short of supplies, and breached by the gunfire of ships that had been able to bombard from positions in Petrograd Bay which the fort's guns had not been intended to cover. The Red Flag again replaced the White over both Krasnaya Gorka and Grey Horse.

*   *   *

Whilst Agar reverted to his courier trips, Cowan was confronted with a new danger; the Admiralty warned him that Germany might refuse to sign the Peace Treaty and renew hostilities. Even if she did not occupy Reval, it would then become untenable as a British base. Since the Armistice terms had allowed Germany to retain eight dreadnoughts, Cowan's ships might have to fight their way out of the Baltic against a much superior force. One cannot doubt that under the Admiral's leadership they would have done so with distinction to the Service. But for all his fighting spirit, he was not foolhardy: " by God's grace," he wrote, " this eventuality did not arise." The truculence of the Weimar Government turned out to be little more than bluff: after a final delay of forty-eight hours the Versailles Treaty was signed on 28th June, 1919, and Cowan was no longer required to cast anxious glances over his shoulder. He also received reinforcements in the shape of four more cruisers. Whilst the *Danae*, *Dauntless* and *Caledon* joined Duff, as we shall see in the next chapter, the *Delhi*, to which Mackworth had transferred from the damaged *Curacoa*, came to Biorko on the 25th when Cowan shifted his flag to her. " I have been very happy in *Cleopatra*," he signalled Little, " and am most grateful for the backing and help everyone has given me, and I hope she will take me back, should I again have to change ships in the Baltic." The Admiral was not, however, to suffer this inconvenience, since the Admiralty realised that, so long as they put their trust in him, they would have to exempt his flagship from the rule limiting the time served in the Baltic by ships from the Atlantic Fleet to periods of six to eight weeks.[1]

Cowan next employed his ships to bombard the Bolshevik front where it reached the southern shore of the Gulf, though he had serious doubts whether the expenditure of ammunition was justified. Rodzianko's jealousy of the Ingermanlanders' advance to the support of Krasnaya Gorka had led him to disarm the remainder of this regiment on the pretext that they planned to establish a republic of their own—this at a time when the White Russian troops were themselves unable to hold the Bolsheviks so that they were being pressed back instead of advancing on Petrograd. The arrival of a number of ships at Reval carrying supplies for the relief of the Tsarist capital was, therefore, somewhat premature. This contrast with the tardy way in which supplies were provided for Estonia and Latvia earlier in the year highlights the Allies' readiness to support White Russia as opposed to their equivocal attitude towards the Baltic States. The Peace Conference had recently declined to settle the future of these in the face of a declaration by Kolchak, who had been formally recognised as

---

[1] To the original reasons for this rule, notably the arduous nature of service in the Baltic, had been added the undesirability of subjecting ships' companies to Bolshevik propaganda for too long. This Whitehall view made no allowance for what the men on the spot saw and heard of conditions under the Red régime, which were quite enough to deter them from being tainted by Communism.

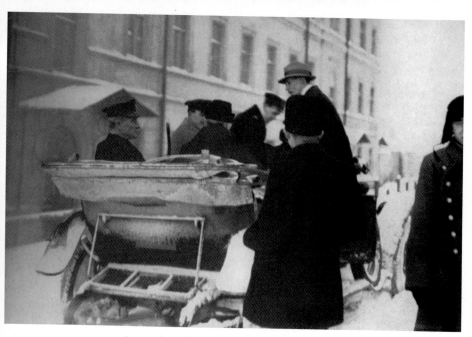

Rear-Admiral E. Alexander-Sinclair *(on left)*,
Commander of the British Baltic Force in 1918, on shore at Reval

The Bolshevik destroyer *Afrotil* flying the White Ensign after
surrendering to the British Baltic Force off Reval in December 1918

Typical of the British light cruisers employed in the Baltic, H.M.S *Caradoc* of 4,120 tons, armed with five 6-inch guns. In background H.M.S. *Princess Margaret* equipped to lay 400 mines

The Bolshevik battleship *Andrei Pervozvanni* of 17,680 tons, armed with four 12-inch and fourteen 8-inch guns

Commander-in-Chief of the
Bolshevik Baltic Fleet in 1919,
A.P. Zelenoy

Captain of the battleship
Andrei Pervozvanni in 1919,
L.M. Galler

First Baronet of the Baltic:
Admiral Sir Walter Cowan, K.C.B., D.S.O. and bar, M.V.O.

General Sir Hubert Gough,
G.C.B., G.C.M.G., K.C.V.O.,
head of the Allied Military
Mission to the Baltic States
in 1919

Admiral Juhan Pitka, K.C.M.G.,
who commanded the Estonian
naval forces in 1919

Royal Air Force planes on Koivisto airfield

The British aircraft carrier *Vindictive* in 1919. Displacing 9,750 tons
and armed with four 7.5-inch guns, she carried twelve planes

Liberator of Finland: Baron Carl
Gustav Mannerheim with his staff

Prime Minister of Latvia in 1919:
Karlis Ulmanis

The German Commander-in-Chief in Latvia,
Major-General Rudiger von der Goltz

Leader of the Twentieth Destroyer Flotilla; H.M.S. *Abdiel* with
painted canvas screens concealing her load of 72 mines

The British submarine *L55* in dock at Kronstadt: sunk by Bolshevik
destroyers in June 1919, she was later salvaged by the Soviet Navy

The Russian cruiser *Oleg* entering Portsmouth Harbour before the
First World War: of 6,650 tons, she was armed with
twelve 6-inch guns

The exploit for which Lieutenant Agar gained the Victoria Cross:
the *Oleg* after being torpedoed by *C.M.B.4* in June 1919

The Bolshevik depot ship *Pamyat Azova* in Kronstadt
Harbour after the British raid in August 1919

Three of the 55-ft. C.M.B.s which attacked Kronstadt
lying in Biorko Sound

The British monitor *Erebus* armed with two 15-inch guns

Three of the six British tanks supplied to the White
Russian North-West Army being unloaded at Reval

The Bolshevik dreadnought *Petropavlovsk* of 23,370 tons,
armed with twelve 12-inch guns

Winter in the Baltic: the quarterdeck of a British light cruiser

"Supreme Ruler of Russia," that his Siberian Government would accept nothing short of a reunited Russia. Although the Allies' attitude was disappointing to Pats and Ulmanis, and discouraging to their armies, their (the Allies') support for Kolchak and Denikin was of considerable indirect help to the Baltic States. As Churchill expressed it on 29th July, "but for these (White Russian) armies drawing off two-thirds of the Bolshevik forces, such pressure might have been brought to bear on the small States created on the Eastern frontier of Europe as would have led to their collapse."

Of more immediate urgency the British Cabinet had to contend with the Admiralty's representations about the insecurity of Cowan's position and the possible inability of his ships to contain an enemy force of which Stalin wrote on 8th July:

It is a subject for congratulation that the Baltic Fleet, which was believed to be non-existent, is being most effectively regenerated. Equally gratifying is the fact that the scourge of venality with which a section of the Russian officer class is afflicted has contaminated the commanding personnel of the Navy least of all. Here we have men who prize the dignity and independence of Russia higher than British gold. Even more gratifying is the fact that the Baltic sailors have become their old selves again, and by their valorous deeds have revived the finest traditions of the Russian Revolutionary Navy.[1]

Minefields laid by the *Princess Margaret* and the Twentieth Destroyer Flotilla, which reached Reval at the end of June, would go some way towards limiting Bolshevik naval activity; but these would not be enough when the Whites advanced on Petrograd, carrying the front to the east of the fields protecting Kronstadt. Cowan had broadcast appeals to the Red ships to leave this fortress base and hoist the White Flag but with no significant success: only the unarmed patrol vessel *Kitoboi* [2] had done so on 14th June, and no other vessel followed her

[1] Stalin, *Works*, Volume IV.
[2] Her captain joined the Estonians and in September was unfortunately captured by the Bolsheviks who promptly crucified him.

example. Lloyd George and his colleagues were therefore reluctantly—except for Churchill—compelled to lift the ban on offensive action and authorise the dispatch of further reinforcements. Cowan was given an adequate number of minesweepers, the First Fleet Sweeping Flotilla reaching Biorko on 16th July, 1919, for hazardous clearance operations which cost the loss of the *Myrtle*, and of the *Gentian* which went to her help, and ten lives. Then came H.M.S. *Vindictive*, commanded by Captain " Dasher " Grace, son of the legendary " W. G." of cricketing fame. This heavy cruiser of the new " Hawkins " class, armed with four 7.5-inch guns, had been partially converted whilst building into an aircraft carrier. Her twelve machines included Griffins, Sopwith Camels and One and a Half Strutters and Short seaplanes under the command of the enthusiastic Major David Donald,[1] Royal Air Force.[2]

The Admiral's desire to initiate air operations suffered an initial setback. On 6th July the *Vindictive*'s officers misunderstood the leading marks for a safe course into Reval, with the result that their ship grounded on a shoal where she stuck fast. Ammunition and fuel had to be disembarked and some of her guns hoisted out to lighten her by some 2000 tons before, with the assistance of camels from Helsingfors, the combined labours of the *Delhi*, *Cleopatra* and three tugs succeeded in towing her off eight days later, " with the God-sent help of a sudden westerly wind which caused an unusual rise of water of about 8 inches." [3] Fortunately the *Vindictive* suffered no appreciable damage and was able to proceed to Biorko where Cowan had already started preparations for her aircraft, and his own flagship's Camel, to work from extemporised shore bases, a 300-yard landing strip for wheeled planes

---

[1] Later Air Marshal Sir David Donald.

[2] The new Service, formed in April 1918, had yet to introduce its own ranks for its officers.

[3] Cowan's words. Minefields apart, navigation in the Baltic was often so hazardous that he was fortunate not to lose any of his ships by grounding. The number of occasions on which his destroyers and submarines touched ground but were quickly got off are too numerous for individual mention in this narrative (*but see Appendix A*).

cleared of virgin forest and granite rocks at Koivisto, and sea-
plane moorings laid off Sidinsari. Having been required to
send the *Dragon* and *Dauntless* back to England, he feared he
might also lose his aircraft-carrier. His apprehension was
unfounded; the *Vindictive* was not required to go farther than
Copenhagen to embark replacement aircraft and stores ferried
so far in H.M.S. *Argus*. But the Admiralty was slow to send
out the oilers and store ships needed by Cowan's growing
force: he was often worried about his fuel supply, whilst the
failure to provide other stores in adequate quantities to meet
the needs of officers and men who had few contacts with civilisation was to have an adverse effect upon their morale.

On 12th July the Admiral had to send the *Abdiel* and five
of her flotilla back to Harwich after laying their first minefield,
but he did this with little reluctance. Agar's attack on the
Oleg had strengthened his belief that C.M.B.s would be the
most effective weapon for use against Bolshevik ships which
declined to be drawn beyond their protective mine barrier.
And when the Admiralty agreed to provide him with a flotilla
of eight of the larger fifty-five-foot craft, commanded by
Commander C. C. Dobson, Curtis went home to tow them
out from their base at Osea Island.[1] Bad weather in the
North Sea sank one boat, but though the tows of the others
broke sixteen times, they managed to reach Biorko on 30th
July where the *Vindictive* became their depot ship. Curtis's
flotilla then resumed their proper task of helping the *Princess
Margaret* to lay minefields designed to restrict enemy sorties,
thereby making the British base secure against a repetition of
the attack on 9th June. This form of protection could not,
however, be effective against submarine attack.

The first of this type of Bolshevik sortie was made by the
Volk on 10th July, but engine trouble obliged her to return to
Kronstadt twenty-four hours later.

The *Pantera* was the next, leaving Kronstadt on the night of
23rd/24th July to attack any enemy ships in Kaporia Bight. (There,

[1] Near Clacton, Essex.

next morning,) a submarine was sighted ahead. Shortly afterwards another submarine was seen. The Captain of the *Pantera* (*A. N. Bakhtin*) kept up-sun to conceal his presence. Seeing that the enemy boats remained on the surface, the *Pantera* closed to half a mile, and fired her starboard stern torpedo at the more distant boat, then turned and fired the port one at the other submarine. Watching through his periscope, the Captain of the *Pantera* saw the first boat get under way and proceed to the south-east, but the second remained stopped. So he started turning to attack her again. Having closed to within 4 cables, the *Pantera* fired both her forward torpedoes, then proceeded towards deep water. The torpedoes ran true, but the enemy boat began to turn and they passed on either side of her. Shortly after firing the second salvo, a torpedo passed along the *Pantera*'s side, apparently fired by the boat which had been attacked. The *Pantera*, to avoid pursuit by an enemy destroyer, returned to Kronstadt.[1]

The British submarine which avoided the *Pantera*'s three torpedoes was the *E40*; the destroyer which attempted a retaliatory depth charge attack was the *Watchman*. As a result of this incident Cowan asked the Admiralty to send out net defences for Biorko, and destroyers fitted with hydrophones. But before these could arrive:

On 27th July the (submarine) *Vyepr* sailed from Kronstadt for Kaporia Bight. (Next morning) a minesweeper and a large destroyer were sighted and attacked without success. Shortly afterwards another British destroyer appeared from the north and, when the *Vyepr* succeeded in again getting within attacking distance of the first destroyer, one of them opened fire on her. The explosion of one depth charge put out the submarine's lights and caused so much other damage that the boat was unable to maintain her depth. But having succeeded in escaping the attack, the crew set about repairing the damage, and set course for Kronstadt which she reached two hours later, although water was beginning to enter the forward hatch and flood the batteries.[2]

The British destroyers involved were the *Valorous* and *Vancouver*. The submarine *L12* also sighted the *Vyepr* but could not manage an attack. The damage already done was,

[1] *Piat Let Krasnogo Flota.*   [2] Ibid.

however, enough to deter further Bolshevik submarine activity for more than a month.[1]

By the end of July Cowan's force, which had been reinforced by half the Third Destroyer Flotilla, was working round the clock. Whilst the ships did all that they could do to contain the Bolshevik fleet by laying minefields, and by maintaining destroyer and submarine patrols, with cruisers (now the *Delhi, Danae, Cleopatra*—and the *Galatea* when not required by Gough) lying at short notice in Biorko ready to support them, they also helped to stem the Bolshevik thrust towards Narva by bombarding the enemy's rear. They were required, too, to carry out more mundane missions, such as ferrying troops, whilst the minesweepers performed their task of making safer the routes through the Russian and German minefields which the British ships required to use. (Despite all this activity, recreation was not forgotten: a successful regatta was held in Biorko on 31st July where the weather was admirable for bathing picnics.) Donald's planes were doing as much at greater hazard by bombing Kronstadt, preventing enemy machines from being too attentive to Kaporia Bight and searching for enemy submarines. They were also carrying out reconnaissance flights and taking photographs to help Cowan with his plans for achieving what must always be a naval commander's main aim, destruction of the enemy battle fleet. Meanwhile, though he had doubts about the advisability of allowing the Kronstadt garrison to be subjected to air attacks, which could only have limited results, before he was ready to carry out a major assault by sea and air on the Bolshevik base, Cowan directed Donald to make the depot ship *Pamyat Azova* and any submarines berthed on her the target for the first of the raids which his planes now began in order (to quote a Soviet source) " to disable the ships and their guns and break down the morale of the Baltic sailors."

---

[1] According to some sources the submarine *Ersh* also made a sortie in which she was sunk by British warships but this does not appear to be confirmed by either British or Soviet records.

On 30th July, 1919, in Operation "DB," so christened by Cowan after his hero David Beatty, two raids were carried out between 0200 and 0400 when, as shore facilities were not complete, the planes took off from the *Vindictive*. Because the wind speed was only twenty-five knots, her forward flight deck was given a wooden extension to provide a safe take-off run of 115 feet. Nine machines carried out the first attack, dropping thirteen bombs, and three the second, dropping three bombs. The subsequent report of Second Lieutenant Chandler, observer in a Short seaplane, is typical of those who took part.

The objective, having two white awnings, presented a very good target. Both bombs were dropped with a two second interval. The first hit the after part of the ship which was observed to be on fire; the second dropped in the foundry near the oil tanks. Besides our own, two bursts were observed in the water close to the wall near the eastern end of the foundry and two in the water on the north shore of Kronstadt. Smoke was observed coming from the dry docks to the eastward of the foundry, and from the foundry. All ships in harbour appeared to have steam up. One light cruiser and one destroyer proceeded out of the harbour but remained in the vicinity of the entrance. A.A. fire was encountered when about 4 miles to the northward of Kronstadt from Fort Alexander, and then from practically every battery and ship in harbour, the *Petropavlovsk* and *Andrei Pervozvanni* apparently using guns of heavy calibre.

Donald summarised the results: " It would appear certain that two bombs (were) dropped on (the *Pamyat Azova*),[1] one on the shed nearest the oil tanks and one on the vessel in the dry dock next to that containing the submarine. Two large fires were started. The A.A. fire was very effective throughout," because the Bolsheviks had obtained prior warning of the raid. To quote one of the *Wallace*'s officers: " No less than three people in Koivisto were rung up by telephone during the (previous) afternoon and asked in broken English when the English aeroplanes were coming."

[1] In fact the ship struck was the tanker *Tatiana* in which one man was killed.

This raid and those that followed it were, however, of little more than nuisance value, for all the courage and determination shown by this squadron of the newly-fledged Royal Air Force. As Cowan realised, their bombs were too small—the largest weighed only 112 lb.—to do any important damage except by some fortuitous chance. They did, however, require Zelenoy to dissipate his resources in " a systematic defence by ships and shore A.A. weapons which compelled the enemy aircraft to remain at a great height and noticeably affected the accuracy of the bombing " [1]—though it did not stop them descending to attack exposed personnel with their machine-guns and to drop propaganda leaflets. But the Bolsheviks' own planes, twelve of various types operating from Oraniem-baum and Peterhof—the British inevitably gave them such nicknames as " Ivan the Terrible " and " Alexander the Awful "—which made a fair number of sorties, chiefly against the ships in Kaporia Bight, were less effective, even though Donald's aircraft, when sent up to thwart these attacks, never arrived in time. The latter had, however, the satisfaction of shooting down Krasnaya Gorka's observation balloon, thereby reducing the effectiveness of the fortress's guns when they fired into Kaporia Bight.

Ashore, the Bolshevik thrust obliged the Russians to allow Laidoner to rearm his Ingermanlanders so that they could effectively defend the Narva flank. Moreover, since Goltz's threat to Estonia had been lifted in circumstances to be related in the next chapter, Pats authorised Laidoner to advance on Petrograd, provided the Whites accepted, and the Allies recognised, Estonia's independence. This was, however, too much to expect of Yudenitch who, rather than allow an Eston-ian advance, refused to order Rodzianko to move forward. Gough laboured to resolve this impasse, though Cowan had his own strong doubts about the capacity of the North-West Army to achieve its aim. They had not yet received sufficient supplies which were slower in reaching Reval than the ships

[1] p. 132 ni., op. cit.

prematurely sent to relieve the starving population of Petrograd. And their morale was poor: their " generals complain of the lack of officers, who appear to be everywhere but with the army in the field. Reval, Libau, Copenhagen, Helsingfors and Stockholm are full of them and there is endless unworthy intrigue going on, much of it with the Germans"—with whose activities in Latvia subsequent to 1st June we must now return.

Chapter Six

OPERATION "RK"

> This is (the) inevitable result of the failure of the Allies to enforce their wishes on the Germans since the occurrences at Libau on 16th April. It is hard to understand how any collection of Statesmen and Soldiers in high office could, in face of the urgent recommendations and reports of those on the spot—all of them consistent and constantly reiterated—disregard and take no effective action in a matter which will lead either to a fresh war or to an ignominious betrayal of the two small States, which were encouraged to rely on our effective support against German domination.

THE QUOTATION comes from one of Cowan's June reports. Strictly, perhaps, he should not have vented his frustration in such words. The Admiral was not, however, admonished by Their Lordships: Wemyss and Ferguson had every sympathy with him since the "Statesmen and Soldiers" in Paris and Versailles seemed unable to restrain a defeated Reich from dominating Latvia and Lithuania, from supporting a Balt invasion of Estonia and from displaying open hostility to British warships. This last intransigence went further than mounting guns that threatened to make Libau an unsafe anchorage for the *Royalist*: Duff was treated with insolent contempt by German troops when he landed to visit Grant Watson who doubted whether his Mission's position would remain tenable for much longer. And in the middle of June Duff was obliged to withdraw the destroyers *Waterhen* and *Vancouver* from Riga for fear that they might be rushed and seized by German troops. One " enquired of my officer of the watch as to what right *Waterhen* had to fly the British ensign when she was a German ship; (others) made gestures with their hands by drawing them across their throats and pointing to the ship," wrote her Captain. The two ships were consequently unable to continue their support for the efforts of the American Mission to restrain the German Commandant from executing a large number of Letts without proper trial.

Early in June Goltz moved his headquarters to Riga so that Duff and Grant Watson were denied direct access to him when he showed no signs of complying with the Allies' latest terms. However, Tallents, very soon after his arrival at Reval, recognised the importance of stopping a German advance into Estonia. Hurrying south to Cecis, where fighting had broken out between Laidoner's troops and the *Landeswehr*, he was able, with the support of French and American representatives, to negotiate a temporary armistice on 16th June. But news that a division of 12,000 German troops was moving north from Riga made him apprehensive of further hostilities.

Cowan, for his part, was especially concerned that a German refusal to sign the Peace Treaty would be a signal for Goltz's guns to open fire on the *Royalist*. He therefore ordered Duff to withdraw to seaward where he was reinforced by the cruisers *Danae* and *Dauntless*. This squadron returned to Libau on 24th June to find that the Germans had withdrawn three miles from the town, leaving it to be garrisoned by Prince Lieven's Russian troops. Since this suggested that Goltz might be about to comply with the Allies' demands, Tallents and Gough met Duff on the 26th, when Niedra unexpectedly arrived from Riga and stated that his puppet government had resigned. The Germans, he said, had withdrawn their support, and since he had been Prime Minister at the time of the atrocities perpetrated against the Letts by both Germans and Balts, most of his fellow-countrymen now looked on him as a traitor. Tallents, Gough and Duff therefore agreed that as a first step towards re-establishing a Lettish Government Ulmanis and his colleagues on board the *Saratov* should land. These stout-hearted Ministers, who had so patiently accepted their water-borne refuge under British protection for two months, came ashore on the 27th and received a great ovation from a large crowd, the proceedings including an official reception, speeches from a hotel balcony and a concert in the evening—not to mention pulling down the monument in Libau's principal square to the Germans' capture of the town in 1915.

Gough and Tallents then left to arrange for Ulmanis to transfer his Government to Riga, which they were obliged to do by way of Reval since the Germans still refused to allow any British representative to travel direct to the Lett capital by rail or road, and since Duff had intelligence that the entrance to the Dvina had been freshly mined against Pitka's ships which were now active in the Gulf of Riga. Thus, by the time the Heads of the British Civil and Military Missions reached their destination, they were confronted with a new problem. As Tallents feared, hostilities had been renewed by Estonian troops and Colonel Zemitan's Lettish force against the *Landeswehr*, supported by a German division. The latter had been routed at Cesis on the 22nd, allowing the Estonians to advance on Riga so that by 1st July, 1919, they were within ten miles of the city. In these circumstances it must be counted one of Tallents's and Gough's greatest achievements that they were able to impose a comprehensive armistice on 3rd July. The Estonian advance, designed to prevent further German-Balt aggression, was halted in the outskirts of Riga and their troops obliged to withdraw. And to ensure that the *Landeswehr* devoted their energies to expelling the Bolsheviks, whom Lettish troops were having difficulties in holding at Latgale, the *Landeswehr's* German commander was removed. In his place Tallents appointed a young Irish Guardsman from the British Mission, Lieutenant-Colonel the Hon. H. R. Alexander, described by Walter Duranty as " the most charming and picturesque person I have ever met and one of two soldiers I have known who derived a strong, positive and permanent exhilaration from the worst of danger."[1]

[1] *I Write as I Please.*

One may wonder how often Field-Marshal Lord Alexander of Tunis, who was thus the only British Army officer to fight in the field in the Baltic States, recalled his command of this German-Balt unit when he held the position of a Supreme Commander in the Second World War. Tallents also removed the German Commandant from his position in Riga and appointed himself temporary Civil Governor until Ulmanis could arrive and assume control. Lastly, but most important of all, Gough, on the evidence of their recent successes, recommended that the task of clearing the Bolsheviks from the country should be left to Estonian troops operating on a common front with the Lettish Army and the *Landeswehr*, in accordance with the agreement which Pats and Ulmanis had reached in February. This allowed Tallents to require Goltz to comply with the Supreme War Council's demand that all his troops should evacuate Latvia as soon as possible: so far as Riga was concerned this was to be effected by 5th July.

Goltz fulfilled this last requirement by pulling back to Mitau. The German garrison also withdrew from Windau. Two days later Ulmanis's Government, now composed of both Letts and Balts in accordance with the wishes of the Allies, who had stressed that it must be broadly based if it was to retain the people's support, arrived in the Dvina on board the *Saratov*. But few supposed that Goltz had abandoned his ambitions, or that the Weimar Government could control him. To quote Duff:

I do not think the (German) withdrawal (from the three ports) should be looked upon as more than a strategic move. There are too many thousands of Prussians who have openly said that they intend to have these provinces. It would appear probable that, if they retire, they hope to arrange that disturbances will occur, and the state of the countries become such that they will have an excuse for returning—this time not on the invitation of the Allies but on account of the danger of Bolshevism in states on their borders. This time they would remain.

The Supreme Council did nothing to resolve the issue when it rejected an American proposal that the United States should assume a mandate over Latvia and Lithuania, Britain doing likewise for Estonia; and then turned down a British proposal that the Allies should make a sum of £10 million available to the three States, largely because France would not allow this to be charged against the reparations they intended to squeeze out of Germany. The Council confined itself to instructing Foch to make a fresh demand on Berlin to withdraw their forces. Goltz denied to Gough that he had received any such instructions from his Government for nearly three weeks, and then said that it would take him two and a half months to evacuate his army, that he would not do it by sea, and that he expected trouble because many were Germans who had volunteered for service in Latvia in return for a promise of land on which they might settle.[1]

Duff also objected to the German troops being evacuated by sea through Libau.

It is feared that the return of the Germans will cause a grave setback. The hatred of the people for the Germans is such that it will be very difficult to prevent occurrences leading to fighting. At the same time the Prussian Army in this country is so accustomed to doing exactly what it pleases that it is anticipated considerable looting will take place (which) there is no force to prevent. I have been doing all that I can to arrange that the evil is minimised. The plan suggested by the War Office, which sounded so simple, is quite impracticable.

Though Gough helped by appointing one of his staff as Military Governor of Libau, Duff was constrained to comment:

The following, I think, is often not realised. The Allies out here may make arrangements which appear to them necessary, but which they have no power to enforce; and if met, as has generally been the case, by a flat refusal to carry out these arrangements, they can only refer the matter to Paris. By the time it has been possible to obtain any decision from there the German has

---

[1] A promise which, incidentally, could not be implemented because Article 293 of the Versailles Treaty annulled all special rights of Germans in the Baltic States.

done what he intended—thanks to having the force to do it; and by the time a decision has been given and action taken from Paris, it has been too late.

A further potential source of trouble was Lieven's Russian force. Notwithstanding the Prince's willingness to co-operate with the Allies, his troops were not popular with the Letts. So long as their number remained limited all might be well, but there was news of 12,000 more Russian ex-prisoners of war coming back from Germany who could be expected to demand that Latvia should remain a Russian province, for whom, moreover, the Letts had no food. So Gough arranged with Cowan for the *Princess Margaret* to transfer the Prince's troops to Reval and join the North-West Army; but Lieven was persuaded by Goltz that this would not be in the interests of a reunited Russia and refused to allow his men to embark. This trial of strength between German and Allied influence was, however, handled with such tact and firmness by Duff that eventually he got most of the Russians away.

The Commodore's destroyers, stationed at Riga and Windau, had their own problems. On 3rd July, for example, the *Vancouver* reported the arrival of the S.S. *Hanover* escorted by two German torpedoboats. Since the Peace Treaty allowed no German warships, other than minesweepers, to be at sea, Duff immediately dispatched the *Danae* to ensure that these craft returned to their own country. Nonetheless, life for officers and men of the British ships was easier now than it had been for some time past. At Libau on 19th July, 1919,

the date of the official peace celebrations, the ships were dressed over all, and in the afternoon a very successful sports meeting was held on shore. A band was hired, and the local officials with their families, the Lettish officers, and the French and American officers and men were invited. A very large number of men were landed from our own ships. Tea was provided for about 600. The afternoon appeared to be a great success. In the evening a short display of fireworks was given by the ships.

Three days before, however, Duff had written:

All reports tend to show that the German Command has halted its preparations for evacuating (Latvia). Troops are returning again from Prussia to Mitau. Colonel Dawley came to see me yesterday (and said) he thought it quite possible that Goltz considered the political situation so unstable that it was worth waiting to see if it might be possible to avoid complying with the order to evacuate the Baltic Provinces.

Goltz, having failed to use Lieven for his purposes, had enlisted the help of one Paul Bermondt. This vain adventurer of dubious Russian origin and uncertain loyalties, who had started his military career in a regimental band and now styled himself Colonel Prince Avalov, was forming a new division out of the expected Russian ex-prisoners of war and German volunteers, which was being supplied by Goltz with all that it needed. " I am to request," wrote the Secretary of the Admiralty to the Foreign Office on receipt of this news, " that the attention of the Supreme Council may be drawn to the urgency of the recall of General von der Goltz." Duff's only weapon was a rigid control of all German shipping visiting Libau, Windau and Riga: no vessels were allowed to arrive at or leave these ports except to remove German troops and their equipment. By continuing to refuse to allow any supplies to be landed, the Commodore had the small satisfaction of knowing that he was causing Goltz some inconvenience.

On 26th July, Duff, having transferred his broad pendant to the *Caledon* which had come to strengthen his force, proceeded to Riga. It was the first time a cruiser had been up the Dvina since Sinclair's withdrawal at the beginning of the year.

Judging by the appearance of the outside of the buildings, (*wrote Duff*) the town has suffered very little from the various occupations it has been subjected to, but, like Libau, it is a depressing sight inasmuch as it has the appearance of a dead city. Practically all the factories are closed (and) most of the houses stripped of their furniture. There are no signs of the prosperous business population which was so marked a feature of the place. The people seen in the streets are mostly of the poorer classes. Although food is reported to be very scarce and prices are enormously high, their appearance did not give the impression that they were suffering anything approaching starvation; though, when the work of the American Food Mission finishes on 15th August, the food question may become very difficult. After the terribly unsettled times the town has been through, the state of nerves of most of the inhabitants is such that the wildest rumours are given credence; this is utilised by German agents (to) hinder the formation of a stable government. The moral effect of seeing our officers and men walking calmly about the town has been of great service in assisting the population to regain some control over its nerves. The destroyer stationed there has been giving regular afternoon leave, and *Caledon* did the same, and the behaviour of our men has been excellent.

Tallents and Gough could not derive as much satisfaction from their discussions with Goltz at Mitau. On 1st August Foch again ordered Berlin to withdraw their turbulent General, and to complete evacuating their troops from Latvia by the 30th under Gough's supervision. But, though those orders were passed to Goltz, Berlin instructed him that he was *not* to co-operate with the British Military Mission. As a result, in Cowan's words, " the German evacuation of the Baltic Provinces continues to be delayed by every shift and evasion which Goltz can engineer; and until this officer is summarily ejected from the Baltic Provinces it is not to be hoped that German intrigue, interference and domination will cease." Seven weeks after the armistice which the two British Heads of Mission had so successfully arranged, Goltz was still in control of the greater part of Latvia except for Riga, Libau and Windau, so that Ulmanis's Government had been unable to make much progress towards the reconstruction of their country. And Bermondt's division was daily gaining in strength —a division which Goltz was deliberately organising against the day when evacuation of his German troops could be delayed no longer.

Since this would not be before October, we may conveniently leave events in Latvia at this point—the first weeks of August 1919—and return to the Gulf of Finland by way of

Lithuania. Though Foch had been unable to persuade the Poles to withdraw their troops from their illegal occupation of Vilna, he had fixed a demarcation line, designed to prevent them encroaching farther on Lithuanian territory, which had avoided any serious clash of arms. Elsewhere, the German Tenth Army retained control but had allowed the Lithuanian forces to launch an offensive against the Bolsheviks with some success. But Voldmaris's Government could make no real progress towards establishing their country's freedom so long as Goltz's machinations in Latvia continued.

*　　　　*　　　　*

KRONSTADT: The fortifications are extensive and were begun by Peter the Great in 1703. Prince Menshikov constructed the works under the direction of Peter and one of the forts still bears his name. Succeeding Governments have strengthened the fortifications and secured the approaches from seaward by sinking ships and erecting batteries, especially after the visit of (*Napier's*) Baltic Squadron in 1854. It has long been the chief station in the Baltic for the Russian Fleet. The dry docks will admit the largest vessels of war, and a splendid steam factory almost rivals Keyham (*Devonport*) in its mechanical appliances.

So wrote the author of Murray's *Handbook for Travellers in Russia*, published as long ago as 1868. As much might be said of Kronstadt in 1919 except that the harbour had been made more impregnable by replacing the sunken ships with massive breakwaters comparable with those at Gibraltar. But the *Handbook* also refers to it as a commercial port visited by 1300 vessels annually, two-thirds of them British, with the consequence that there was a " British Hotel," a British chapel and a British Seaman's Hospital and " even the *drojky* drivers are able to converse in ' pigeon [*sic*]-English ' "; and all this had been outdated. A deep water channel had been dredged and a canal constructed which allowed large vessels to proceed up to St. Petersburg, saving the inconvenience of transferring cargoes to lighters, and allowing shipyards to be built in the capital. By the First World War Kronstadt was to the Russian Navy what Portsmouth was to the British. On the other hand, Kotlin Island, five miles long and at most a mile wide, on whose south-eastern end Kronstadt stands, was more than this. Conveniently sited fifteen miles to seaward of the Neva delta, its eight forts had been supplemented by a chain of nine, similar to those at Spithead, across the six-mile wide channel separating the island from the mainland to the north, and a further six across the four-mile wide channel to the south, the water in both being no more than two fathoms deep. And a mine barrage to seaward of Tolboukin Lighthouse, designed to keep enemy ships outside gun range, made it unlikely that any of those batteries would be destroyed by naval bombardment. Kotlin was thus the core of a defensive system that rendered Petrograd virtually impregnable from the sea—just as Krasnaya Gorka (and Fort Ino before it fell to the Finns) protected it against land and sea attack—whilst Kronstadt Harbour provided a secure base for the Russian Baltic Fleet. Indeed, until the Treaty of Brest-Litovsk, the German Navy never approached so close to it as Cowan's ships after their arrival at Biorko, and its defences were never seriously challenged until Donald's aircraft carried out their first raid at the end of July. Even then, since their bombs could do little damage, Zelenoy's ships might have remained safe under the cover of Kronstadt's guns and protected by its breakwaters, if Cowan had not realised, largely as a result of the sinking of the *Oleg*, that C.M.B.s (which had been devised in the latter half of the First World War for comparable attacks against the German coast) were a weapon whose high speed and shallow draught might be used to breach such formidable defences.[1]

---

[1] To-day (1963) Kronstadt, which is easily seen by the traveller approaching Leningrad by sea, since the deep water channel passes two cables off the harbour, is much the same as it was in 1919, with a modernised dockyard serving as the main base of the Soviet Baltic Fleet, for which reason no foreigner may now visit Kotlin Island. The two chains of forts are, however, only ruins, many having crumbled beneath the surface of Leningrad Bay.

The Admiral's aim was the destruction of the Bolshevik ships, notably the battleships *Petropavlovsk* and *Andrei Pervozvanni*, so that they no longer presented a serious challenge to his own force, and so that they could not menace the flank of the Estonian and Russian North-West Armies when their advance on Petrograd carried them to the east of the minefields. To this end Cowan planned Operation " RK," so named after his friend Keyes who had given the dragon's tail such a " damn' good twist " at Zeebrugge.[1] Having no staff apart from his Flag Captain, Secretary and Flag Lieutenant, to do the manifold work which operating and administering his now sizeable force involved, he enlisted the help of his flagship's able Executive Officer, Commander Clark, assisted by Agar who provided invaluable knowledge and personal experience, and by Dobson and Donald. These two made a number of reconnaissance flights over Kronstadt, whilst air photographs also showed where the Bolshevik ships were berthed. The targets selected, in addition to the two battleships, were the depot ship *Pamyat Azova*, to reduce the effectiveness of the enemy submarines, the cruiser *Rurik* because she was reported to be carrying 300 mines whose detonation would destroy much of the dockyard, the cruiser *Avroras* or *Diana*, and the caisson of the Nikolayevsky dock. A secondary target would be the destroyer on patrol outside the harbour. Surprise being vital, a night air-raid would divert the attention of the defences. Under its cover six C.M.B.s would penetrate the harbour, using guncotton charges to cut a passage through the boom across the fifty-yard wide breakwater entrance, and fire their torpedoes. And against the possibility that the attack might

---

[1] A closer, but more recent parallel is Cunningham's attack on the Italian battle fleet in Taranto (1941). Cowan considered attempting to close Kronstadt with blockships, as Keyes had closed the canal to Bruges, but after the sinking of the *Oleg*, rejected this method as too difficult to execute and less certain of success. In particular, blockships would have had to be swept through the mine barrage. Moreover, it would have been necessary to wait until mid-September for nights long enough to allow the necessarily slow approach to be carried out under cover of darkness.

provoke a sortie by the enemy, Cowan's cruisers and destroyers would lie in wait to seaward of the mine barrage.

Everything was ready by the middle of August 1919, a fortnight after the C.M.B.s' arrival from England, since Cowan was convinced that he could only ensure surprise by carrying out the operation with the minimum of delay. The boats' hulls had been overhauled after their 2000-mile tow, their 1500 h.p. petrol engines had been tuned and their torpedoes shipped in their stern firing troughs with the ready help of the crew of the *Vindictive*. Rehearsals, too, had been staged in Biorko Sound, but, as always seems to happen on such occasions, the summer weather broke: a strong westerly wind and heavy rain prevented an attack on the 15th and 16th. However, Sunday, the 17th, dawned fine and clear, when Cowan, having ordered the operation to be executed that night, visited the *Vindictive* and spoke to all who were to take part.

At 2200 Dobson's flotilla left Biorko: their gallant captains, all in their twenties, each of whom took the wheel of his own craft, must be named: *No. 24*, Lieutenant L. E. S. Napier; *No. 31*, Lieutenant R. Macbean (with Dobson on board); *No. 62*, Lieutenant-Commander J. T. Brade, R.N.R.; *No. 72*, Sub-Lieutenant E. R. Bodley, R.N.R.; *No. 79*, Lieutenant W. H. Bremner; *No. 86*, Sub-Lieutenant F. Howard, R.N.R.; *No. 88*, Lieutenant A. Dayrell-Reed. Each boat carried another officer, whose main task was to fire its torpedo(es),[1] and a chief motor mechanic to nurse its twin engines. All seven proceeded to a rendezvous off Inonini Point where they were joined at midnight by Agar in his own boat. He was to lead the flotilla through the chain of forts and up to the entrance to the harbour, though each captain also had the help of a Finnish smuggler as pilot: by virtue of their "trade" with Petrograd, they knew the way. The night was cloudy with a calm sea, a light wind and no more than a new moon when the eight boats, proceeding at fairly high speed, altered course for Kronstadt.

[1] *Nos. 24, 72* and *79* carried one, *Nos. 31, 62, 86* and *88* two.

148

Shortly after midnight Cowan in the *Delhi* brought the *Danae* and *Cleopatra* out of Biorko. The three cruisers were preceded by the Second Destroyer Flotilla, led by H.M.S. *Spenser*, Captain Colin Maclean, which had just arrived from England to relieve the *Wallace* and Campbell's First Flotilla. These ships were destined to play an unspectacular part: they had no more than a distant grandstand view of the attack from the west of the mine barrage. By 1000 on the 18th they were back in Biorko.

The C.M.B.s had difficulty in keeping in touch with each other as they ran in towards the North Channel. " Boats astern were dropping behind and only three could be seen," wrote Lieutenant Gordon Steele, second-in-command of *No. 88.* " After about half an hour's run, land could be seen to starboard which we knew was (Kotlin) Island. The first large fortress loomed up, (then) the chain of small forts which guard Petrograd Bay. They rise right out of the sea and looked unpleasantly close together. We seemed to be in sight of (them) for an interminably long time. I began to feel quite drowsy and had to keep awake by constantly reminding myself that any instant those black objects might change into flashes of gunfire. Indeed, from the noise our engines were making and (the) large sheets of flame coming from the exhaust pipes of the boats ahead, we ought to have been spotted at any minute." The flotilla intended to pass between Forts Nos. 8 and 11 but, according to Agar, " Dobson and the two boats following him (Bremner's and Dayrell-Reed's) lost sight of us. His smuggler-pilot, finding himself too close to the (eastern) end of the Kotlin shore, turned parallel to the chain of forts and slipped in between Nos. 7 and 10, a passage not previously used, and on which they would certainly have stuck had it not been for the extra water under their propellers due to the temporary rise of the water level. [1] Luck was so far with us."

---

[1] The strong westerly wind which had blown during the previous forty-eight hours raised the water three feet. This phenomenon occasionally lifts the level of the Neva until it floods much of Leningrad, as Pushkin describes in *The Bronze*

To quote Steele again: " The seconds seemed like hours; it appeared outside all possibility that they would not see us. I stood by the Lewis gun pointing it at the fort as we passed— not that it would be of much use, but it gave one confidence." Two of the forts did open fire on some of the flotilla but failed to pass the alarm to Kronstadt, so that by 0100 all the boats were off the eastern extremity of the island with the lights of Petrograd visible in the distance. There, whilst Kronstadt slept on, they formed up in two groups for the attack. Dobson was to take *Nos. 79, 31* and *88* into the enemy harbour first. They were to be followed by *Nos. 86, 72* and *62.* Napier's *No. 24* had to deal with the destroyer *Gavriil* which was anchored outside the entrance.

Meanwhile, back at Koivisto, on the landing strip which the men of Cowan's squadron had slashed out of Finnish forest, mechanics had swung the propellers of Dobson's machines; and a dozen " stick and string " biplanes had taken off into the night. Fifteen minutes later, flying at little more than sixty knots, they were over Kronstadt; and shortly before 0130 they came in over the harbour from many directions. The defences were alert: searchlights swept the sky: the guns of the warships and shore batteries put up a firework display of shrapnel and tracers. The planes, nonetheless, dropped their bombs, two apiece, none weighing more than 112 lb., and sometimes had the satisfaction of seeing a yellow detonation followed by a flickering red flame. This done, they continued to hold the enemy's attention by diving again and again down the searchlight beams. Judged as an air raid, the attack was to small effect: the R.A.F. had had little experience of bombing by night. But it served its purpose well: " we knew," wrote Steele, " that our faithful supporters, the Air Force, were taking the enemy's attention off us and getting a

---

Horseman. The British Home Fleet experienced similar conditions when it paid an official visit to the city in 1955, the first since Beatty's battlecruisers went to Kronstadt in June 1914.

warm reception themselves in consequence." They were doing more than that; they compelled the greater part of the garrison, the men who were supposed to man the lookout posts and the guns of the forts to repel an attack from the sea, to remain under cover whilst the C.M.B.s made their final approach.

The first group was led by Bremner whose boat carried the explosives and other gear needed to deal with the boom: Macbean, with Dobson aboard, followed: then came Dayrell-Reed. Their boats approached in line ahead, with their engines throttled back to cut noise and eliminate the white streak of bow waves. " The entrance to the middle harbour could now be seen to starboard, and ahead of us the guard-ship," wrote Steele. " She looked quite peaceful at anchor and it was hard to imagine her as an enemy ship guarding the entrance to an enemy harbour. Our three C.M.B.s glided past her and arrived at the entrance without a shot being fired at us. We stopped engines to give the two boats ahead of us time to get in." Bremner found no boom to bar his way—a deficiency to which some Soviet authorities ascribe the British success. Opening his throttle he roared into the main harbour, which was less than half a mile square, and headed for the *Pamyat Azova*, berthed off the jetty extending into the centre of the basin. Swinging round to starboard he discharged his torpedo which struck the depot ship. She listed rapidly and as quickly sank. Dobson, following close behind Bremner, swung to port towards the dreadnought *Petropavlovsk*. " His attack," records Agar, " was a more difficult manœuvre; he had to stop one engine, turn the boat, and gather speed quickly again before firing. This requires great judgment and coolness, but he did it; his torpedoes found their mark."

The roar of these explosions brought the garrison from their shelters. " As Dayrell-Reed's boat entered the harbour," noted Steele, " fire was opened on us, first from the direction of the dry dock and afterwards from both sides. We (headed) for the corner where our objective, the battleships, were berthed.

151

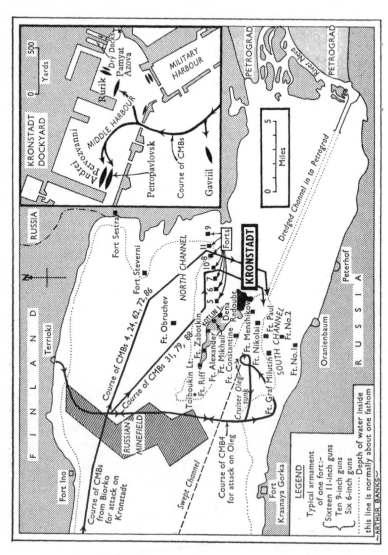

The Approaches to Petrograd

Almost simultaneously we received bursts of fire from the batteries and splashes appeared on both sides. Instinctively I ducked as the bullets whistled past. I turned round and was just about to remark to Dayrell-Reed, ' Where are you heading? ' as we were making straight for a hospital ship, when I noticed that his head was resting on the wooden conning tower top in front of him '': *No. 88*'s captain had been shot through the head. Despite Reed's considerable weight, Steele managed to lower him into the cockpit: " at the same time I put the wheel hard over and righted the boat on her proper course. We were now quite close to the *Andrei Pervoz-vanni*. Throttling back as far as possible, I fired both torpedoes at her, after which I stopped one engine to help the boat turn quickly. As I did this we saw two columns of water rise up from the side of the (*Petropavlovsk*) and heard two crashes. I knew they must be Dobson's torpedoes which had found their target. (Then) there was another terrific explosion nearby. We received a great shock and a douche of water. Looking over my shoulder, I realised the cause of it was one of our torpedoes exploding on the side of the (other) battleship. We were so close to her that a shower of picric powder from the warhead of our torpedo was thrown over the stern of the boat, staining us a yellow colour which we had some difficulty in removing afterwards. (Missing) a lighter by a few feet (we) followed Dobson out of the basin. I had just time to take another look back and see the result of our second torpedo. A high column of flame from the (*Andrei Pervozvanni*) lit up the whole basin. We passed the guardship at anchor again. Morley (*No. 88*'s mechanic) gave her a burst of machine-gun fire as a parting present and afterwards went to see what he could do for Reed.''

The *Gavriil* was still there because Napier had the mortification of missing her with *No. 24*'s torpedo: it passed under the destroyer's bottom. Moreover, Sevastyanov's crew retaliated so promptly that a shell split *No. 24* in half and sank her. Brade was equally unfortunate: as his boat was coming in she collided with Bremner's as it was leaving the harbour, the latter being nearly cut in two. Brade, who had realised that he was not required to carry out his main task—attacking the battleships if Dobson or Dayrell-Reed failed—then displayed great presence of mind. By going full speed ahead he kept his boat and Bremner's locked together, whilst the latter first fired the fuse of the guncotton charges he carried to deal with the boom, before clambering to safety with his crew. The charges exploded and destroyed Bremner's boat after Brade had drawn clear, when he turned to fire his torpedoes at the *Gavriil*; but like Napier's, and for the same reason, both missed. Brade's boat was then likewise sunk by Sevastyanov's gunfire.

Howard and Bodley, in *Nos. 86* and *72*, who had hoped to deal with the *Rurik* and the caisson of the Nikolayevsky dock, suffered ill-luck. Howard's engines broke down as he was about to begin his run in at the head of the second group, so that he suffered the frustration of being unable to take part in the attack. And as Bodley was approaching the entrance a shell splinter damaged the firing gear of his torpedo. With his boat deprived of its sting he had to withdraw; but he found Howard and, though under fire from Kronstadt's forts, towed his boat safely away, a fine piece of courageous seamanship. Agar, who had fired his torpedo into the harbour from just outside the entrance, was the last to leave the scene as dawn was breaking, when a hail of enemy shell pursued his boat and those of Dobson, Bodley and Howard as they returned to Biorko.[1]

As soon as Donald's pilots, their unselfish task of acting as decoys so well done, had landed at Koivisto and refuelled their planes, they took off again and returned to reconnoitre the scene of the action. They rejoiced to find that the *Petropavlovsk*, the *Andrei Pervozvanni* and the *Pamyat Azova* had all been sunk, though there was insufficient water to submerge their

[1] The quotations from Agar's and Steele's accounts of the attack are from *Footprints in the Sea*.

hulls, and the floating dock had been damaged by a bomb. Subsequent intelligence revealed that the *Petropavlovsk* had been struck by two torpedoes so that it was a long time before she could be salvaged; and that, whilst the *Andrei Pervozvanni* had only been struck by one, so that she was quickly raised and moved into dry dock, she would require extensive repairs.

A Soviet account of this raid (in which the times differ from those in the British version) has its own interest:

On 18th August at about 0100, five British C.M.B.s left Biorko, and a little later two similar craft left Terrioki. They all made a rendezvous in the vicinity of Fort Ino, and proceeded in company by the North Channel to the rear of Kronstadt. At 0400 they were sighted in the proximity of Fort Obruchev. After this, the craft proceeded between Forts Nos. 3 and 4, and passed Kronstadt. At 0345 aircraft appeared over Kronstadt and "strafed" the ships and harbour basins with tracer bullets and dropped bombs. At 0420 the destroyer guardship, *Gavriil*, anchored in the roadstead, which was returning the fire of aircraft attacking her, sighted two boats and simultaneously heard a large explosion in the harbour close to the workshops of the Baltic Yard. The *Gavriil* opened fire and with her first shot sank one boat, while the other disappeared behind a defence-work. The explosion in the harbour was caused by a torpedo which had missed the *Gavriil* and had struck the basin wall.

The *Gavriil* also sighted two or three boats entering the harbour at very high speed and firing their machine-guns at the ships berthed there. She could not fire at these boats for fear of damaging our own vessels. They torpedoed the *Pamyat Azova* and almost simultaneously, at 0425, the *Andrei Pervozvanni* was blown up, after which the C.M.B.s nipped out of the harbour towards the south. During their exit two boats were sunk by gunfire from the *Gavriil*, which quickly sent a boat to save 3 officers and 6 ratings. The C.M.B.s which had sunk the *Pamyat Azova* and *Andrei Pervozvanni* continued to fire with their machine-guns.

As already mentioned, the C.M.B.s got through the North Channel, where four were sighted by Fort Obruchev, moving at very high speed. As the fort was then returning the fire of attacking aircraft it could not open fire on the C.M.B.s, though they sprayed it with machine-gun fire. The fort immediately telegraphed to the Fortress Staff who in turn informed the Staff of the Active Squadron

Command. But the latter could not do anything on this belated information because its reception coincided with the *Gavriil* opening fire. The passage of the C.M.B.s was also seen by Forts Nos. 3 and 4 but they could not do anything because the first had no guns whilst the other was replacing her weapons and was restricted to rifle fire. Allowing for the 40 knot speed of these boats, it is clear that everything happened with unaccustomed rapidity, in darkness and during an air raid. Moreover the very idea of an attack by C.M.B.s was completely unexpected both in its conception and the boldness of its execution. Not until after the boats had broken through did the forts switch on their searchlights and go to action stations, and by that time the C.M.B.s were to the rear, where most of the guns were unable to train.

On their way back the C.M.B.s, moving in two groups at full speed, again by the North Channel, were picked up in the beams of the searchlights, and came under heavy machine-gun fire from the forts. They also came under gunfire, but this was unsuccessful. Thus out of eight attacking C.M.B.s, three were sunk by the *Gavriil*'s fire and five got away. From the moment when the C.M.B.s left the harbour the air attacks, which had been delivered almost at masthead height, ceased. The din of their engines and their machine-gun fire were of great assistance to the C.M.B.s, for the A.A. weapons were fully occupied with aerial targets, and super-fluous personnel were sent below decks or under shelter.

The torpedo which struck the *Andrei Pervozvanni* displaced four armour plates on the port side, two of them being torn away some two feet from the side. The compartments between Nos. 4 and 13 frames up to the second armoured deck were flooded, and between Nos. 13 and 15 frames to the orlop-deck, one man being killed and two injured.

The Commission of Enquiry reached the following conclusions on the reasons for the success of the attack:

(*a*) The complete unexpectedness of the idea of a C.M.B. attack on Kronstadt.

(*b*) The complete confidence in the impossibility of any sort of naval operation by way of the North Channel.

(*c*) The complete distraction of the attention of the forts, batteries, signal station and ships, by aircraft.

(*d*) The shallow draught of the boats which allowed them to proceed on the surface at 40 knots.[1]

So much for the Soviet point of view. From the British

---

[1] *Piat Let Krasnogo Flota.*

there was no doubt about the result; at the cost of three
C.M.B.s, Operation " R.K." had achieved Cowan's purpose.
Of Zelenoy's active fleet only a handful of destroyers and
submarines remained. There was no longer any major threat
to the British Baltic Force, or to the seaward flank of Laidoner's
and Yudenitch's armies—unless the Bolsheviks managed to
commission some of the heavy ships which lay idle in the
shipyards of the Neva. " Deeds of this kind have in times
past built up the fame of the English Navy, and this feat has
once more shown the world that when England strikes it
strikes hard," wrote Mannerheim who fully appreciated the
implications of Cowan's success for his own country's future.
The Estonian Foreign Minister [1] was " especially jubilant over
this success." Madden said: " This successful enterprise will
rank among the most daring and skilfully executed of naval
operations. On no other occasion has so small a force inflicted
so much damage on the enemy. Rear-Admiral Sir Walter
Cowan deserves generous recognition for the able foresight,
planning and preparations which led to this great naval
success." But not all those who carried out this enterprise
returned to " enjoy the fruits of their labours." Six officers
had been killed, including Brade and Dayrell-Reed, and nine
ratings,[2] whilst Bremner and Napier were among the three
officers and six ratings rescued by the *Gavriil*'s boats who had
to endure Bolshevik prisons (though they were not seriously
ill-treated) before they were released. Cowan, in his speech
to the survivors, said: " The losses are heavy, but there is not
one single incident to regret or one which could have been
avoided. The three boats which were lost went most gloriously,
fighting indomitably to the finish. I venture to think that their
end will have as great an effect in keeping the remainder of
the Bolshevik Navy quiet as will the devastation you have
wrought in their harbour—the strongest naval fortress in the
world, ravished and blasted by under fifteen splendidly

[1] Jan Poska.
[2] The Soviet Government later returned their bodies to Britain for burial.

disciplined and dauntless Britons." " They all deserve the
V.C.," wrote the *Cleopatra*'s navigator. Two were awarded,
to Dobson and Steele; Agar and three other officers received
the D.S.O., eight officers the D.S.C., whilst all the ratings were
decorated with the C.G.M. in recognition of their valour in
striking a blow which, in one brief hour, achieved Cowan's
aim, destruction of the enemy battle fleet. " After this nothing
bigger than a destroyer moved again." [1]

Almost everyone was pleased—except the British Cabinet.
Wemyss wrote:

I have been awaiting further news of your brilliant action
before writing, but can wait no longer to congratulate you and all
concerned. It appears to have been an extraordinarily gallant and
successful attack, and I am in hopes that you may get some permanent relief from the strain of the Baltic. I have, as you can
imagine, been thinking about you and yours constantly, and I
think I can realise the difficulties of your situation. You probably
also realise how almost impossible it is to get real help or guidance
from our so-called Cabinet with their slipshod methods and want
of definite policy which inevitably leads to difficulties. The permission for you to attack was obtained, so to speak, on a snap vote
and I took the opportunity. But they don't or won't understand
the situation. [2]

The Admiral who went to announce the success of the attack
to the Cabinet met, greatly to his surprise, with a far from
cordial reception. The sinking of the Baltic Fleet was the
last thing they desired when, though openly disavowing the
Bolsheviks, they were secretly negotiating for the withdrawal
of British forces from Archangel. Wemyss was so disgusted
by this example of political opportunism that he tendered his
resignation. But he had either done this, or threatened it,
too often in the past six months,[3] to be taken seriously.[4]

[1] Cowan in his *Despatch*.
[2] *The Life and Letters of Lord Wester Wemyss.*
[3] A previous instance is mentioned in Chapter 8.
[4] Although the Kronstadt raid was so disastrous for the Bolsheviks, it reacted
in their favour in one incidental respect. As in Petrograd, where there had been
strikes among the factory workers in March, there was much discontent
among the Kronstadt garrison which led to serious disturbances in April. Though

This removal of a major impediment to a military advance towards Petrograd and to the operations by Cowan's force did not, however, allow the British force to relax. Ships and submarines continued their patrols and minelaying against sorties by Bolshevik destroyers, minelayers and submarines which the Admiral warned his captains were likely to be intensified in retaliation for the Kronstadt raid, in addition to bombarding the seaward flank of the Red Army in support of the Estonians. Their work was, to quote Cowan, " tireless, dauntless and never-ending and with never the relaxation of lying in a defended port with fires out and on full rations; in cramped navigational waters necessitating the almost constant presence on deck of the captain, and always within range, and often under fire of the guns of Krasnaya Gorka." Donald's planes likewise carried on their frequent raids against Kronstadt, where their principal target was the docked *Andrei Pervozvanni.* In all they made some sixty raids on the Bolshevik base. On 3rd September, 1919, one of their bombs exploded only thirty yards from the docked battleship. Next day a bomb splinter wounded a man on board a minesweeper. On the 14th, two bombs damaged an auxiliary vessel; on 8th October, one struck another ship; and six days later the destroyer *Svoboda* and submarine *Tigr* were strafed whilst out exercising, when the former vessel suffered slight damage and casualties. " From these results it may be concluded that the damage caused by enemy air raids was generally insignificant,"

Cowan was never encouraged to believe that the garrison would change sides since his appeals to the Bolshevik ships to hoist the White Flag had had such small results, this was certainly a possibility, especially at the time of the abortive revolt in Krasnaya Gorka. The men of the Baltic Fleet were, however, so angered by the success of the British raid on Kronstadt that they no longer agitated against the Red régime: they were now opposed to welcoming the ships of a foreign power that had struck such a blow against Holy Russia. (The major Kronstadt revolt in February 1921 had an entirely different complexion: the sailors of the Baltic Fleet then mutinied in protest at Lenin's New Economic Policy which, though very necessary if the U.S.S.R. was to recover from the disastrous effects of the Civil War, was a major retreat from the Communism for which they had fought and suffered so much.)

was a Soviet historian's conclusion. It is not, however, a reflection on Donald's men, for the same writer gives the reason: " the bombs used by the British were quite inadequate for their purpose." [1] Moreover, he implies that their other activities were of considerable value when he refers to the efforts made by Bolshevik planes, albeit unsuccessful, to locate and attack Donald's airfields. But, as Cowan pointed out to the Admiralty on 20th August, none of his ships carried guns of sufficient calibre to deal with the major obstacle to an advance by Laidoner's and Yudenitch's armies, Fort Krasnaya Gorka, for which reason he asked that he might be provided with two long-range monitors. He had, however, to add that the Estonian Army would not advance so long as the Allies refused to recognise their country's independence; indeed, that in the absence of this the Estonian Government was seeking to arrange an armistice with the Bolsheviks.[2] The Admiral also said that the Russian North-West Army, though it had recently been reinforced by six British tanks,[3] was unlikely to make their much vaunted advance in view of " their disobedience and disregard of General Gough's suggestions, their perpetual quarrelling amongst each other, and intrigue amongst themselves and with the Germans." The Admiralty's reply to Cowan's request for monitors was to the effect that, since all experience showed that fortresses could not be reduced by naval bombardment alone—the Dardanelles were foremost in their minds—such vessels would not be sent to the Baltic until Laidoner's or Yudenitch's armies might begin a serious advance on Petrograd—if, indeed, they should do so before the winter called a halt to naval operations in the Gulf.

Towards the end of August Agar's two small C.M.B.s made their final venturesome trips into Petrograd Bay. Fully aware

[1] p. 156 n., op. cit.

[2] The negotiations were conducted by Poska with Chicherin, Soviet Commissar for Foreign Affairs.

[3] Manned by British volunteers since the Russians were not considered competent to do this. These were the only British troops to fight with Yudenitch's army, notwithstanding Soviet statements to the contrary.

that they could not hope to continue them much longer before
the Bolsheviks learned of their activities and took counter-
measures, their purpose was to bring out S.T.25—Paul Dukes
—whom the Government had ordered to leave Russia before
he tempted fate too far.   They also wanted this singularly
brave man's first-hand report on conditions in Petrograd in
order to contest the growing opposition of the Labour leaders
who viewed the Reds through spectacles as opaque as they
were rosy.   Agar was all but successful on the 23rd, Dukes and
a friendly Russian midshipman being in sight of *C.M.B.7*
when their skiff sprang a serious leak and they were obliged to
swim for the shore.   Dukes then decided against risking this
route again and that he would leave Russia by another: he
managed it across the Latvian front, reaching Helsingfors on
7th September.   Before this, however, Agar, unaware of Dukes's
changed plans, made a further attempt to bring him off by
sea on 26th August.   This time *C.M.B.7* was detected by the
forts in the North Channel which opened fire.   A shot carried
away the boat's tiller ropes so that, out of control, she ran on
to the breakwater joining Fort No. 5 to Kotlin Island.   By
superhuman efforts Agar and his crew managed to get the
boat off and plug the holes in her bottom.   Then, using an
improvised sail, and baling hard all the way, they somehow
managed, notwithstanding daylight, to complete the hazardous
return voyage to Terrioki in just under twelve hours.   This
achievement is as remarkable as the Bolshevik's failure to
impede it.   " Was their escape a miracle," wrote Agar, " or
an answer to prayer?   I am sure it was both."

Having destroyed *C.M.B.7*, Agar closed his Terrioki base
and went to Biorko to collect the repaired *C.M.B.4*.   In her
he led two of the larger C.M.B.s by night into the swept channel
leading to Kronstadt to lay four small submarine mines.   This
operation was, however, seen by the Bolsheviks who sent out
minesweepers, escorted by the *Svoboda*, to clear them on
4th September.   After this Agar and his small band who,
almost unique for naval officers and men, had been directly

employed by the British Secret Service, returned to England.[1]

At the end of August Zelenoy achieved some small revenge for the Kronstadt raid. On the 31st, after six weeks of inactivity, the *Pantera* left Kronstadt and,

having passed Tolboukin Light, submerged to periscope depth. At 1430 a four-funnelled destroyer was sighted to the S.W., but she quickly disappeared. Investigating the area, now moving deep, now watching through her periscope, the submarine next saw two destroyers anchored to the east of Seskar Island and decided to attack them. (*These were the* Abdiel *and* Vittoria, *Lieutenant-Commander Hammersley Heenan, which were on patrol. Cowan's instructions allowed them to anchor during reduced visibility by night and Curtis had decided to take advantage of this in order to give his officers and men some relief from the strain of war watchkeeping.*) The *Pantera* steered to get closer to the shore and attack from the north-west, because the destroyers were anchored in relatively shallow water: after the attack it would be essential to escape quickly into deeper water: it was also preferable to make the approach from up-sun. At 2110 the *Pantera* went in to attack the destroyer anchored further to seaward and at 2119 fired two torpedoes from her forward tubes. She then dived to 80 feet and touched bottom. Half a minute after firing a big explosion was heard, but the submarine was below periscope depth so that the result was not observed. (*The* Pantera's *torpedoes struck the* Vittoria *which sank in five minutes; fortunately the* Abdiel *was able to rescue all but eight of her crew.*) Shortly after this several shots were heard, evidently fired by the second destroyer. On surfacing a little later, however, it was too dark for the *Pantera* to see anything. So, having again dived to 40 ft., she set course for Kronstadt. Not until 1120 the following day, when Tolboukin Light was abeam, did the *Pantera* surface. By this time the pressure within the submarine was so great that the measuring instrument's needle was off the end of the scale, the air was so foul that a match would not light, and it was extremely difficult to breathe. She had spent more than 28 hours under water making good 75 miles.[2]

[1] *C.M.B.4* was for a time in the Imperial War Museum and then returned to her builders, Messrs. Thornycroft, who kept her for many years at their yard on Platt's Eyot, Hampton-on-Thames. However these closed and Vosper-Thornycroft, as the firm now is, do not know what became of her. *RMB*

(for non-Thames people Eyot is pronounced Eight)

[2] p. 156 n., op. cit.

Cowan was understandably angry with Curtis when he learned
how the loss of the *Vittoria* had occurred, but his remarks on
the report of the subsequent court of inquiry so far recognised
the good work which the Twentieth Flotilla was doing that
Curtis escaped with no more than Their Lordships' severe
displeasure.

The British force suffered another loss four days later:
the *Verulam*, Lieutenant-Commander G. L. Warren, struck a
British mine off Stirs Point and sank with the loss of twenty-nine
of her crew. But she belonged to Maclean's Second Flotilla
which, to quote Cowan, " has scarcely yet become accustomed
to the difficult conditions of maintaining the patrols under the
cramped conditions of manœuvring space which must obtain
whilst we remain here." The rest of September passed with
few incidents in the Gulf worth specific mention. Minelaying
by the British ships was abandoned in the middle of the month
when the *Princess Margaret* and half the Twentieth Flotilla
returned to England, Curtis taking the remainder of his ships
down to Libau to augment Duff's force. The Second Flotilla
maintained the necessary regular patrols and continued bombarding the southern shore. Extracts from a diary kept by
a member of the crew of the *Westminster* show what this
involved:

With *Vectis*, *Walpole* and *Valentine*, left harbour, *Walpole* and
selves making straight for the Estonian coast. Our duties are to
patrol the flank of the troops ashore. Bolshevik forts are plainly
to be seen, but make no effort to fire at us. During the afternoon
an Estonian destroyer suddenly made a quick dash right in under
the land, loosed off a few salvoes and as quickly nipped out again.
No reply from the shore to this greeting. . . .

With *Walpole* off Estonian coast; at 1645 *Walpole* opens fire
on battery ashore, keeping up 4-inch shell fire for half an hour or
more. Battery returns an accurate fire but falling short. *Walpole*
must be anchored just out of range. *Walpole* gets under way and,
moving along the coast, opens up a fine bombardment with all
guns on what appears to be a factory with tall chimney. We
could see the fall of shot and the firing was very good. *Walpole* had

further gun practice later but we left the area to escort *E39* to patrol area. . . .

Spenser signals coming out at 0600 to assist bombardment. We again escort *E39*, then join up with *Spenser* and *Walpole*. At 1045 we closed up at action stations to do a little bombarding on our own account. *Spenser* ceased fire but *Walpole* continued until *Westminster* opened up. Shore guns now turned from *Walpole* on to us. They gradually got our range but fall of shot was well astern of us. We opened fire at 11,000 yards and selected the tall chimney, which was apparently being used as an observation post. We found the range as 10,800 yards and claimed some hits though the chimney still stood. After a final 12 rounds of lyddite we returned to patrol.

The British cruisers, of which the *Danae* had been relieved by the *Phaeton*, had nothing so interesting to occupy them. "It's very boring being here now," noted the *Cleopatra*'s navigator. The depot ship *Maidstone*, Captain Max Horton,[1] reached Reval with a fresh submarine flotilla to relieve the *Lucia* and Nasmith's boats but this new blood was to have no opportunity for action. Donald's planes raided Kronstadt several times a week, usually with six Camels, to some effect. And the Swedish *Eskstuna III* eluded the British blockade of Petrograd with a cargo of handsaws, but was intercepted on her return with a load of flax. Having orders to turn back neutral ships approaching from the west, but no authority to seize one if it came from the east, Cowan solved the problem by handing her over to the Finns. The Admiralty appreciated that this was unsatisfactory and pressed the Foreign Office to obtain a clear ruling from Paris. As a result, on 10th October, 1919, the Supreme Council announced a formal blockade of Petrograd which Cowan was authorised to enforce notwithstanding its questionable legality, in that, despite hostilities, war had not been declared between Britain and Soviet Russia so that technically neither was a belligerent power.

---

[1] Who had commanded a submarine operating from Reval against the Germans in 1915 and was to become Admiral Sir Max Horton, Commander-in-Chief Western Approaches for most of the Second World War.

From " the other side of the hill," there is likewise nothing of significance to record up to the end of September. Notwithstanding the *Pantera*'s success, Zelenoy made no further attempt to attack Cowan's force, or to interfere with the support which it was giving to the Estonians in Kaporia Bight. In the words of a Soviet historian, the British ships " had continuous command of the Gulf," a proper tribute to the work of Cowan and all who served under him.

On land, in the same period, there was no advance—but there were political developments. On 14th August Gough managed to form a Russian North-West Government in Helsingfors with Yudenitch as Minister of War and Commander-in-Chief. Gough's reasons for this step, which was taken with Tallents's approval, were three; (*a*) the critical condition of the Russian North-Western Army, (*b*) the seriousness of a threat by the Estonian Army to refuse to participate further against the Bolsheviks unless Estonian independence was granted and (*c*) the need to fuse democratic and reactionary parties into a whole-hearted attack on the Bolsheviks. And this new Government quickly displayed its willingness to co-operate by issuing a declaration recognising Estonian independence and calling on the Allies to do likewise. For this action, which London and Paris viewed as contrary to Allied policy, Gough was recalled to report. He went under the impression that the German evacuation of Latvia was progressing well, and that Bermondt had agreed to serve under Yudenitch. Though he was mistaken in both these matters, the War Office did not hesitate to issue a lengthy report summarising Gough's work since his arrival in June which expressed considerable satisfaction with all that he had achieved in the face of many difficulties. No doubt this document was inspired by the militant Churchill who had his own views on the need to recognise the independence of the Baltic States. For on 20th September, 1919, he wrote to the Prime Minister urging that this should be done at once, " for in a little while it would be too late to secure terms for these small States which had given aid against Bolshevism." But with unusual frankness Lloyd George answered:

> You want us to recognise their independence in return for their attacking the Bolsheviks. (But) in the end, whoever won in Russia, the Government there would promptly recover the old Russian Baltic ports. Are you prepared to go to war with perhaps an anti-Bolshevik Government of Russia to prevent that? If not, it would be a disgraceful piece of deception on our part to give any guarantee to those new Baltic States that you are proposing to use to conquer Russia. You won't find another responsible person in the whole land who will take your view, (so) why waste your energy and your usefulness on this vain fretting? [1]

Whilst all this was happening, the Bolsheviks, wishing to divert their Seventh Army to help compass the early defeat of Kolchak's and Denikin's forces, had decided to forego their claims to the Baltic States. They were therefore encouraging overtures for armistices from both Estonia and Latvia, with the result that Curzon instructed Grant Watson to request that the Latvian Government " will take no action in the direction of peace. His Majesty's Government would deplore individual action being taken by them and trust that they will conduct their foreign policy only as part of a concerted plan with the Allied Governments." Unfortunately the Allies had no plan—at least none which recognised the Baltic States' demand for *de jure* recognition. However, on 25th September, Curzon sent an important document to Tallents:

---

[1] Lord Beaverbrook's *The Decline and Fall of Lloyd George*, makes clear that this was far from being the only problem on which Churchill was at odds with the Prime Minister. The two men shared a bitter hostility for each other. Nor was Churchill alone in this; the whole Cabinet was rent by dissension. This was aggravated by Lloyd George's capacity for shifting his ground from, for example, full support for the Whites to conciliating the Reds, whichever seemed more likely to enable him to retain his position at the top. " He must be Prime Minister. He did not seem to care which way he travelled provided he was in the driver's seat." This unhappy quagmire of intrigue continued until Lloyd George had settled the intractable Irish problem; the Conservatives then seized upon his bellicose handling of the Chanak crisis to bring the post-war coalition to an end.

The numerous requests for assistance and for a definite declaration of policy that are continually addressed to H.M. Government on behalf of the Baltic States, have required the former to reconsider the question. It now appears that none of the States concerned wishes to act separately, and that concerted action is contemplated. Indeed, a conference has been summoned for this purpose on 29th September. H.M. Government have already recognised the autonomous existence of the Baltic States, and have dealt with them as such. The question of (their) *de jure* recognition is one which it is impossible for them to decide upon their own responsibility. The Peace Conference alone, or the League of Nations sitting in sequel to the Peace Conference, can arrive at a definite decision. The principal menace by which a settlement is threatened is the presence of German forces under Goltz. Foch has already requested the German Government to order their immediate withdrawal, and in view of their failure to comply, steps are being taken to apply measures of coercion.

H.M. Government are asked whether they can continue to supply military material and stores to the States. The reduction of the available stocks consequent upon the termination of the war and the shortage of shipping unfortunately renders this impossible. This is not intended to imply abandonment of the States in the event of their existence (being) imperilled by an invasion of Bolshevik forces. H.M. Government might (then) be prepared to reconsider their decision as to the supply of war material. As regards the provision of credit, it is impossible for H.M. Government to assume a financial responsibility which they have hitherto been unable to accept. While they have exerted themselves to aid the States in the provision of loans from independent quarters, they cannot, in view of the grave financial straits in which the entire world is placed, depart from their attitude in this respect.

In these circumstances H.M. Government feel that they are not entitled to exercise any pressure upon the free initiative of the Baltic States, and that their Governments must be at liberty to decide upon such action as may be most conducive to the preservation of their own national existence. It is for them to determine with unfettered judgment whether they should make any arrangement, and if so of what nature, with the Soviet authorities; and if, as seems to be in contemplation, they decide to act in unison, the effective control of the situation should be within their power.

Of the likely outcome of the conference to which Curzon

referred, Horton noted: " All the Baltic States' delegates, with the Finns as well, are meeting to-day to discuss whether they are going to make a combined peace with the Bolshies or not. I expect it will come off, for everyone seems tired of scrapping and the conditions are certainly damnable." But he forgot Goltz, of whose return to Mitau after a visit to Berlin to ensure that the Weimar Government supported his plans for Latvia, Cowan had recently written that it " makes the German situation very serious, and if the Allies persist in allowing this officer to defy them and go where he likes in the Baltic, there can never be any satisfactory solution to any question out here."

*   *   *

Reverting to the middle of August, Duff in the *Caledon* at Libau had the assistance of the *Royalist*, with destroyers from the Third Flotilla and Brisson's French sloops to help him at Windau and Riga—a force which was augmented by Curtis's Twentieth Flotilla in the middle of September. Up to the end of that month these ships were not involved in any serious incident: Duff and his captains were chiefly concerned to support Ulmanis's Government in the face of Goltz's determination to achieve his own ends, and the Allies' failure to enforce his removal.

On the evening of 24th August (*wrote Duff*) the Germans held a demonstration at Mitau against evacuating Latvia, asking Goltz to keep command and to separate from the German Government. The Lettish garrison were disarmed, their headquarters entered, and a safe pillaged. The Commander of the (German) division addressed the demonstrators and signified that evacuation would not be insisted upon. The German Command states that soldiers refused to entrain owing to promises of land in Latvia. This has the appearance of carrying out the policy that Goltz is reported to have threatened, viz. stating that he can no longer control his troops; and, instead of evacuating them, to allow them to break away and by pillage and destruction reduce the country to such

168

a state that it will be necessary for some organised armed force to occupy it. And since Germany appears to be the only country that is ready to do so, and will say that it is impossible to have Bolshevism on her borders, she will probably reoccupy it.

Duff also noted that many Germans were joining Bermondt's growing force, whose leader publicly denied the Russian North-West Government's authority and, notwithstanding instructions which he received from Kolchak in his capacity as Supreme Ruler of Russia, refused to obey Yudenitch's orders, from which it was clear that an advance on Petrograd was not his purpose.

In the middle of September the Supreme Council considered a draft note which the French proposed should be sent to Berlin, once again demanding evacuation of the Baltic States. If not complied with within a month, steps would be taken to enforce it by economic restrictions, a renewal of the blockade, stoppage of the repatriation of prisoners and, if necessary, force. Foch declared that he did not believe this would have any effect: it amounted only to a further postponement of the question. Gough, who was called to give his views, stressed that the German danger was far more serious than the Bolshevik. Goltz, he said, was plotting to form

a large German army outside Germany, in alliance with the non-Bolshevik Russians, to seize the Baltic States and eventually Russia itself. The liberty of those States would be destroyed and the independence of Finland threatened. This German and Russian force might well become the most powerful in Europe and be used against the Allies. The population of the Baltic States was democratic, not Bolshevik, but it would rather be under the Bolsheviks than under the Germans. He thought that these States should be allowed to make peace with Russia if they wished. It was not true that the German troops would not obey Goltz. It would be easy to oblige the Germans who were with the Russian troops to rejoin their own corps in Germany, as, in the absence of a German army in the Baltic States, they would be murdered if they remained there. The German Government was waiting to see whether the Allies were prepared to show firmness.

The British Representative [1] then reminded the Council

that it was Lloyd George who had urged the necessity of getting the Germans out of the Baltic States. The original plan was to send an ultimatum and back it up by military force, but it had to be discarded owing to American opposition. The substitution of a threat of some undefined economic action seemed so completely to alter the character of the measure contemplated that I seriously doubted the wisdom of resorting to another ultimatum to the three already sent. Apart from this I could not commit my Government to the adoption of the coercive measures proposed. I anticipated great difficulties in stopping the repatriation of our German prisoners, nor could I say whether H.M. Government was prepared, or even in a position to reimpose drastic restrictions on trade and intercourse with Germany, involving a renewal of the blockade. I therefore suggested that the Conference should defer a decision so as to allow each delegation to obtain from their Government a statement of the precise measures which (it was) prepared to take. If we could agree on (these), I thought the best course would be to take them at once instead of merely threatening.

However, notwithstanding Crowe's realistic appraisal, the Council, when they next met four days later, decided only to send Berlin a strongly worded note demanding, under threat of sanctions, an immediate evacuation of the Baltic States, this to include all Germans in Bermondt's corps. Three days later the Wilhelmstrasse replied that it was replacing Goltz by Lieutenant-General Magnus von Eberhardt who would supervise the evacuation. But once again, Goltz and Berlin were a step ahead of the Allies. Although the " Prussian fox " ostensibly transferred his command to Bermondt, who had formed his own West Russian Government in Mitau, he was not recalled from Latvia: he remained there in the background manipulating both Eberhardt and Bermondt with the intention of restoring Niedra's puppet régime.

Such was the position on 28th September, 1919, when the *Dauntless* arrived at Libau and, as Madden had suggested, Duff went home in the *Caledon* for leave and rest. This left

[1] Sir Eyre Crowe.

Curtis as British senior officer in Latvian waters. Realising that the comparative quiet which prevailed there was too uneasy to last, and that when the explosion came it would centre on Riga, he took the *Abdiel* and two of his flotilla five miles up the Dvina to join the French sloop *Aisne* in the centre of the capital so that he could be in the closest possible touch with Tallents and Burt.

Meanwhile, in Lithuania, although a French Mission had fixed a provisional demarcation line in June intended to stop the Poles from enlarging their hold on the Vilna area, they had moved farther forward. This compelled Foch to intervene; in July he fixed a second line farther to the west which, for the time being, checked Polish aggression, though clashes still occurred. Notwithstanding this pre-occupation, Voldmaris's Government had managed, despite German obstruction and refusal to supply equipment, to mobilise a force sufficient to launch an offensive in May against the Bolsheviks to the north of Vilna; and by the end of August these had been driven back nearly to the frontier. The greater part of the country remained, nonetheless, under German occupation. There was also a Lithuanian " Bermondt," by name Virgolich: against the day when the Allies compelled Berlin to evacuate their troops, Goltz had encouraged him to recruit a force of Russian ex-prisoners of war, providing it with German instructors and equipment. And this had been swollen by German volunteers until it numbered 2000 men with modern arms and transport as ready as Bermondt's corps to do Goltz's bidding.

Chapter Seven

BERMONDT AND YUDENITCH

The Latvian National Council has received with deep joy
the news that the offensive of our Army is being assisted by
the English and French Fleets, and expresses its most sincere
gratitude to the brave English and French sailors who have
helped the cause of the Latvian soldiers. The Latvian
Army fights its last hard battle against Prussian militarism,
and the Latvian National Council expresses on behalf of
the whole Latvian nation its full satisfaction that the Allied
Fleet has prevented them destroying Courland.

*Message received by Cowan from
the President of Latvia*

ON 1st October, 1919, the *Phaeton* relieved the *Dauntless* of the
task of maintaining the Allied blockade of Libau against
German shipping. Her captain's responsibilities were light
compared with Curtis's at Riga. Goltz and his Government
had to forestall the deadline which the Allies had given for
the evacuation of their troops. " At 0945 on 8th October,"
wrote Curtis,

three German aeroplanes appeared over the town and dropped
a few small bombs on the outer defences. The troops in the streets
and in the defences opened fire with rifles, with no result. At the
same time the Russo-German forces under Bermondt commenced
their advance on Riga, which the Letts opposed; hostilities therefore commenced simultaneously with the air raid. Fighting
continued during the day and by the evening the Letts had been
compelled to fall back on their main defensive line.

Bermondt, who had some 15,000 men, had launched a third
of this number through the western suburbs of the capital,
towards the left bank of the Dvina, to capture the only two

bridges so as to prevent the Letts retreating by this route.[1] The rest of Bermondt's force would then attack the main part of the city, which lay on the right bank, from the south. Initially the Letts had 9000 men to garrison a fifteen-mile defence line, but when the attack began, Balodis, now a general, increased this number to 12,500 by withdrawing units from his eastern (Bolshevik) front where Alexander remained in command of the *Landeswehr*.[2] There was, therefore, no great disparity between the two sides; the Letts might not be so well equipped nor trained as Bermondt's troops, but they fought with a patriotic fervour which never inspired the German mercenaries. Curtis's report continued:

9th October. At 0200 the Germans made a desperate attack on the Mitau Road and forced the Letts back to within two miles of the bridges. At 0800, however, the Letts made a violent counter-attack and forced the Germans back, capturing about 100 prisoners and 14 machine-guns. Although aeroplanes circled continually over the *Abdiel* and *Aisne* and dropped a few bombs in the river, no offensive measures were taken against them, in accordance with previous arrangements that Allied warships should remain neutral (so as to be) of use to the Missions should necessity arise. (Later) the Germans again broke through the Letts on the Mitau Road and, as the Letts were seriously outnumbered, their whole line fell back and entered the town over the bridges during the night. The ship at this time was berthed alongside the Customs Quay.

10th October. At 0800 the German forces arrived at the western ends of the bridges crossing the Dvina and spread down the river and opposite the *Abdiel*. The Letts lifted sections of the bridges so that none could cross, and a furious battle began across the river. The *Aisne*, which was alongside about 500 yards south of the *Abdiel*, finding herself under fire from three directions, proceeded

---

[1] When news of this attack reached the Foreign Office, Curzon suggested that the French should postpone ratification of the German Peace Treaty. Unfortunately it was too late to take this step.

[2] Who could not be employed against Bermondt since German could not be expected to fight German. Indeed, there was at one time a possibility that they would *join* Bermondt under the leadership of Alexander's Chief of Staff, the Baltic Baron von Taube. Fortunately wireless messages between the latter and Bermondt were intercepted by the Letts which enabled Alexander to forestall this danger.

downstream. I noticed that the Germans ceased fire when the *Aisne* left the jetty, and did not resume again until she was clear, which led me to think that they were respecting the neutrality of the Allied ships. Later, when the Germans brought field-guns up and the battle gradually spread down both sides of the river, the *Abdiel* came under very hot fire, the bullets rattling against the sides, luckily not penetrating. Then field-guns began to drop shells into the town over our heads until I began to suspect that they were dropping them near us intentionally, and at 1030 I moved down river about 500 yards to keep out of the way. I remained in this position until 1115, by which time the Germans had started bursting shrapnel immediately overhead and dropping projectiles from field-guns in the water close to the ship. The battle was still spreading down the river on both sides, with parties of men firing machine-guns at each other across the river. As it became apparent that they were trying to hit the ship, I again weighed and moved half a mile farther down, anchoring in the middle of the river.

At 1240 I was obliged to move again as shells were falling close and shrapnel bursting near. There was no doubt that the Germans were firing at the ship, as they pitched shell after shell ten yards short on either quarter but never made an actual hit. There were no casualties. The *Aisne* (which was) anchored near, also moved down river and (was) fired on. The shelling continued until we were out of range (when) I anchored at the mouth of the river. After dark I moved up the river and sent away a motorboat protected with mattresses and manned by a volunteer crew to try and reach Riga by back channels and get into touch with the Mission. This they were successful in doing through finding a telephone. I ascertained that the Germans had not yet crossed the river and that the Missions were safe though the town was being fired on.

11th October. Remained at anchor in midstream, Germans still attacking the town. During the afternoon it became apparent that they were occupying the left bank as far down as Fort Dunamunde. During the night they extinguished the harbour lights and started firing at tugs and neutral ships. The French *Garnier* and *Marne* arrived, also H.M.S. *Vanoc.* I anchored the *Marne* near the river mouth to watch the river and to prevent any serious irregularity taking place on neutral shipping.

One can have nothing but admiration for the courageous restraint with which Curtis and his officers and men supported

Tallents's and Burt's Missions in such provocative circumstances. When his report was received at the Admiralty,
Ferguson commented " Captain Curtis evidently adds other
qualities to those which he was known to possess ": and
Beatty added " This shows that a difficult situation was well
handled by Captain Curtis. Officers and men behaved well."
For reasons to be related, Cowan could not be drawn by the
sound of these guns, but he sent the *Dragon*, *Cleopatra* and
Princess Margaret to Riga. He also retaliated by ordering the
arrest of all German vessels sighted at sea in the Baltic, eight
being quickly taken by British or French warships, whilst
those in Libau were seized by the Letts.

In Riga, Balodis's troops still held the bridges four days after
Bermondt launched his attack.

12th October. At 1330 a tug went alongside the *Marne* and
asked who was in command of the Allied ships. An officer of the
Marne brought (the tug) up to me (Curtis). In the tug was Baron
von Roenne (who) stated that he was in command of artillery in
this sector, and that his guns were covering the position in which
we were anchored. Should the Letts begin to annoy the Germans
by firing across the river, which is only 400 yards wide at this point,
he would be obliged to open fire, and would not guarantee not
hitting us. He said he wished us to go away altogether (which) I
refused to do. He then suggested that if we would anchor off Fort
Dunamunde, he would guarantee that we were not fired on. I
agreed on condition that Allied ships' boats should be allowed to
go up and down the river to the town without molestation, either
by day or night. Before this officer left the ship, Yudenitch's
proclamation [1] was read to him and seemed to have some effect.
I moved the whole of the destroyers down to an anchorage opposite
Fort Dunamunde. After 2100 all (our) boats were employed
bringing off refugees and members of the British Missions for
transfer to the *Princess Margaret*. This was safely accomplished
though all the boats were fired on by the Germans on all trips.

[1] " As Bermondt has not fulfilled any of my orders and information has been
received that he has started military action against the Lettish Troops, I declare
him a traitor to his country and exclude himself and his troops from lists of forces
on the German front." Yudenitch was particularly angry with Bermondt for
using his troops to attack Riga instead of for an advance on Petrograd.

13th October. I placed all refugees and members of the Missions on board the *Princess Margaret* during the forenoon and, on return to the anchorage, placed myself under the orders of Commodore Brisson, who had arrived in the *Lestin* during the night. During the forenoon Burt sent a request to Cowan that an ultimatum might be sent to Bermondt to remove his forces from Fort Dunamunde as they were a menace to Allied shipping. This ultimatum was duly delivered. The Germans in the fort continued to molest shipping by firing on them, and even attempted to take possession of a small Lettish steamer, which was prevented by the *Vanoc*.

To ensure that he was acting according to Cowan's wishes, Brisson signalled him: " In the event of the ultimatum to the Germans to evacuate Fort Dunamunde not being complied with, may I bombard the fort, afterwards occupying the position with Lettish troops, observing that, although this is directly assisting (them), the operation will be useless unless it is done? " The Admiral replied: " Most certainly." His ultimatum, for which he obtained the Admiralty's approval (which Wemyss had the courage to authorise, informing the Supreme Council afterwards) took the following form:

> *To Officers Commanding German Forces at Mitau and Dunamunde from British Admiral.* I require you to withdraw your forces imme-diately from positions near Dunamunde, which are now a threat to Allied vessels in River Dvina, by noon on 15th October, after which I shall take what action I think fit.

Eberhardt, doubtless inspired by the wily Goltz, answered: " There are not and never have been any German troops near Dunamunde. Try the Chief of Russian Voluntary Western Army." Bermondt replied:

> Our wireless station has informed me of your message to Officer Commanding German Troops. Dunamunde is occupied by First Russian Regiment of my Army. As Chief of the Russian Army, and as representative of nation allied with England, have given necessary orders.

This did not satisfy Cowan who wirelessed:

> I wait for your report of withdrawal from all Riga positions and

a cessation of hostilities between your troops and the Letts, and your explanation for bombarding positions near where Allied vessels were berthed, before giving other directions to Allied war vessels.

But before this, at 1215, since the Germans showed no signs of evacuating the fort, Brisson had ordered the Allied ships to open fire. Half an hour's bombardment had the desired effect: Curtis thought it

silly to blow the enemy out of the fort and not occupy it, and not having enough men to do it ourselves, I asked the Military Mission if they could raise a force to storm the fort and suggested, if a big enough force could be sent, they could attack the flank of the German line and establish a front of their own. We could act as artillery. They agreed and a large collection of ferry boats, pleasure steamers, launches and tugs crowded with troops came down the river and made for the fort under our barrage which we lifted at the proper time. The crews of all these craft were women and they handled them well. We then weighed and steamed slowly up river, shooting at the Germans who were bolting across country pursued by the Letts, who established a line across country from a mile or two up river diagonally to the sea. We anchored up river off the end of their line. The Letts took 300 prisoners.

During this bombardment the *Vanquisher* and *Windsor* arrived and joined the Allied force at the river mouth; so did the *Dragon* and *Cleopatra*, the latter's return to England being temporarily deferred. Both cruisers anchored to the west of the river mouth and shelled the Germans with their 6-inch guns.

Although this bombardment had been deliberately provoked by the Germans, Bermondt sent a defiant plea to the Allied Missions:

There was a time when Bolshevik forces were attacking Riga and the ships of the Allied squadron made haste to reach the sea, leaving the town to the Bolsheviks. Today, when the Russian Army is forced to fight the Bolshevik hordes, the Allied squadron has twice crushed my First Regiment of Cossacks; and the civil population declare that it is in this way that Russian blood pays for the heroic help given (to the Allies) during the prolonged struggle against Germany. I can but understand these acts to be in support of the Bolsheviks. I will never give up the position I hold and my army and myself will fight for the salvation of Russia to the last drop of blood.

Needless to say the Allied Missions were not to be hoodwinked: the only Bolsheviks in Latvia were being held by Lettish troops many miles from Riga. At the same time Bermondt signalled Cowan:

Having established the present strategic base for undertaking an offensive against the Bolsheviks, I offered an armistice to the Letts on 10th October. I beg you to realise (that) my troops directed their fire solely against the enemy. I thought the ships of the Allies, being friendly with Russians, would not help Lettish troops who are fighting against friends. I beg you to send a representative with full powers, and in order to save useless bloodshed, I demand that the fire of the Allied ships directed against my troops and the civil population cease.

This was followed by another message:

Reference your signal in which you warn me that my forces must be withdrawn from Dunamunde by 1200 on the 15th, destroyers opened fire notwithstanding I informed you Dunamunde was occupied by Russian troops. I am surprised and perturbed that you permitted fire to be opened and allowed blood of Russian soldiers to be shed. I have issued orders to fire on ships that fire on my forces. Your action shows that you are supporting Lettish insurgents to detriment of Russian Army which is fighting for restoration of Russia.

Cowan's answer was very short and splendidly to the point: " I recognise no Russian commander who fights under German direction or in opposition to General Yudenitch."

In sum, Bermondt's first attack on Riga had failed. When the gallant Letts prevented his troops from seizing the Dvina bridges, the Germans provoked the Allied ships into supporting the Letts, with the result that the Germans were driven well back from the left bank. Consequently, Bermondt had to cancel his main assault from the south: Balodis's troops held their defence line with no more than minor clashes with the enemy. And during the rest of the month they were able to push them well back towards Mitau. It was, however, too much to hope that the Allied warships would be able to continue their support without suffering casualties. Curtis wrote:

17th October. Established a captured wireless set at the divisional headquarters of the Letts; constant communication between the front line and the destroyers was established. There was intermittent fighting on the Lett line during the day, which remained firm. At 1730 a land battery opened fire on H.M.S. *Dragon*, hitting her four times, killing nine men, and wounding one officer and three men. She replied and is reported to have put one gun out of action. She and the *Princess Margaret* then shifted three miles from the entrance to the river out of range.[1]

23rd October. At 1345 German guns started shelling the flotilla. Position of guns could not be located, and as they were making good shooting, *Venturous* being straddled and two men wounded, the flotilla moved down to an anchorage off Fort Dunamunde.

24th October. Situation still unchanged. H.M.S. *Versatile*, *Voyager*, *Vortigern* and *Velox* arrived as reliefs for Twentieth Flotilla. At 1700 the Flotilla moved up river and carried out bombardment on the gun which shelled this part of the anchorage. The scheme of firing was a controlled, concentrated barrage, 1500 yards deep, 1200 yards wide. The enemy gun dropped a few shells in (our) direction when the bombardment started, but suddenly ceased and, it is hoped, was silenced. The *Dragon* also bombarded a battery and (another) point where two guns had been reported. These had been firing all the afternoon but ceased after a few rounds had been fired on them, *Dragon*'s firing being spotted from front line trenches and signalled to her by wireless.

25th October. All quiet. The reliefs for the Twentieth Flotilla took over their duties and at 0900 on the 26th (we) sailed for England. In concluding this report I wish to mention the extraordinary good behaviour of officers and men under fire. There was no difficulty in getting men on deck to work cables, etc.; in fact my greatest concern was the casual way in which they exposed themselves in spite of repeated orders to keep behind cover. I wish

[1] The situation had improved enough to allow the *Cleopatra* to be released: she had sailed for England earlier in the day.

also to mention the officers and men who formed the motorboat's crew who ran the gauntlet of rifle and machine-gun fire up the river, not only on the night of 10th October, but on many subsequent occasions. I could not have wished for a more considerate and competent Senior Naval Officer than Commodore Brisson. His far-seeing tact and willingness for British and French to act together in perfect accord produced the greatest efficiency.

Notwithstanding Bermondt's failure, Balodis could not afford to be complacent; Goltz's henchman could be expected to make another and stronger attack on the capital and, if this was delayed more than a few weeks, ice might have compelled the Allied warships to withdraw. For the present, however, though the *Princess Margaret* sailed on 27th October, the *Dragon* and four British destroyers remained in the Dvina with Brisson's ships. And from Libau, Captain L. Dundas of the *Phaeton* warned Cowan that Bermondt was planning an attack on that port. The Admiral instructed him that in such an event he was to evacuate all civilians from the vicinity of the Naval Harbour " so that you can direct as heavy a bombardment as your forces are capable of on this (area), without preoccupation as to its results to the friendly population, but you should avoid destroying the church. It is important that you should lose no opportunity of inflicting severe punishment on any (Russo-German) force attacking Libau."

*   *   *

Why, for once, had the " sound of the guns " failed to draw Cowan? Why did he decide against leaving Biorko to take personal charge of the Allied action against Bermondt's force, more especially since Duff was absent from Lettish waters?

After Kolchak's attempt to reach Moscow through the Urals in the early summer of 1919 had failed, Denikin began a new drive for the Bolshevik capital from the south in August.

On the 17th his cavalry broke through the Red Army front: on the 23rd he captured Odessa, and a week later Kiev. By 21st September his troops had moved north through Kharkov to Kursk: at the beginning of October they were marching on Voronezh and Orel, the latter only 200 miles from Moscow. This success, coupled with the possibility that Estonia might sign a separate armistice with the Bolsheviks and deprive the Russian North-West Army of its principal base, compelled Yudenitch to launch a serious attack against the Red Army to the north of Lake Peipus. This obliged Pats to break off his armistice negotiations and allow Laidoner's troops to advance in order to avoid a salient potentially dangerous to Estonia. The Estonian flank depended upon Cowan's ships for artillery support and for protection against an assault from the sea for which Zelenoy could use several modern destroyers. And the British Admiral judged that this situation was potentially more important than Bermondt's assault on Riga.

Yudenitch's advance, with some 40,000 men under Rodzianko's command, began with considerable *élan* in the second week in October, though even at this juncture many White officers were on leave in Stockholm and elsewhere. Moreover, Rodzianko refused to establish any effective liaison with the Estonians on his northern flank.[1] However, the Reds, who had no armour of their own, were unnerved by the six British tanks which drove all before them. At the same time, bombardments by the *Delhi, Dauntless* and destroyers enabled the Estonians to push forward along the shore of the Gulf until, on 21st October, Cowan reported: " The Russian advance towards Petrograd is going well and the Estonians are fighting very hard for Krasnaya Gorka, (but they) have now advanced further east than our guns will reach until we can sweep in through the mines."

On this anniversary of Trafalgar, when the Whites

---

[1] Yudenitch showed as much contempt for Pats and his colleagues by the wholly ineffective gesture of appointing a Russian Governor to Tallinn, contrary to his August recognition of Estonian independence.

were only eight miles from Petrograd, disaster struck the Red Fleet.

During the operations of Yudenitch's army against Petrograd, enemy (*i.e. British*) destroyers and light cruisers systematically bombarded positions on the right flank, remaining out of sight of our batteries and posts behind Cape Dolgy Nos. This made effective return fire against the enemy ships impossible (and) had a pernicious effect on the morale of the Red Army units operating there, a counter-attack on 19th October being paralysed by enemy naval gunfire. So, to prevent the enemy approaching the bombardment area, the Baltic Fleet Command decided to lay a mine barrier on a westerly line from Cape Dolgy Nos, the destroyers *Azard*, *Gavriil*, *Konstantin*, and *Svoboda* being detailed for this operation. They sailed from Kronstadt on 21st October, but at 0545 ran into an enemy minefield about three miles off Cape Dolgy Nos, the *Gavriil*, *Konstantin* and *Svoboda* being lost with all hands. The *Azard*, after remaining in the area until 0620, succeeded in getting out of the minefield and returned to Kronstadt.[1]

The simultaneous sinking of these three destroyers, which Zelenoy could ill afford to lose at this critical juncture, is of sufficient importance to warrant quoting another Soviet source:

To oppose the English and Estonian ships, the Baltic Fleet Command decided to lay minefields in the region of Cape Dolgy Nos. To carry out this mission the destroyers *Gavriil*, *Svoboda*, *Konstantin* and *Azard* moved into Koporsky Bight very early on 21st October. At 0545, off Cape Dolgy Nos, the destroyers hit a minefield laid by the enemy. Three were blown up and sank, only 25 men being saved.[2] The *Azard*, which brought up the rear, escaped destruction and returned safely to Kronstadt. A Committee of Enquiry decided that the main reason for the loss of the destroyers was the crew's inadequate knowledge of the situation in the area where the hostile attack was to be made. The Committee noted the unparalleled heroism of the crews of the lost ships and particularly of the commanders and the commissars: " the officers took all measures in their power to ensure the safety of their ships and crews, caring nothing for their own safety." [3]

---

[1] *Piat Let Krasnogo Flota.*
[2] Six were picked up by an Estonian vessel.   [3] *Baltiisky Flot.*

Notwithstanding this disaster, the men of the Red Fleet were instrumental in saving Petrograd. Whilst the Bolshevik leaders in Moscow feared for the safety of their new capital—since Denikin's troops had captured Orel on 13th October—and counted the old one as good as lost, there were many others determined to defend it to the last. The dreadnought *Sevastopol*, berthed in the Neva, might not be able to steam, but from 20th October her 12-inch guns bombarded the White Russian lines. So, too, did the smaller weapons of the likewise immobile destroyers *Vsadnik* and *Gaidamak*. More important, Commissar N. I. Martinov hurried to Kronstadt and called for volunteers from the Fleet to reinforce the Red Army. As many as 11,000 seamen were landed near Peterhof, their arrival doing more than stem Yudenitch's advance: by 28th October his troops had been pushed well back from Petrograd. The Estonians might then have abandoned their attempt to take Krasnaya Gorka but for a recent Admiralty decision. In response to an urgent plea from Cowan, the 15-inch gunned monitor *Erebus*, Captain J. A. Moreton, homeward bound from the White Sea, had been ordered to Biorko where she arrived on 24th October.

Three days later, a member of the *Westminster*'s crew noted in his diary:

At daybreak the *Delhi* and *Dunedin* screened by the *Spenser*, *Mackay*, *Winchelsea*, *Walpole* and *Vectis* join us at Kaporia. At 0700 the *Erebus* and Estonian destroyers proceed inshore. Our destroyers circle them as an anti-submarine screen. At 0730 the *Delhi* opens up bombardment with a salvo of 6-inch followed by the *Erebus* and *Dunedin*. Until 0900 these three kept up a steady fire on the Bolshevik positions, the *Mackay* and *Shakespeare* moving inshore and opening up at 0800. A big gun ashore replied with about six shots, doing no damage. At 0830 two C.M.B.s join the squadron. Seaplanes were also up spotting. At 0915 the cruisers returned to harbour and the *Erebus* anchored.

This put fresh heart into the Estonians, but whether on this or subsequent days the *Erebus*'s heavy shell did any serious damage to Krasnaya Gorka (or Grey Horse) is questionable.

It certainly did not dislodge the hard pressed garrison: to quote a Soviet source:

> Since they were unable to seize the forts with troops, the Interventionists tried to overthrow them with ships' gunfire. On 27th October an English naval force, including the *Erebus*, armed with 15-inch guns, entered Kaporia Bight and began firing at Krasnaya Gorka. Although their fire was spotted by aircraft, the fort did not fall. Only 20 shells fell near Krasnaya Gorka, of which a significant number failed to explode. The answering fire from the forts compelled the ships to cease fire and leave. On 30th October, enemy ships including the *Erebus* and Estonian destroyers again opened fire on Krasnaya Gorka without result, and were likewise driven back by fire from the fort. For their stoic courage the garrison was awarded the Red Star of the Revolution. For three weeks on end they had stood by their guns for twenty-four hours a day and only their skilful firing made it possible to repulse repeated enemy attempts to break through the front.[1]

Be this as it may, the *Erebus* had arrived too late. On 31st October, by which time the Red Army had recaptured Orel, thereby stemming Denikin's advance (and his troops were never again to be so close to Moscow), and Kolchak's troops had been evicted from Tobolsk, Cowan had to write:

> The Petrograd advance is checked and unlikely to reach its objective, for the chief reason that there was no co-operation or liaison between Yudenitch's columns and the Estonians; the Russian columns received little, if any, direction from Yudenitch once they were launched forward; and no attempt was made by the Russians to provide for, or assist, in the capture of Krasnaya Gorka, without which it was madness to hope for the capture of Petrograd. When the Bolshevik resistance stiffened, the Russians incontinently fell back with no word to the Estonians, thereby exposing their right flank and compromising the slight hope remaining that they might take Krasnaya Gorka with the help of the *Erebus*'s guns. The *Erebus* again carried out a very accurate bombardment, assisted by seaplane spotting yesterday, but no infantry attack followed and she is now out of ammunition. Yudenitch and all his commanders have relied on the tanks with their British personnel achieving the impossible on every sector of

[1] p. 182 n3., op. cit.

the front, in the same spirit that they have often inferred that my force of light cruisers and destroyers should steam through the mines, past the forts at point blank range, and up to Kronstadt and its forts, to capture but not injure the warships there and then hoist the Russian flag for them, this with no intention of doing anything in the way of attacking these forts themselves from the land. The only hope now of getting to Petrograd is the intervention of the Finns.

But, as the Admiral had previously reported, " the Finns, as soon as they think it a certainty will undoubtedly join in, but they will not ' get off the fence ' in order to turn the scale whilst the result is still in doubt."

All this time Cowan was without Gough's help and guidance. When the General had been called home in mid-August, the War Office had expressed the view that he had done all that was required of him, notwithstanding his refusal to support Churchill's strong anti-Bolshevik attitude by, for example, encouraging the Finns to launch an attack on Petrograd. Nonetheless, he had pursued a policy towards the Baltic States contrary to the Cabinet's. " Yet independence was the only sensible and realistic policy at that time," he wrote. " I was (however) hated for (it). The White Russians were furious, accusing me of dismembering their country. A general, Gorky by name, paid me a visit and expressed his indignation in very fierce language. (And) the large number of Russian nobility who were still seeking refuge in these border States, as well as in Denmark, in Sweden and in England had the ear of Lloyd George and Churchill. I was accused of being a Bolshevik myself. As a result of (this) intrigue, Lloyd George peremptorily recalled me." [1] When Cowan learned this he evinced unusual restraint:

Following the decision that General Sir Hubert Gough is not to return—which decision has been withheld for two months—his Chief Staff Officer and the rest of his Staff are now ordered home. All this has happened during the time it was of vital importance

[1] *Soldiering On.*

for the success of Yudenitch's operations that there should be continuous military advice and direction by British officers who were *au fait* with the situation; and, on the spot here, it is impossible to see the wisdom of such a step if the money we have spent on military supplies for these armies is expected to bear any fruit at all.

The Cabinet was not, however, withdrawing the Military Mission, only those who were Gough's supporters. In his place came General Sir Richard Haking who, after meeting the Admiral, hurried to see Yudenitch. " I have great hopes," wrote Cowan, " that he will induce him to avoid the gross military mistakes which have precluded all hope of success up to now."

Haking met Yudenitch, Laidoner and Pitka on 2nd November when, to quote Cowan,

it was announced by Yudenitch that he was unable to continue his advance on Petrograd owing to increased pressure on his right flank, and the consequent necessity of withdrawing troops for its support. Laidoner also stated that he could not now capture Krasnaya Gorka, even with all the assistance our ships could give, and that he must withdraw his line back to Kaporia Bight at once. This ends the hope of relieving Petrograd this year, to prevent which has been one of Goltz's chief aims; and it must be a source of deep satisfaction to him that the forbearance of the Allies to thwart his plans in any degree during the whole of this year has made his task such a simple one; his stroke against Riga, at the critical time, having the effect of withholding reinforcements from the North-West Russian and Estonian fronts just when they might have turned the scale against the Bolshevik defence of Petrograd.

Since the Russian North-West Army was now a spent force, Cowan's considered judgment on its offensive is worth quotation:

Yudenitch insisted on advancing straight for Petrograd without first making his main objective the capture of Krasnaya Gorka, which would have laid Kronstadt open to attack, and would have enabled my ships to sweep in and bombard from the sea. The attack on Krasnaya Gorka was left to a weak force of Estonians;

and with no attempt by either Commander to co-operate in any degree whatever, until—as happened—one or other of them got into difficulties, when recriminations ensued, but no effective support was given. It would be difficult to recall any offensive effort ever conducted, which has showed such an utter lack of intelligent leadership, or in which greater military mistakes have been made. Yudenitch thought that our tanks on land, and our ships off the coast, would do everything for him. His advisers and subordinate commanders are far too impregnated with German leanings and influence to leave me very sure that he really meant this effort to succeed.

Haking remained in Helsingfors for just long enough—a fortnight—to determine that no other policy than that followed by Gough would work. Then he, too, returned to England, though for a different reason. Until now the Allies had believed that the Whites would be able to overthrow Lenin and his supporters and could be persuaded to establish a new democratic Russia which the Baltic States would willingly rejoin. But the failure of Denikin's and Kolchak's drives on Moscow, and Yudenitch's on Petrograd, undermined this conviction. Whilst continuing to incite the Whites in the hope that they might yet triumph, the British and French began to guard against a Red victory. On 23rd October Clemenceau formulated his doctrine of a *cordon sanitaire*: the Baltic States' desire for independence should be encouraged so that, with Finland and Poland, they would form a barrier between Communist Russia and Western Europe. The British Government readily accepted this: a large proportion of the electorate favoured allowing the Russians to settle their own affairs; the dismissed Gough was not the only man on the spot who had stressed that *de jure* recognition of the Baltic States was the only realistic policy when Britain was so firmly against sending a military force to Russia; and it accorded with the help which the Royal Navy had been giving these countries for almost a year. Clemenceau was, however, determined that, if the Baltic States were to be independent they should be closely aligned with France. When, therefore, the

Supreme Council decided on 28th October to replace the Baltic Military Mission by an Inter-Allied Commission charged with the task of ensuring that the Germans did not further delay the evacuation of Latvia and Lithuania,[1] the French insisted that it should be headed by their nominee, General Niessel. The British Cabinet treated this as an undeserved insult, though their failure to support Gough made it difficult to contest the appointment. The rift between the British and French Governments was, however, more serious than this: on 8th November, 1919, Lloyd George publicly declared that, whilst he now favoured an independent bloc of Baltic States, they should be under British influence and serve as a bridge —not a barrier—between England and Soviet Russia. And, fortunately for this attitude, not only had the Royal Navy already laid firm foundations for friendly relations with the Baltic States, but Niessel's actions were so lacking in wisdom as to wreck any possibility that Clemenceau might achieve the same dominant position for his country as he had already achieved in Poland.

*   *   *

Before, however, Niessel's Commission [2] could reach the Baltic, the battle for Riga was renewed. Three weeks of comparative quiet had allowed Balodis to redeploy his troops for an attack designed to forestall a fresh assault on the city before winter compelled the Allied warships to withdraw from

[1] The Commission's instructions stated that " the carrying out of the provisions of Article XII of the Armistice includes not only the withdrawal of the organised German units at present in the Baltic Provinces, together with their staffs and administrative services, but also the recall of all German soldiers who, after being demobilised, shall have singly or in groups joined the Russian units organised in the said Provinces. Similarly, German diplomatic and civilian officials will be required to leave the Baltic Provinces at the same time as the troops. Control will also apply to the checking of material taken away by the German troops, with a view to preventing the removal of material and supplies not properly belonging to the said troops."

[2] With which the Weimar Government had agreed to co-operate by appointing Admiral Hopmann as their representative.

188

the Dvina area. The Letts were ready by 3rd November when they advanced through the western suburbs against Bermondt's division, with the support of the guns of the *Dragon*, four "V & W" destroyers and Brisson's sloops anchored near the mouth of the Dvina.[1] Fierce fighting followed for eight days and nights during which the Letts repelled every counter-attack and slowly drove the Germans back, whilst the British and French ships kept within range by moving along the coast of the Gulf of Riga. Then, on the 11th, Bermondt's troops were reported withdrawing in some confusion all along the front, and it was clear that Balodis and his gallant countrymen had gained a considerable victory, that Riga was safe, and Brisson could order his own and the British ships to cease fire—which was as well since they had nearly exhausted their ammunition. The Letts had saved their capital by their own exertions, but they were in no doubt of the debt they owed to the Allied Navies: in the words of a Lett who was there, " the fleet's artillery greatly helped the courageous soldiers throughout those days, shelling enemy positions and rear lines. The liaison and co-operation arranged at the beginning of the attack worked well. The Allied fleet rendered irreplaceable help to the fighters for freedom against the stubborn invader." [2]

Meanwhile all was not so well at Libau where Dundas in the *Phaeton*, together with the *Dauntless* and the destroyers *Winchester*, *Whitley*, *Valorous* and *Wryneck*, had for some weeks expected Bermondt to attack the small Lettish garrison. The Germans began their advance on 4th November when the British ships opened a steady fire which only ceased at sunset. The *Winchester* was then sent to Windau to reconnoitre, whilst the Allied Political and Military Missions were embarked in the *Watchman* and evacuated to safety. That night was quiet, but the renewed German attack next day was followed by

---

[1] The French had ordered the armoured cruiser *Gueydon* to the Baltic to reinforce Brisson. But she was too big: she grounded on the way to Riga and had to return damaged to Copenhagen.

[2] *The Adventure of Bermondt-Avalov.*

intense activity during the night of the 5th requiring a British counter-bombardment. The *Winchester* returned with disquieting news that the Windau garrison of only 300 men faced an imminent attack by 600 Germans. So Dundas dispatched the *Wryneck* with 150 reinforcements, all that the hard-pressed Commandant of the Libau garrison could spare. The German attack on the latter port was renewed on the 6th and 7th but made little progress against the gunfire of the British cruisers and destroyers berthed in the harbour, when a German aeroplane which attempted to bomb them was shot down by the Letts. The onset of winter prevented a further attack on the 8th: " this is considered to be due to the ice on the lakes having been cut and the temperature rising to 30 degrees," wrote Dundas: " it appears in abeyance until the lakes freeze hard and the ice becomes thick. Snow is falling," he added ominously. But against this he could write, " H.M.S. *Erebus* has arrived and suitable targets are being prospected for." On receipt of news of the German attack on Libau, whose value to the Allies had been stressed time and again, the Admiralty suggested to Cowan that this heavy-gunned monitor would be better employed there than in a further assault on Krasnaya Gorka—but Cowan had already ordered her south. With her arrival Captain Moreton became the Senior Naval Officer in the Libau area. On the same day, 8th November, the British ships were able to replenish their magazines and shell rooms. Next morning the *Erebus* joined the other British ships in countering German gunfire on the port.

The ensuing four days were relatively quiet whilst the Germans, having failed in their first assault on less than 2000 Letts, doubled their original force of some 4000 men. On the 14th these launched a new attack soon after dawn. Although the British ships and the French sloop *Ancre* replied with heavy fire, the Germans succeeded in capturing the fixed defences and in penetrating the outskirts of the town by 1000. Half an hour later the Letts counter-attacked so fiercely behind a lifting barrage laid by the ships that, by 1450, the

Germans had been driven back two miles behind the line which they had held for the past five days. According to a member of the *Erebus*'s crew, " we opened fire at a range of about a mile and a quarter which, for the 15-inch, was almost point-blank. Firing at first was at fairly long intervals and for quite a few rounds the 4-inch guns' crews had to pull on a lanyard to open the breech, as the water put on the mushroom head to maintain the gas-tight seal had frozen solid. (However) the rate of firing and the range soon increased until, when it ceased at about 1400, the range was over twenty miles. We learned afterwards that as soon as the Germans started to run, the men of Libau went after them by cart, car, tram or anything on wheels, armed with anything from rifles to spades and pick-axes." Since this success was achieved with no more than twenty-five Letts killed against some 8000 Germans, it is not surprising that Moreton reported the Letts to be still " full of fight." He had, however, cause for anxiety should the Germans make another attack: the *Valorous* had exhausted her ammunition, the other ships were running short, and there were no further supplies in the port. Fortunately the Germans continued to fall back on the 15th and 16th, notwithstanding an impertinent demand calling on the garrison of Libau to surrender by noon on the 17th, whilst the force which had been menacing Windau was reported to have withdrawn. And by that time Cowan had been able to send an ammunition ship to Libau: he also diverted the *Galatea*, homeward bound with Haking aboard, and her escorting destroyers to Libau to transfer the contents of their magazines to Moreton's force. To quote the member of the *Erebus*'s crew again: " After that there was no more firing and we began to think we had a chance of being home for Christmas."

Though this was not to be—Cowan did not finally sail the *Erebus* from Copenhagen until 29th December—Bermondt's repulse from Libau on 14th November, coupled with the defeat of his attack on Riga on the 11th, marked the beginning of the end of his Baltic adventure. As the Germans withdrew through Mitau, the Letts outflanked and attacked them on successive days until their position was so desperate that Eberhardt relieved Bermondt of his command. And on the night of 18th November the former asked for an armistice. But Balodis had had too much experience of the Germans to agree to this; on 21st November he captured Mitau. Niessel then proposed that the fighting should cease and the now demoralised Germans be allowed to evacuate the country. Cowan had other views: "The situation (in Latvia) is satisfactory," he wrote,

but the German threat may at any time recur owing to what seems to me an incredibly short-sighted and injudicious attitude by the Mission under General Niessel. This Mission, after visiting Berlin, are now functioning from Memel, and have evidently listened to the German side of the question, and are disregarding the most urgent representations that I can make to them, to the effect that there should be no cessation of hostilities until either all the Germans are hunted back into Prussia, or they have unconditionally surrendered. General Niessel is doing his utmost to bring about what the Germans most urgently need, i.e., a twenty-four hours' cessation of hostilities, and this is madness, as anyone who has followed and suffered under the German situation, and the extreme weakness and vacillation of the Allied policy out here to the extent that I have, can very quickly realise.

Fortunately Balodis was of the same mind: he ignored Niessel and by the end of November had driven the last German soldier from Latvia, Goltz and Eberhardt with them.

Though the problem of removing them from Lithuania remained, Balodis was free to transfer the greater part of his victorious force to the eastern front where his troops had recently captured a whole Red regiment. "Being hard up for food themselves they decided they'd have to shoot the lot," noted one British officer. "However, the Lettish battalion told off for the job couldn't stick it and refused to go on, so they called up a woman's battalion who cheerfully scuppered the lot with hand grenades"—which may or may not be true; but if it was, who shall blame them after all that their countrywomen had suffered in Riga and elsewhere during the past year. More important, this success presaged well for the Letts' determination, following their success against the Germans, to drive the Bolsheviks from their country.

Chapter Eight

"A SUDDEN FLOOD OF MUTINY"

So the man, machine-ly treated, and whose hopes are fast aground
In the " Proper Service Channels . . ."
When he's strained will fracture badly . . .

Admiral Ronald Hopwood

COWAN first went to the Baltic as a junior rear-admiral with a couple of cruisers and half-a-dozen destroyers. Within a year his force comprised every type of war vessel, except for capital ships, and was of a size rarely commanded by an officer of his seniority. His initial purpose was to encourage Estonia and Latvia to resist Bolshevik aggression. It became a campaign against a hostile fleet whilst helping four separate states to maintain their newly declared independence against virulent Bolshevism, Prussian imperialism and White Russian ambitions; and he was required to do it with his hands tied by the ambivalent attitude of the Allies towards Intervention and reluctance to enforce a German withdrawal. But though Cowan's fleet, tasks and responsibilities came to exceed those which a rear-admiral is expected to shoulder, his supersession by a more senior officer was never seriously considered. There could be no clearer evidence of the Admiralty's confidence in him, for all that they required him to remain subordinate to the Commander-in-Chief Atlantic Fleet. Since the Baltic Force was to all intents an independent command directly under the Admiralty, akin to a foreign station except that it depended for its ships upon frequently changed detachments from home waters, greater justice would have been done had this been recognised and Cowan granted acting higher rank, even if he could not be accorded the title of Commander-in-Chief.[1]

This interruption to the thread of our narrative is prompted by the need to deal with certain incidents which increased the burden of Cowan's task. History and legend have combined to give an ugly connotation to the word mutiny, defined as a combination of two or more persons to defy authority with *or without* violence. It may amount to the wholesale usurping of power involving bloodshed;[2] more often it is limited to passive refusal of duty, akin to a workmen's strike, aimed at the redress of grievances which men believe they can relieve in no other way.[3] Since Cowan's detractors ascribed to him responsibility for the mutinies which occurred in the Baltic Force in 1919, more especially when they were able to add the trouble he later experienced in the *Hood* to what he had previously suffered in the *Zealandia*, justice to a unique man requires the record to be set aright.

There were more mutinies in the British Services in 1919 than those which occurred in the Baltic. The high standards of morale and discipline of Britain's Armed Forces are based on years of peace-time training. In war those standards are the backbone of forces multiplied many times by officers and men whose training is measured in weeks, when patriotism and kindred factors ensure that they are proof against the " slings and arrows of outrageous fortune." Morale is, however, strained and, when the fighting is done, may be subjected to influences sufficient to disrupt discipline.

Since the Armistice of 1918 had to be enforced until a peace treaty was signed, and order had to be restored in countries ruptured by the war, there could be no sudden reduction of the Services to their pre-August 1914 size. But there was no need to maintain them at their war strength; as

---

[1] Notwithstanding the precedent of Sir Samuel Hood who held the appointment of Commander-in-Chief in the " Windward and Leeward Charibee Islands " in 1804 when no more than a commodore.

[2] e.g. the *Bounty* (1789) and at the Nore (1797).

[3] e.g. at Spithead (1797) and Invergordon (1931).

many men as possible had to be released to restore Britain's economy. Unfortunately, lack of experience, together with a cessation of hostilities earlier than expected, led Lloyd George's war-winning Coalition Government to authorise a demobilisation scheme in which priority was given to those who were most needed in industry. But men who had been torn from their homes and chosen careers, who wanted to return to them as speedily as possible, were no more interested in this requirement than they understood the need to maintain large forces when they believed they had beaten the Hun. Equity meant " first in, first out." This was the main reason for the mutinies in the Army in 1919, when troops refused to return from leave in Britain to the Army of Occupation on the Rhine, and similar protests in transit camps in France.

For the Navy there was no longer a need for a massive battle fleet in home waters when the High Seas Fleet was interned in Scapa Flow. A large force of sweepers would be required until the seas around Britain could be cleared of mines; otherwise the Fleet could be reduced to near its peacetime size; i.e. one battle fleet in home waters, which would suffice to provide the ships temporarily required in the Baltic and the White Sea, another in the Mediterranean, and cruiser squadrons elsewhere. And this could be done with some 250,000 officers and men—those of the regular Navy (146,000 in 1914) augmented by volunteers from amongst reservists and " hostilities only " ratings. But demobilising the rest could not be effected overnight. All had to be given ten days' post-war leave. The ships for the post-war fleets and squadrons had to be chosen and their reservists and " hostilities only " officers and men, who might number as many as eighty per cent of their complement, replaced by regulars, who could only be found after other ships had been reduced to reserve. And men impatient for release found it difficult to appreciate how much these difficulties bedevilled the Admiralty's implementation of the demobilisation scheme which added to their discontent with its fundamental unfairness to those who had served the greater part of the war at sea.

There was, however, a more weighty reason for discontent in the Navy. In 1852, the basic rate of pay of an able seaman had been fixed at 1s. 6d. per day: in the ensuing sixty years it had risen by no more than 1d. In 1912 Churchill, as First Lord, had persuaded the Government to grant a further increase of 1d. This might have been adequate at the time, but the outbreak of war, with the consequent rapid rise in the cost of living, called for a further rise, especially for those with wives and families to support. This was met in 1917 by additions, of 2d. per day in the case of an able seaman, plus a separation allowance of 10s. 6d. per week for wives. These amounts had, however, little relation to reality; the increases of more than 200 per cent which had to be given in 1919 are damning evidence of the nation's injustice to those who loyally fought on until the Armistice was signed. Then their resentment blazed. But the Admiralty took two months to set up a special committee [1] to examine the problem, and a further month to wring a temporary increase from the Treasury of 1s. 6d. per day in the case of able seamen and *pro rata*. Before this, first at Devonport and later at the other home ports, the Lower Deck was constrained to set up their own committees whose proposals were, for the most part, so sound that they were adopted by the Jerram Committee. Accepting that strike action was wholly out of place in the Services, they never suggested a resort to Labour's weapon for coercing employers. Their patience was, however, sorely tried. Though the Jerram Committee reported at the end of March, the Admiralty then appointed another departmental one to examine its recommendations. This meant that the long awaited new rates of pay (which brought the basic rate of an able seaman up to 4s. per day) were not announced until May,[2] when the Fleet's gratification was tempered by the

---

[1] Headed by Admiral Sir Martyn Jerram.

[2] After Wemyss had threatened resignation in order to obtain Cabinet agree-

knowledge that some recommendations had been rejected, notably that the increases should be backdated to 1st October, 1918, and that adequate provision should be made for widows and children.

There was also discontent over the payment of war gratuities: whilst officers were given these at the same rate for service ashore and afloat, ratings were awarded more for service afloat than ashore, which, however logical, was resented on the grounds that this had been beyond their control. So there were, for example, mutinies in January 1919 aboard minesweepers at Rosyth, and in the patrol boat *Kilbride* at Milford Haven, when the Red Flag was hoisted. And though the pay problem was largely resolved by the end of May, it left a legacy of discontent which, coupled with the unfairness of the demobilisation scheme, could not be quickly removed. These points should be borne in mind as we now turn to the mutinies which occurred later in the year in ships of the Baltic Force.

When the First Destroyer Flotilla came home from the Baltic in the second half of August it was, to quote Cowan, " a model of discipline and cheerful, high war spirit." Yet on 12th October, on hearing that they were about to return to the Baltic, 150 seamen broke out of their ships at Port Edgar, one losing as much as a third of her crew. Half of the flotilla sailed on the 14th with its crews made up from Atlantic Fleet battleships,[1] and most of the deserters soon gave themselves up, or were arrested in Edinburgh. But forty-four men made their way to London to present a petition to Whitehall. These were arrested at King's Cross by half-a-dozen policemen and escorted to Chatham.

The Commodore Atlantic Fleet Destroyers reported:

---

ment. Officers had to wait for a separate committee, which was set up in March, whose recommendations for increases of the order of 75 per cent were announced in July.

[1] They went to Riga and Libau. The remainder reached Biorko on 10th November when the Second Flotilla sailed for home.

The causes of the unrest are due to many minor grievances which the destroyers have made their own; they carried their full share of the burden of the war and they felt that they were entitled before anybody to a spell, and undoubtedly expected to be sent early to their home ports: as a matter of fact, they were the last to leave Rosyth. There was considerable feeling on the subject of the naval (victory) march through London: the destroyers had led the battleships throughout the war and expected, if not to lead, to have a definite place in the parade: it was unfortunate that they were placed at the rear. There is discontent (because) many men in barracks and in reserve ships have had almost continual leave since the Armistice and they consider that these should have a turn at the Baltic. The fact that the S.N.O. in the Baltic promised this particular flotilla seven days' extra leave on arrival in England, and that it was not possible to grant this leave was mentioned.[1] These minor grievances, taken separately, are of no importance; but the agitators are quick to pick them up and foster a sense of injustice; the dislike of Baltic service is seized on by the leaders of unrest. Some of these destroyers are making their third visit to the Baltic.

The subsequent court of inquiry reported that there was no evidence that the mutiny was prearranged, and added more important reasons for it: that the men were being employed on arduous service without being at war, for which they were not receiving extra pay as was the Army fighting in North Russia, and the Merchant Navy working in the Baltic, likewise ratings engaged in mine clearance; that they were under the misapprehension that service in the Baltic should be restricted to volunteers; and that they suffered a shortage of provisions and canteen stores. By 21st November ninety-six offenders had been arrested and punished, ten by sentences of imprisonment. Most of the remainder were later dealt with similarly.

Another mutiny occurred on board the *Vindictive* at Copenhagen in November when she was secured alongside the collier *Jenny*, which in her turn was secured to the *Argus* from

---

[1] Cowan told Campbell that he would recommend the Admiralty to grant this additional leave. Through some misunderstanding Campbell informed his ships' companies without waiting for Admiralty approval, which was not given.

which the *Vindictive's* seamen and marines were transferring provisions and stores. Due to bad weather the *Vindictive* had steam up and two anchors down. To quote Captain Grace's report:

Special leave had been given to one watch on Monday, but owing to the state of the sea and the work in hand, no leave was granted on Tuesday. Also, men who broke their leave seriously on the previous stay of the ship at Copenhagen were informed that they would not be granted leave. Some of these took advantage of the situation to persuade others, principally young stokers, that they were being harshly treated. At 1330 a party of about 40 fell in on the quarterdeck demanding to see the Commander. They were told that (he) would see some of them singly, but they refused to go away. I was (there) at the time and, thinking they would pay attention to me, said that they could only be seen singly, and ordered them away. When they paid no attention, I had two men placed below under arrest. After a few minutes, the master-at-arms and some petty officers persuaded (the others) to leave the quarterdeck. Shortly afterwards, however, they returned and fell in shouting, " We want some leave." I ordered the Marine detachment to be fallen in. When the men saw that they were still unsuccessful, they dispersed and went to their messdeck where they remained singing and cheering.

The weather was steadily getting worse, and at 1530 I was forced to shift billet. While the ship was under way the Senior Engineer Officer informed me that he had caught two of the stokers, whom I had reason to believe were ringleaders, (trying) to stop the fan engines,[1] and that he had posted petty officers to prevent any recurrence of this.

After evening quarters, when the ship had anchored, Lower Deck was cleared and everybody ordered aft when Grace told his officers and men what had happened, giving the reasons for the disturbance—lack of canteen stores, mess traps and other comforts, the failure to give leave that afternoon, and

---

[1] Thereby showing a callous disregard for their shipmates tending the boiler furnaces from which there might have been an oil fuel flashback as a result of the drop in the boiler-room air pressure. The loss of steam pressure to the engines would also have endangered the ship; with a gale blowing in such a confined harbour the *Vindictive* might have been stranded. These two men were justly sentenced to five years' penal servitude.

objections to serving in the Baltic, with special reference to the campaign being waged by certain English newspapers against Intervention: one went so far as to describe the Navy in the Baltic as " worse than the Hun baby-killers who bombed London." [1]

I dealt with these, pointing out the reasons for them. I told them that I relied upon their loyalty to prevent any disturbance by a small section of discontented men of indifferent character. I then ordered the two men who were caught at the fan engines to stand forward: they were immediately arrested and marched below. The opinion of the ship's company was obviously on the side of law and order; the whole matter was carried out in silence without a murmur from the malcontents. I continued my speech, saying that leave would be given next day if possible, but that no men who had taken part in the disturbance would be allowed ashore. I also told them that I intended to punish such of these men as I considered necessary.

On the following morning, many of these men did not turn to, so I arrested five of the worst, charged them, and sent them off to England for 90 days' hard labour, after which I trust that they will be discharged from H.M. Service. I (then) arrested six more, and followed the same procedure. Next morning, 14 men still refused duty; these were at once arrested. Finally, late on Thursday evening, two seamen refused duty. I dealt with them at once. There has been no further trouble.

Likewise in November 1919 the " hostilities only " crews of the minesweepers operating in the Baltic refused duty because they had reached the end of the year for which they had volunteered for service after the Armistice and because, when doing so, it had been expressly stated that they would not be involved in further hostilities.

Lastly, there was a mutiny in Cowan's flagship. Though circumstances denied the *Delhi* the usual shake-down and work-up period after commissioning before she left England in May, her West Country crew's success at sport and other activities in Biorko showed that she was as well set for a

[1] Inspired, no doubt, by a singularly infelicitous question in the House of Commons: " Are British battleships murdering Russians at the present time? " —to which, needless to say, no reply was given.

successful commission as any other ship, notwithstanding their captain, Mackworth's, unpopularity. By December, however, they had further grievances—a fear that the ship would not return to England when the Gulf of Finland was frozen, a shortage of Arctic clothing, and the knowledge that the ship was not fitted with any special heating equipment. To these men who were expecting a bleak Christmas amidst the desolation of Biorko, came the heart-warming news that the *Delhi* was to proceed to Reval. One of her officers remembers:

As usual Walter Cowan was ashore within a few minutes of anchoring. " Off to see old Spitkid," we said; such was the rude nickname we had given Admiral Pitka. About 1100 the barge was seen returning, whilst the Commander was discussing with some of us what leave should be given. Up the gangway tripped the trim little figure of Walter Cowan. He was, of course, received at the top by the O.O.W., the Commander and Mackworth. As he came over the side he barked out in his little nasal voice, "Prepare for sea at once, please, Captain Mackworth; we are returning to Biorko." Even the most loyal among the ship's company felt that this was " a bit 'ard." No Christmas shopping, no run ashore, nothing but an immediate return to bloody Biorko. So when the Commander ordered, " Both watches prepare ship for sea," the response was very poor; only about 25% of the ship's company obeyed the bugle.

The next few hours are a jumbled kaleidoscope in my mind: anxious consultations between the various wardroom officers, briefing of divisional officers by the Commander advising us how to try and get our divisions to work, interviews with senior ratings, deputations going here and there, false alarms of worse things— and of better—a general feeling of malaise and unreality. But towards the end of the afternoon enough confidence was felt to sound off, " Both watches prepare for sea " again, this time with nearly complete success. There were a few laggards, but the majority soon put them straight. Thereafter we had no trouble.

The superficial commentator might ascribe this trouble to Cowan; that his order to the *Delhi*'s captain was given too hastily. But the real fault was Mackworth's; if he had pointed out the disappointment this change of plan must mean for his ship's company, and asked for an explanation which he could give them, they would have responded with nothing worse than the sailor's traditional toothsuck. As it was, Mackworth's swift echo of " his master's voice " produced a regrettable refusal of duty. But—and this is important when considering the question of Cowan's alleged responsibility for mutinies in ships in which he served—this trouble in the *Delhi* was not so serious as those which occurred in the First Destroyer Flotilla and the *Vindictive*, for which Cowan could only be held responsible on the grounds that he took insufficient steps to represent to the Admiralty the grievances which the men suffered. But there is no evidence to support this; on the contrary, the Admiralty in part, but chiefly the Government, persisted in refusing to recognise that service in the Baltic amounted to war, and so to authorise measures for relieving the hardships of the men in the ships serving there.

So the surprising thing is not that there were a few mutinies in Cowan's force, but that there were no more. This may be countered with the argument that there was only one naval mutiny at this time in the White Sea area,[1] and none in the British Mediterranean Fleet supporting the White forces in South Russia, where the discipline of the French Navy proved so bad that its ships had to be withdrawn. But the just view, surely, is that any other admiral in Cowan's position would have been as badly plagued by such influences beyond his control and that some might have been unable to prevent them disrupting the campaign; whereas Cowan, by his insistence on the highest standards, coupled with a tolerance of human frailty which was recognised by the men who served under him, though he cloaked it by outbursts of temper, managed to maintain discipline in the face of great provocation in all but a very few cases.

Let Cowan's denigrators also read this from a memorandum which, amid all his heavy responsibilities, he found

---

[1] In the gunboat *Cicala*, which is to the Navy's credit since the British Army, and the Royal Marines working ashore there, suffered serious disaffection, though the extent to which the men concerned were provoked into this was recognised by the commutation of sentences of death to one year's imprisonment.

time to write in October 1919—an extract which will serve to recall us to the main stream of our story:

Our role is to keep order and prevent oppression in the Baltic until stable and humane Governments are formed by all peoples on its shores. You will agree with me that our service out here is hard and disagreeable (when) so many have well earned rest and happiness; yet our Navy has scarcely ever had a worthier aim or, if it succeeds, one which will bring it more honour and affection in the world, particularly out here among the peoples who have been kept from oppression and saved from starvation. So I ask you to help me to see it through with the same splendid staunchness that I have had from you all through my nine months' service here; and I hope that what I have said will remove the perplexity which must be in many of your minds. In one word, we are the police of a very disturbed district, and our great hope is to end as the saviours of thousands of lives by winning our way through the minefields with food for Petrograd.

Chapter Nine

THE PRIZE OF ADMIRALTY

I believe that both the Estonian and Lettish Governments owe their existence directly to the support of British sea power and that, without that support, the territories controlled by them would long ago have been in either Bolshevik or German hands.

Lieutenant-Colonel S. G. Tallents

AFTER Yudenitch's admission that he was unable to continue his advance, Cowan wrote from Biorko on the 6th November, 1919: " The situation has been fairly quiet for the last day or two, and it appears that there may yet be a thrust against Petrograd over the Finnish frontier by a mixed Finn and Russian force; but I have no great hopes of its success even if it eventuates. A British or a German general will, in the end, lead into Petrograd, and I sincerely hope it will be the former. He would need no more than a division, provided they were British troops, and there would be plenty of native troops to thicken his line once he lands and they know his intentions and objective." But the Admiral was hankering after the impossible. Opportunist, ambivalent, equivocal, were all adjectives which could be used of most aspects of the British Government's policy towards Bolshevik Russia, but they had never deviated from their determination not to send troops to the Baltic. Nor had they been pressed by the Allies to do so. Moreover, by this time they had all but withdrawn their forces from North Russia, a venture to which they had been committed in very different circumstances before the Armistice.

Although Cowan must, therefore, have known that it was

too late for a British general to be sent to the Baltic to any purpose, he could not forbear to express himself (to the Admiralty) on the subject once more on 25th November:

It is very difficult to think, or write, with moderation of the folly and short-sightedness of it all. My suggestion in January was inexpensive, i.e., a few cargoes of equipment, and the pay of a general and his staff. It was non-committal: I was well aware of the Government's reluctance to throw a small expedition into Russia, with the preoccupation of possibly having to send a larger one to extricate it—as happened in the north. But a British general and staff could have been extricated by a destroyer at any moment. Both the Sudan campaigns of 1898–99, and South Africa 1899–1901 were made necessary because, years before, the Government of the day failed to grasp the nettle; and the German threat in the Baltic could not well have been more obvious after the occurrences at Libau last April.

This pungent criticism was followed by an interesting constructive idea:

If the advice of soldiers and sailors on the spot is not considered by the Government of sufficient value, then the remedy would seem to be to send out some high and trusted civilian member of the Government to get a true and level view; and to sum up whose counsel is worth taking, and what military operations are necessary, and by whom to be undertaken, and under what direction. And let him also bear always in mind that it is elementary ignorance to hope that ships can act with permanent effect and success against land forces and shore defences, unless supported by adequate occupying detachments, as well as the necessary mobile columns.

Cowan's wisdom was proved in the Second World War when the appointment of Ministers with Cabinet rank to headquarters abroad did much to ensure effective co-operation between Service Commanders and Whitehall.[1]

The casualties suffered by Yudenitch's army during its October advance were relatively small, especially when

---

[1] e.g. Mr. Oliver Lyttleton was sent to Middle-East Headquarters in 1941 to "represent the War Cabinet on the spot." Mr. Harold Macmillan subsequently filled the same role in Algiers.

compared with those sustained by Estonian troops. The Red Army had offered little resistance to the Whites until they reached the outskirts of Petrograd, whereas the Estonians had tackled the formidable defences and heavy guns of Krasnaya Gorka and Grey Horse. The story was different when the Bolsheviks stood their ground and, reinforced by sailors from Kronstadt and supported by the guns of their fleet, counter-attacked and drove the North-West Army back. The Estonians had no alternative but to retreat with them as far as their frontier, nor did this run counter to Pats's policy. They moved back along the coast in good order covered by Cowan's ships, without serious loss. Not so with Rodzianko; he attempted an orderly withdrawal, but the consequence of inadequate leaders proved devastating. His troops lacked the morale to accept a retreat, especially when neither side showed any mercy to their prisoners. As they marched westwards the casualties grew until, on 14th November, the Bolsheviks inflicted a defeat at Yemburg which was not only decisive but calamitous. The retreat became a rout, the men were neglected and the survivors who fled into Estonia were decimated by typhus.[1]

Meanwhile Pats had not been idle in the interests of his own country. Though Yudenitch's advance had obliged him to break off negotiations with the Bolsheviks, he had not lost sight of the need for peace if his country was to secure its independence. At their October conference all three Baltic States had agreed that this should be their policy, especially when the Allies supported Clemenceau's *cordon sanitaire*. So, as soon as Pats realised that Yudenitch's venture had failed, he reopened negotiations with the Bolsheviks who were only too willing, notwithstanding their successes against Kolchak and Denikin. Lenin knew that there was much more to be

---

[1] The figures given by various authorities for the casualties suffered by the North-West Russian Army, by the Estonian Army and by the Red Army during October and November vary to such an extent that they are not worth quoting. All that can be said is that both sides lost many thousands in killed, wounded, taken prisoner, desertions and died of disease.

done before the Civil War could be brought to an end in a country so vast as Russia in which there were still all too many who had not accepted the Soviet régime. Pats did, however, have to agree to one condition imposed by the Bolsheviks, albeit with little reluctance in view of Yudenitch's consistently hostile attitude: the disorganised remnants of the North-West Army were to be disarmed and interned. This was effected at the beginning of December when, with the opening of formal talks at Dorpat for a peace treaty, the Russian North-West Army ceased to exist. Such was the inglorious end of one patriot's dream of restoring the old régime to a reunited Russian Empire. But it was not the zenith of Yudenitch's own misfortunes: in January he was arrested by his own officers for misappropriating his army's funds. To save his life the Allies intervened, secured his release and arranged for him to spend the rest of his days in the melancholy obscurity of the White Russian colony in France where he died in 1933.

*　　　　*　　　　*

On 31st October Cowan wrote: "The weather has become very severe in the last few days, and I should think is the beginning of winter." A fortnight later one of the *Wallace*'s officers noted in his diary:

Twenty degrees of frost today: a slight amount of snow at intervals. We are having trouble with water pipes and tanks and the engineers have had to fit steam pipes in them. The glycerine and water mixture for the Poulsen (*arc*) W/T has frozen, as also the hydraulic release gear for depth charges, (which uses) a glycerine mixture. All water that goes on the upper deck or over the ship's side is frozen solid almost at once. Ships that have been under way keep a permanent record in the shape of a frozen bow wave. The seaplane patrol has had to be given up: they can't get the engines started in this weather. *Waterhen* reported ice in the water bottles of her torpedoes in spite of steam heating. The sea (has) started to freeze over all round the ship in places and there are large chunks all over the harbour.

And on 25th November Cowan reported: " As far as can be ascertained there is solid ice between Kronstadt and the northern shore." But despite a climate which made a nightmare of much of the work of his ships, he did not abandon his task. He must first be sure that the Bolshevik Fleet was iced in for the winter, for the southern side of Kronstadt was still clear " and since yesterday it has been thawing." His judgment was proved on 1st December when the *Wallace*'s officer wrote: " The thaw has been going on for ten days now. There is no sign of frost. The experts say this place won't freeze till after Christmas." Understandably he added: " I sincerely hope they are wrong," since skating and occasional games of ice hockey were the only relaxation now available at an anchorage which was daily becoming more depressingly desolate as the Arctic winter sought to grip the British base, where the sun did not rise until after breakfast and went down again before tea.

Fortunately for morale there was still more than enough work for the British Force. Throughout November the *Delhi*, *Dragon* and *Dunedin*, and more often the destroyers, were required to carry out bombardments in conjunction with Estonian ships to relieve Red pressure on Laidoner's troops in the Narva area. The *Princess Margaret*, before she was diverted to Riga, laid more minefields to the west of the Russian barrage to hinder forays by Bolshevik vessels. Minesweeping had to continue. Campbell's destroyers maintained their ceaseless patrols. So, too, did Horton's submarines. Much of this work was unspectacular, but it was not without its anxieties and excitements. There was intelligence that the *Sevastopol* was in commission and would leave Petrograd. From time to time, smoke rising from Kronstadt suggested that Bolshevik destroyers were about to sortie. More often there were signs that Red submarines were active; periscopes were sighted, suspicious propeller noises were detected by hydrophones or the indicator lights were fired on the net protecting Biorko Sound. Out of these " alarums and excursions " the

Sevastopol rumours proved groundless and the few serviceable Kronstadt destroyers did no more than exercise under the guns of their fortress base. But Bolshevik submarines were more active than they had been for months past, several making sorties as far as the approaches to Reval during November, though their few attacks on British vessels were no more successful than the latter's counter-measures.

This is not to belittle the work done by Cowan's ships, more often than otherwise in darkness, fog, snow and biting cold which made it necessary to reduce the customary four-hour deck watches to two. Rather is it a measure of the success of the British blockade, of the Admiral's determination to confine the enemy fleet to waters where it was powerless to exercise any influence on the freedom already achieved by Finland and soon to be consolidated by Estonia and the other Baltic States. To the continuing need for British naval support both the Finnish and Estonian Governments testified on 30th November. In a debate in the House of Commons Lloyd George, with astonishing ignorance of the facts, stated that the blockade was no longer being maintained by Cowan's ships and that ice and mines were doing this task for them. The implication that the Royal Navy was about to be withdrawn caused so much alarm in Helsingfors and Reval that both Governments sent urgent requests to Whitehall that it should be allowed to remain. Cowan agreed: " It will be necessary to maintain a patrol from Reval after we have to leave Biorko, until the ice is as far west as our minefields. The Finns (*and, he might have added, the Estonians too*) are nervous of something breaking out of the ice after we have gone." The R.A.F. had, however, been compelled to abandon its sorties: snow made it impossible for them to use their landing ground at Koivisto. By the end of the month the *Vindictive* had re-embarked all her aircraft and their crews and sailed for Libau. There she landed three Camels which were sent to Riga, with two officers to train Letts to fly them.

At the beginning of December, with peace talks under way,

the Reds relaxed their pressure on Laidoner's troops, and indicated that they did not intend to advance beyond the Estonian frontier. Cowan then received this tribute:

In (its) struggle against numerically superior and technically better equipped forces His Britannic Majesty's Fleet has never failed to render valuable aid at the most critical junctures, and the Estonian Government wishes to convey to you the expressions of its deepest gratitude in the name of the entire Estonian nation, for the inestimable help rendered by you and your men. They will never forget the bravery and gallantry shown by the British bluejacket, who has always gone into action with the greatest dash whenever occasion offered, and has not hesitated to risk his life on behalf of our country. You may rest assured that he will always be a welcome guest in our ports.

Now the British ships were no longer required to carry out supporting bombardments; and, as the ice spread, the Admiral was able to reduce his patrols. " There have been no observed movements of enemy ships (during the past fortnight)," he wrote on 16th December. " It has been freezing for a week, to-day eight to ten degrees, and this anchorage (Biorko) is frozen over. In Petrograd Bay the ice is now as far west as Karavelda Point, but of no great thickness." One week later, when his ships were, in the words of one of his officers, " all white from truck to waterline, a mass of frozen ice and fog and fug from living spaces," Cowan reported:

On 18th December the frost suddenly became very severe, and as Biorko anchorage had already been frozen over for two days, I evacuated it at dawn on 19th December and fell back to Reval, leaving patrols to the eastward. The thermometer fell quickly to below zero, and the ice extended up to, and to the westward of Seskar Island. I feel that the Baltic Force may now be reduced to three light cruisers and eight destroyers, provided that H.M. Government considers that the Allies are able so far to control the German nation that their threat against the Baltic States is at an end. As to whether the Estonians will make peace with the Bolsheviks, or not, hangs in the balance, and therefore it will be very necessary to keep ships here so long as the ice conditions permit, as it will be advisable to carry out occasional patrols to Narva Bay and the eastward. It is unlikely that Reval will be finally closed by ice until the middle of January.

The *Princess Margaret*, the *Maidstone* and her submarines, and several other units of the British Baltic Force then went home, whilst the Fourth Destroyer Flotilla, of " S " class boats, came out to relieve the First.

*   *   *

In mid-September 1919 Madden had asked how many ships he would be required to maintain in the Baltic during the winter, and suggested that Cowan should be relieved of his heavy duties. The Admiralty had been obliged to answer:

> It is not possible to give you any reliable forecast of the naval policy to be pursued in the Baltic during the coming winter. (It) is dependent on the general policy to be decided by H.M. Government, but beyond an expression of hope that, when the ice sets in, the Baltic will automatically cease to be a field for naval operations, the Cabinet have not made any pronouncement. It is possible that this country will continue to maintain Military Missions in Finland and other Baltic regions during the winter, in which case it will be necessary to keep ships in the Baltic, but the force will be considerably reduced. My Lords (therefore) agree with your proposals as to relieving Rear-Admiral Sir Walter Cowan.

Two months later the situation had clarified. When Duff returned to the Baltic in the *Caledon* in the last week in November his orders stated:

> You are to proceed to the Baltic and place yourself in communication with the Rear-Admiral (Cowan). You will act under his orders until such time as the British Force is withdrawn from the Gulfs of Finland and Riga, when the Rear-Admiral will return home. You will then assume the duties of Senior Naval Officer in the Baltic. The force under your orders will consist of two light cruisers and five destroyers. (Your) object will be to watch events, and to afford moral support to the Allied Missions to the Baltic States. Any operations which you may undertake should be strictly confined to assistance to the local Governments against external

aggression. Such operations should only be undertaken with due consideration to the small force at your disposal, and you should be careful to raise no hope of any military assistance from the Allies. The British Government has decided that no military force is to be sent.

Duff was not instructed as to how he should treat Bolshevik ships: the Admiralty assumed that they would be iced in by the time he relieved Cowan.

Soon after Duff reached Libau on 26th November, 1919, he held a meeting with Burt from Riga, and members of Niessel's Commission from Memel, at which he learned that, though Latvia was almost clear of German troops, there was a large force of them in Lithuania within fifty miles of Libau. The Lithuanian Army was in no position to emulate its northern neighbour when it had to hold in check both Red and Polish invasions. Moreover, the Military Party which was in control in Konigsberg, and with typical Prussian arrogance prepared to ignore Berlin,[1] had well-equipped reinforcements available which it was truculently threatening to send into Lithuania, whence they would be able to re-invade Latvia. Nor was this all; the country was also troubled by the remnants of Bermondt's mercenaries, and an equally unruly local *Baltische Landeswehr*. However, Niessel was in no doubt that these would be of small importance once the German troops had been withdrawn: his Commission was therefore concentrating on negotiating and enforcing this.

They made good progress, " with the usual lawless exceptions that one has come to expect from the Prussians in this part of the world," until 6th December. The Germans having withdrawn as far as Shavli, then started pillaging, blowing up ammunition dumps and causing other disturbances, which

---

[1] " East Prussia does not realise that Germany has lost the war." (*Brigadier-General A. J. Turner, the British representative on Niessel's Commission.*) The Weimar Government was more realistic; " All the woes that pelted us this autumn would never have occurred if the German Nationalists had not convinced the troops that they were strong enough to hold the Baltic States against a victorious world " (*Minister Eric Koch-Weser*).

made it necessary for Niessel to recall his officers when they were in the middle of arranging a further withdrawal to Tauroggen. One division followed up this revolt by marching across country towards Memel. Being in Prussia, this move was believed by some to herald a military *coup d'état* designed to overthrow the German Government, but Duff was more concerned that these troops who " for the past nine months have been accustomed to ravage and pillage the Baltic Provinces unhindered," might turn north and seize Libau. However, after ten uneasy days, in which Niessel's Commission achieved an orderly evacuation of all the other German troops, it became clear that this rebellious division had made no more than a last, lone gesture of defiance.

The successful removal of the Germans from Lithuania inside three weeks must, therefore, be counted to Niessel's credit, notwithstanding Cowan's comments to the contrary— and even though he elected to return to Paris without resolving the issue of the unruly division in Memel. This, however, was of small concern to Duff once the threat of a German advance on Libau had been removed. Now he could afford to reduce his force by sailing the *Vindictive* and *Erebus* to Copenhagen, though he was less happy when ice obliged him to withdraw his last destroyer from Riga so that he had no direct communication with the British Missions.

Some two months earlier Cowan had written, in the spirit of Drake's immortal prayer: " Should the question of my relief occupy Their Lordships' attention, I would ask that I may be permitted to remain until, in my judgment, the situation in all parts of the Baltic permits me leaving it with a quiet mind." News of the German revolt at Shavli nearly drew the Admiral south to Libau, but his fears that " Goltz (nominally Eberhardt) will shortly defy and probably eject the Allied Commission " were proved unfounded before the last week of December when " ice formed very rapidly all over the Gulf of Finland almost as far west as Hogland." There could be no further Bolshevik naval activity before the spring.

On 28th December, 1919, Cowan left Reval in the *Delhi*, taking the *Dragon* and the First Destroyer Flotilla with him. Of all the force that had so successfully clipped the wings of Soviet naval power in the Baltic, only the *Dunedin* and half the Fourth Flotilla remained in the Gulf of Finland. And when the Admiral met Duff at Libau he knew that, at least for the winter months, the new Baltic States were safe from invasion. The Germans had completed their evacuation, and the Bolsheviks had done more than agree to withdraw from Latvia and Lithuania; they were discussing peace terms with delegates sent by Ulmanis and Voldmaris as well as with Pats's emissaries. In these circumstances the lesser problems of ensuring the future loyalty of the *Baltische Landeswehr*, and of disbanding the last remnants of Bermondt's force, were such as the two Governments could be expected to resolve without undue difficulty.

So the time had come when Cowan could leave the Baltic with an easy mind. On 1st January, 1920, he sailed from Copenhagen: three days later the *Delhi* entered Plymouth Sound. As she passed the breakwater Cowan received this signal:

The Board of Admiralty desire to convey to Rear-Admiral Sir Walter Cowan and to the officers and men of the Baltic Force now returning to England their marked approbation of the manner in which the work of the Force has been performed. The Baltic Force has during the past year cheerfully endured trying conditions, and when occasion offered has attacked the enemy with the utmost gallantry. It has prevented the destruction of States which have upheld the Allied cause, has supported the forces of civilisation when menaced by anarchy, and has worthily upheld the honour of the British Navy. This record is the more praiseworthy because it comes after the long previous strain of war, at a time when the other forces of the Crown have for the most part been enjoying a relaxation of effort. The Board's gratification is to be made known to all concerned.

" The Baltic Force are most grateful for Their Lordships' message," was Cowan's modest reply. " What service they have been able to render has been very gladly done." And this service cannot be better summarised than in the final paragraphs of his dispatch:

In conclusion, if Their Lordships will permit me, I would like to say that, throughout the time I have served in the Baltic and Gulf of Finland, such difficulties and perplexities as have confronted me, I have been able to face and deal with with an untroubled mind, owing to having been made conscious of Their Lordships', and the Commander-in-Chief's, intention to trust and support me whenever the situation has made it necessary for me to act as seemed best to me at the time. My aim was throughout the year to prevent any Bolshevik warships breaking out into the Gulf of Finland—and the ice has now relieved me of this responsibility—and also to frustrate by every means the most evident design of the Germans to overrun and dominate the Baltic Provinces and then to advance on Petrograd; and their repulse from both Riga and Libau in October and November by the Lettish troops under cover of the bombardment of our ships has, I think, put an end to this also, and all German troops were back into Prussia by 15th December.

But what of the Soviet point of view? How do their historians explain the failure of the Bolshevik Navy to dominate the Gulf of Finland? These are the conclusions of Professor Goncharov: [1]

(*a*) The passive character of the Baltic Fleet's operations was due to the marked superiority of the enemy naval forces.

(*b*) The Baltic Fleet's lack of shallow-draught vessels prevented minelaying and other operations which would have limited the enemy's sphere of activity.

(*c*) The enemy's superiority enabled him to bottle up the Baltic Fleet in Kronstadt and thus prevent timely operations in support of the Red Army. In spite of this the Fleet gave considerable support in a limited area, where and when they possessed temporary command of the sea.

(*d*) The maritime defence of a coast cannot be secured by submarines and minefields alone, without the support of surface forces.

(*e*) The enemy's operations demonstrated the help which a

[1] In *Piat Let Krasnogo Flota.*

fleet can render to an army by flank support and landing operations.

(f) The economic conditions imposed by the War and the Revolution, together with the need to provide forces for the land battle and on the rivers, did not allow the formation of a Baltic Fleet strong enough to retain command of the sea on the Army's flank.

(g) The effectiveness of the Fleet was severely restricted by Kronstadt's position near the frontier; the harbour possessed only one exit (and that a shallow one) which permitted an enemy based on Biorko to keep it under continuous control, or even blockade it.

(h) The presence of the Baltic Fleet did, however, act as a deterrent to an enemy attack on Petrograd from seaward, which could not have been undertaken without the risk of severe losses.

Of these conclusions only one need be disputed, that Cowan had a much stronger force at his disposal than Zelenoy. The Professor could not have paid the British Admiral and his officers and men a greater, albeit unintentional, tribute for, as this book has shown, the Russian Baltic Fleet included capital ships, and was operating close to a fully defended base with all the resources of a modern dockyard: Cowan, on the other hand, had nothing larger than light cruisers, and his ships had to work from an anchorage with no better than improvised defences only fifty miles from Kronstadt and a thousand from a British dockyard. But, as Napoleon wrote, " morale is to material as three is to one." Cowan's officers and men had all the skill and determination with which they had so recently confined the German High Seas Fleet to its harbours for more than four years. They were inspired by five hundred years of maritime tradition—two hundred and fifty since the schisms of the English Revolution and Civil War —sustained by a humane and understanding discipline, and imbued with the offensive spirit by which ships and squadrons of the Royal Navy had so often defeated more powerful forces. Against these priceless assets the Russian Fleet had nothing but revolutionary fervour to offset a recent complete break-down of discipline, the massacre of many of its officers, little maritime tradition, a legacy of annihilating defeats at Port Arthur and Tsushima, and the same fallacy—that war at sea can be won by remaining on the defensive.

As important, whilst the Russian Baltic Fleet was under the command of the inexperienced Zelenoy, whose every move was subject to the fierce scrutiny and criticism of Bolshevik commissars who were wholly ignorant of maritime war, the British Baltic Force was commanded by an admiral who had proved himself an outstanding war leader and whose moral and physical courage and devotion to duty never ceased to be a shining example to those who served under him. Not for nothing was Rear-Admiral Sir Walter Cowan created Baronet of the Baltic. His campaign had, in the words of the First Lord, added " lustre to the great Service of which you are so distinguished a member." [1] But the Admiral never forgot how much his success was due to every officer and man who so stout-heartedly enabled him to wrest command of the sea from a more powerful enemy force. Their unswerving constancy of purpose shone with all the brilliancy of a search-light beam when contrasted with the flickering candles of indecision that illuminated the corridors of Whitehall, Paris and Versailles. The peoples of Finland, Estonia, Latvia and, to a lesser extent, Lithuania, were in no doubt of what the Royal Navy achieved in the Baltic during that memorable year: their freedom was the prize of admiralty.

*   *   *

Duff in the *Caledon*, with the *Dunedin* and the Fourth Destroyer Flotilla, remained behind after the Admiral had gone.[2] Using Copenhagen as his base, the Commodore divided his ships between Libau, Reval and Memel. Their task was that of watchdogs for the Allies: with the Red Fleet

---

[1] In a letter to Cowan after reading his Despatch. Beatty's comment has been quoted on p. 70.
[2] So, too, did three small French warships.

iced in, with peace talks making progress at Dorpat, and the German Army clear of all three Baltic States, officers and men had no active operations to compensate them for the severities of life afloat in a Baltic winter. Fortunately for them, the Admiralty maintained its policy of limiting the time spent by ships in this sea to about six weeks, so that those named above were relieved at the end of February by others from the Atlantic Fleet. But the need to do this caused Madden concern: allowing for ships refitting and giving leave, the Baltic was absorbing nearly all his light cruisers and destroyers. He was even more worried about the coming spring, when he estimated that the Bolsheviks would be able to deploy a force of four battleships, two cruisers, fifteen or more destroyers and seven or more submarines. He was averse, he told the Admiralty, to trying again to contain them with nothing larger than light cruisers: " it may be expected that Kronstadt will be absolutely protected against C.M.B. attack by floating booms and other means." He proposed a balanced fleet headed by two or four battleships: " it is preferable to send a moderate force, consisting of all types of vessel, than to station nearly the whole of our light forces in one area, whilst retaining the heavy ships in another." This pre-supposed the continuation of hostilities between the Bolsheviks and the Baltic States: should there be peace " it will still be desirable to send a British naval force into the Baltic periodically during 1920 to support and encourage our trade, and to accustom the Baltic Powers to our presence and influence in these seas." The Admiralty discounted Madden's estimate of the likely future strength of the Red Fleet in the Baltic: many of its ships were in a deplorable condition, and all would suffer a grave shortage of fuel so long as Denikin controlled the Baku area. So they told the Commander-in-Chief: " The question whether a British naval force will be required in the Baltic in 1920 depends on the ruling of H.M. Government. Their Lordships fully realise the disadvantages attaching to the present composition of the force, but the many objections to the employment of heavy ships in (the Baltic) are held to outweigh the desirability of their presence there."

Cowan gave the Admiralty his own different views on how the Bolshevik Baltic Fleet should be neutralised in 1920:

The atmosphere of the negotiations now going on between the Estonians and the Bolsheviks is that the Bolsheviks are anxious to secure the neutrality of the Finnish Gulf, and thereby an amelioration of the blockade conditions, i.e., that Allied war vessels should not enter Petrograd Bay. In return for this they are prepared to destroy their whole Fleet, and probably also to submit to controlled imports of locomotives, machinery and foodstuffs, and to exclude war material. It is probable that the French and Americans may not agree to this; but as neither of these nations has taken any hand in containing the Bolshevik Fleet during the past year, I do not consider that they have a right to interfere with, or question, any decision that the British Government may come to regarding the disposal of the Fleet.

The Bolsheviks put forward alternatives such as selling this Fleet to the British Government, interning it in British ports, or being allowed to remove it to Vladivostok. I could not advise agreeing to any of these, as all would entail these ships remaining in being until the commencement of the next campaigning season, by which time German or White Russian influences may permit these ships to remain a factor disturbing the balance of power. I regard the prospect of these ships again coming under the control of the White Russians as a danger second only to that of the Germans gaining possession of them. I consider our Government should inform the Soviet Government that they must either accept the condition of destroying their Fleet in return for such relaxation of the blockade as it is thought fit to grant them, or they must be prepared to endure the same conditions that have obtained through the present year. It should further be insisted on that if by a certain date, (and I recommend that this should not be later than 1st February), every warship in Kronstadt (and) Petrograd is not destroyed and submitted to the inspection of a British Naval Commission, they should be informed that this offer will automatically lapse.

In the event, however, both Madden's proper concern and Cowan's drastic recommendations were proved academic exercises. In January 1920, Balodis, with an army of 33,000, and Alexander, with a *Landeswehr* of 6000, cleared the Red Army from Livonia, while 20,000 Poles came north and liberated the fortress of Daugavpils: before the end of the month the whole of Latvia was free. On 2nd February the Letts' northern neighbours achieved their triumph: Pats's delegates signed a peace treaty by which Soviet Russia " voluntarily and for ever " renounced its sovereign rights over the territory and people of Estonia. This was in line with a decision of the Baltic Conference held in Finland from 13th–22nd January at which representatives of Poland as well as the Baltic States decided that they wished to live at peace with Soviet Russia. Nor was it contrary to the wishes of the Allies: on 16th January the Supreme Council had decided to relax the blockade; the Allied and neutral countries were authorised to exchange goods on the basis of reciprocity with Soviet Russia. This decision, which amounted to a tacit acceptance of the Bolshevik régime, was logically followed on 24th February by an Allied statement having a more direct reference to the Baltic States.

If the communities which border on the frontiers of Soviet Russia, and whose independence or *de facto* autonomy they (the Allies) have recognised, were to approach them and ask for advice as to what attitude they should take with regard to Soviet Russia, the Allied Governments would reply that they cannot accept the responsibility of advising them to continue a war which may be injurious to their own interests. Still less would they advise them to adopt a policy of aggression towards Russia. If, however, Soviet Russia attacks them inside their legitimate frontiers, the Allies will give them every possible support.

This had its repercussions on the British Baltic Force. The battlecruisers *Hood* and *Tiger* which were on their way to Reval, with a flotilla of destroyers, as reinforcements for the summer, were ordered home as soon as they reached Copenhagen in May 1920. And before the ice melted at Kronstadt the Admiralty signalled Duff: " Offensive action against ships of Soviet Russia is *not* to be taken." This ended the undeclared naval war: with the lifting of the blockade of Petrograd Bay, the Bolshevik Fleet made no hostile move, even when the Red Army launched a major offensive against Poland. So there was no need to augment the British Force: throughout 1920 it remained a mere handful of light cruisers and destroyers; and by the time it was finally withdrawn in 1921, it had been reduced to a single light cruiser and two destroyers.

Well before that, on 30th June, 1920, Lithuania had signed a peace treaty, followed by Latvia on 11th August and by Finland on 14th October. As with Estonia, Soviet Russia " voluntarily and for ever " renounced its sovereign rights over the territories and peoples of these states. Only the problem of Vilna remained. Though the Lithuanian Army was able to occupy this holy city in August 1920, the Poles recaptured it in October in open defiance of the League of Nations. In these circumstances it is hardly surprising that the Lithuanians declined to recognise the League's decision of February 1923, that Vilna should belong to Poland, right down to March 1938, notwithstanding their valuable acquisition of an outlet to the sea: after three years' administration by a French Commission, the port of Memel was handed over to Lithuania in January 1923. However, except for this lamentable dispute between two countries which had once been so closely aligned, 1920 brought both peace and freedom to the Baltic States. And on 26th January, 1921, Lloyd George, in the face of Curzon's objections, agreed with the French and Italian representatives on the Supreme Allied Council, that Estonia and Latvia should be granted *de jure* recognition as sovereign independent states. Lithuania had to wait for this seal on her sovereignty until December 1922; but before that, in September 1921, all three countries were admitted to the League of Nations.

*   *   *

Seen against the whole tapestry of history the Baltic troubles of 1918–20 were but an appendage to the First World War.

Nonetheless, they teach a lesson as old as Cicero, that " whoso can hold the sea has command of the situation." British sea power had an effect out of all proportion to the strength of the force employed and the few casualties incurred. The words which Edmund Waller wrote of Britain's war with Spain in the seventeenth century, are as well applied to the Royal Navy's operations against the Red Fleet in 1919:

> *They that the whole world's monarchy designed*
> *Are to their ports by our bold fleet confined*

The story has been well summed up by a disinterested American writer:[1]

During the early post-war years Great Britain virtually ran the Baltic area without any real aspiration to control the Baltic States. She supplied (them) with arms, ammunition and foodstuffs. The British Fleet offered both moral and military support. From British ships sprang the high prestige which England later enjoyed throughout the Baltic. Each British ship was a visible instrument of British power, however diluted in the Baltic where it had to meet still potent and conflicting German and Russian forces. It is amazing to consider what function a few scattered Englishmen who found themselves representing their country in the enemy-infested Baltic during 1919 and 1920, were discharging. Extreme pains and skill were required to lead the Baltic States out of troubles discovered at almost every corner (of) that part of the world after the First World War. The zigzagging, meandering and wavering of policy toward the Baltic States could be partly explained (by) the considerable disagreement among the Allies in regard to the future of those countries, and partly (by) the disagreement between the British military men and diplomats, and even among the diplomats themselves. Those who fought for the independence of the Baltic States finally won. Within a period of three years Great Britain managed to replace both Russia and Germany as the dominant power in the Baltic by establishing a block of states between Russia and Germany under her leadership.

As a result, to quote the same objective source, Britain

enjoyed great prestige and economic hegemony in the Baltic States which were grateful to her for their independence. British policy regarding the Baltic States could be described as benevolent. She

[1] Edgar Anderson in *British Policy towards the Baltic States, 1918–1920.*

supported them morally, but did not commit herself politically or militarily. The Baltic area was isolated from Great Britain and she did not want to assume any risks; (but) the Baltic people greatly prospered under British influence and the next decades showed the influence of Anglo-Saxon culture.

The tragic events that removed the Baltic States's independence during World War II are outside the scope of this book. The Soviet Union first claimed bases in 1940 but then in its usual way forcefully extended its influence so that by 1945 all three were part of the Soviet Union.

But not, it would seem, a very willing part. Those who were able to keep their ears to the ground knew that there remained significant nationalist undercurrents. In 1962 the Lettish patriot Anton Gramatins wrote

> Of the Allied countries which helped the Baltic States to liberate their territories from their enemies, Great Britain, indubitably, played the leading part. Therefore the Latvians have always had great respect for the British nation. In fact the Latvian people at the end of the Second World War, so highly unfortunate for them, fanatically expected the British Fleet in the Baltic Sea to start a new war of independence.

That had been out of the question. In 1945 Britain was an exhausted nation economically and physically and, despite the vigorous approach taken with the Soviets when possible by the great Foreign Secretary Ernest Bevin, there was little practically that could be done to halt Soviet expansion, not only in the Baltic but also across Eastern Europe. The Iron Curtain was firmly in place.

However there is a verse from an Estonian poet, Lydia Koidula, which calls on people to have faith in the future.

> Take then hope. . .
> Better time shall yet arise!
> Firmly Walk! Keep head erect!
> Time will put all things aright.

And time did. But it took until the 1980s for the Soviet Union and its Communist party to start to implode. Thankfully, under the outstanding leadership of Mikhail Gorbachev, aided considerably by the skilful handling of the situation in the West by Margaret Thatcher and Ronald Reagan, it was all relatively peaceful.

In September 1990 all three states and their six million peoples were recognised as independent again and admitted to the United Nations.

It may be hoped they recall how much they owe to the British navy for what it did in 1919, especially to the man who led them so far along the "golden road" to liberty, Rear Admiral Walter Cowan, First Baron of the Baltic.

ADDENDUM TO THE BIRLINN EDITION

WHEN ANY such book as this appears the author will almost certainly get correspondence which sheds new light on the story. Soon after *Cowan's War* was first published, Dr D.C. Halliwell, writing from Jersey, revealed that as a young surgeon-lieutenant he had been the author of the item from *Baltic Bits* which opens this book. He said that the event had been an interesting part of his life which he would not have missed.

The book attracted a significant number of reviews, mostly complimentary, but not adding anything significant to the sum of knowledge, though one did draw attention to the correct spelling of Rear-Admiral Fergusson's name with two s's (pages 89, 90 137, 75 & index).

An interesting point that emerges from his papers is that my father radically revised his view of Cowan, whom he never met, as he wrote. Initially he had believed he was an unpopular martinet; this view was in part based on memories of what he had heard early in his career when serving in the Mediterranean, where Cowan's time as C-in-C a few years before had not been smooth. However a number of those who remembered him well, in particular Admiral-of-the-Fleet Viscount Cunningham, who wrote him two useful letters just before his death in 1963, led him to revise his view significantly, though he was still aware there were some who disliked him cordially. One problem he seems to have had in the Baltic was communicating even with quite senior officers, let alone the lower deck, the purpose of the exercise. One former seaman wrote that only after he read this book had he understood why they were there; he recalled a notice on his ship's board just saying they were in the Baltic to 'police the seas' — that was all.

Also my father received several letters from some who had been in the action. These included Captain Augustus Agar V.C., and Vice-Admiral Berwick Curtis, who commented that it was 'an excellent book'.

Perhaps most informative was the long letter from former Signalman George Sinclair, who had been in charge of a watch on *Caradoc*. In 1917 he had been transferred from H.M.S. *Cordelia* of the 1st Light Cruiser Squadron to the brand-new *Caradoc* under Captain Munro Kerr. After working up they joined with *Cardiff, Cassandra, Calypso* and *Ceres* at Scapa to form the 6th Light Cruiser Squadron under Rear-Admiral Sinclair (no relation) flying his flag in *Cardiff.*

Signalman Sinclair was clearly an educated man. He was later a civil servant, who had kept a detailed diary and also afterwards formed something of an informal old comrades' association, keeping in touch with a number of the others involved, in particular Captain Kerr, who, he says, ran a very happy ship, and his first-lieutenant, D.B. Fisher, both future admirals. On reading this book, which he called 'fascinating', he carefully checked all the details he could against his own records and sent a list of corrections, some of which he accepts were 'trivial'. I am sure my father regretted that he had not heard about him before he wrote and, as he indicates he accepts most of the comments, I will summarise them.

Page 33 paragraph 2. The Light Cruiser Squadron did not sail 'next day', but five days later, on 26th November 1918. Signalman Sinclair says that there were some very disgruntled 'hotheads' among the 'hostilities only' ratings at missing anticipated end-of-war leave, but he managed help keep a lid on trouble,

Page 35 line 6. They spent five days, not forty-eight hours, in Copenhagen and sailed for Libau on 3rd December.

Page 38 paragraph 2. Rear-Admiral Sinclair took his ships to shell the Bolshevik's rear on 14th, not 13th, December. Signalman Sinclair had kept his copy of the signal he received at 0820 by semaphore:

OBJECT OF THE OPERATION GENERALLY TO BOMBARD ENEMY'S LINES FROM THEIR REAR. 'CARDIFF' WILL TRY AND LOCATE THEIR BATTERY TO

DESTROY IT. ONE DESTROYER WILL BE DETAILED TO SPOT FOR 'CARADOC'. THE REMAINING DESTROYERS WILL CLOSE LAND WITH CAUTION BETWEEN LCS AND FIRE ON ANY ENEMY SEEN RETREATING. ENEMY'S PRESENT APPROXIMATE POSITION IS NORTH AND SOUTH LINE IN NEIGHBOURHOOD OF MAHOLM CHURCH. DAMAGE TO PROPERTY SHOULD BE AVOIDED UNLESS ENEMY IS USING IT FOR SHELTER. ESTONIAN ARMOURED TRAIN WILL BE ON EAST AND WEST RAILWAY TO PREVENT ENEMY RETREATING INLAND. FIRE NOT TO BE OPENED UNTIL 'CARDIFF' HAS OPENED FIRE OR SIGNAL IS MADE.

He then records that *Cardiff* opened fire at 1020, with C*aradoc* following half an hour later and they both ceased at 1115.

Page 46 line 3 *et seq. Caradoc*'s only visit to Helsingfors was on 3rd January 1919 and she left the following day.

Page 46 line 6. *Wakeful* took no part in this action but *Vortigern* did.

Page 50 penultimate line. *Caradoc* reached Rosyth on 8th, not 10th, January.

Page 53. The Grand Fleet ships met Sinclair's on 7th, not 6th, January.

Page 59, first para. Signalman Sinclair was on the bridge of *Caradoc* in the Bight on 17 November 1917. He says that Cowan did not press the pursuit until *Caledon* was hit, but had simply obeyed a signal from Admiral Sinclair in *Cardiff* calling off the pursuit when the German battleships loomed up. As *Caledon* turned she was hit by a shell which glanced off without exploding. He believes this has sometimes been exaggerated, in particular in Cowan's obituary in *The Guardian*, which overemphasised his commitment to pursuit and also made the exaggerated claim that *Caledon* had been 'badly hit'.

He recalled that on Christmas Day 1918 they received a signal sent to the whole navy with a message from the king, which began with the observation that, at last, their was 'no longer fighting', which they received with wry amusement.

He says he has no regrets at not serving in the same ship as Cowan, whom he saw occasionally at close quarters. He heard much about his tantrums and believed him to be 'martinet and pretty ruthless as far as the lower deck was concerned'.

He also records that on 13th March 1920 he received his share of the prize money for *Avtroil* and *Spartak* (Chapter II).

Rodney M. Bennett

COWAN'S SECOND WAR

Soon after this republication was arranged I talked with former commando, Chief Petty Officer Bill Mellow, who had a vivid memory of encountering Sir Walter Cowan when he was sent for boat training to Inverary in 1940: 'I soon spotted this clearly elderly but very wiry and fit looking Commander [the rank Cowan had been given for the job] and wondered who he was. Someone told me he was a retired Admiral who had come back for the war. We called him "Titch" Cowan. He was a real bolt of lightning and always kept things moving along.'

As more information has now surfaced about Cowan's unusual World War II career it is worth recording the gist of this. In North Africa he virtually attached himself to an Indian regiment, the 18th King Edward's Own Cavalry, which had only abandoned the horse in favour of mechanisation in 1939, and was still only modestly equipped with bren-gun carriers (small, open, tracked vehicles).

Nonetheless they consistently raided the Italians and Cowan particularly admired the audacious Jats, Rajputs, and Hahimkhanis, in particular their night-raiding skills.[2] Despite language limitations he became a great favourite of the *sowars*. One Indian Risaldar commented to his British squadron commander, 'If your young old men are like this what hope can the Germans have of beating you.'

My father has (page 62) printed Cowan's own account of his capture by the Italians. Initially he and all those taken with him had a difficult time as their captors had only limited facilities in

---

[2] Much of this information comes from an article in the 10 November 1991 issue of *Sanik Samachar*, the official magazine of the Indian armed forces. In addition an article on the repatriation in the short-lived magazine of the 1980s, *World War II Investigator*, has been helpful.

the desert to accommodate them. Quite a few of the men managed to escape but a close watch must have been kept on the officers for, if given half-a-chance, Cowan would surely have done so also.

Eventually Cowan arrived in Benghazi, where he was put on a plane for Italy. It was only the second time he had flown; the previous occasion being when he had made just a short hop in a sea-plane before World War I. Initially he was placed in the centre of the plane with an officer in charge, but soon after they had taken off the pilot received a signal which led him to invite Cowan to sit alongside. He realised that the Italians now had some idea who he was.

When he arrived in Rome the Italian navy continued to show him considerable respect and treated him well, though he was interrogated to try and discover how on earth an elderly retired admiral had been fighting with some Indian cavalry. After a couple of weeks they concluded he would not, indeed probably could not, give them anything of serious interest and he was sent to a POW camp at Veano, near Piacenzia in Lombardy, where he had the consolation of being able to talk with a number of fellow commandos. However his captors made periodic comments about his age and indicated they were considering repatriation.

What made this possible was a rather unusual situation that had developed in the Red Sea after Italy entered the war in 1940. At this time there were a number of ships of the Italian navy in Massawa, the port of the then Italian colony of Eritrea. A number of vessels, such as submarines, attempted – some successfully – to make it back to Europe around the Cape, but this was not practical for some destroyers and other smaller vessels. Instructions were sent from Rome for them to be scuttled, but the local commander was not prepared to do this without some show of defiance first.

Unfortunately for him this was not very successful and in early April 1941 about 800 Italian seamen had to make their way ashore in neutral Saudi Arabia. This was most unwelcome to the Saudis, who, under the Geneva convention, were bound to intern them, which they did in a camp near Jeddah. Providing a diet they found acceptable was a particular headache for the Arabs, so they soon made approaches to see if there was some way they could be rid of them.

In June the also neutral Turks offered their services and the British, wary of a significant body of enemy men not so far from Egypt when Rommel was making significant headway in his desert campaign, indicated they welcomed this. Contact was made with the Italians via the Turks and eventually, in early 1943, it was agreed that all the men should be returned unconditionally in exchange for a similar number of British officers and men of equal rank held in Italy.

This did not at all go smoothly. A British merchantman, S.S. *Talma*, was sent to Jeddah to collect the Italians, but on her way with them to the Turkish port of Mersin, where the exchange was due to take pace she was bombed by a passing Italian plane, despite having a large union flag painted on her side. The bombs all missed, however, and a vigorous British protest led to a senior Italian officer making a personal apology to the captain of the *Talma*.

At the same time the equivalent British party, including Cowan, were brought to the same port on the Italian hospital ship *Gradisca*. Presumably the Italians considered his effective rank commander; there were no full admirals among their men. A minor hiccough came when one of the Britons died of blood poisoning soon after setting sail from Bari, but the British agreed not to make anything of this.

Most of the 800 men were soon back in the United Kingdom, many at the naval barracks in Portsmouth. Usually under the Geneva convention those freed in this way are not supposed to become combatants again, so the question arose whether they were now entitled to return to normal duties. Though it had been agreed that this exchange was unconditional, some of the men said they had signed papers which they believed constituted an undertaking not to be involved further in hostilities. The commodore of the barracks conducted an enquiry and, after talking with the senior officer among those freed, Commander

W. Brown, and a number of the men, he concluded they had given no such undertaking and that the men with concerns must have misunderstood the papers they signed, which were in Italian.

Cowan returned directly to North Africa and resumed his activities. However the following year, when he was 72, he began to realise that none of us are immortal and time was at last beginning to take its toll. So he returned home. His bar to his D.S.O., almost certainly the oldest man ever to received this, was gazetted that autumn and he formally retired again the following year at the end of hostilities in May.

It was two years later, in 1947, that he received the invitation from India to be honorary colonel of the 18th King Edward's Own, an honour that he said gave him the greatest pride and pleasure among all those he had received. It is almost certainly unique for a British naval officer to receive such a distinction. He was able to visit them at Eisalpur in the North-West Frontier Province accompanied by his daughter, Martha. At a champagne reception Ris Maj Azam, Ali Khan expressed his warm appreciation at the long journey he had made and continued:

You first joined the Regiment in the field of battle and you fought most gallantly with us. We all know of your great exploits and it is a matter of great pride that our Honorary Colonel is a man whose bravery is renowned and recognised the world over. . . .When at Bir Hacheim on 27 May 1942 the Regiment was captured, you valiantly risked your life for the honour of the Regiment. We shall never forget this.

Some years later, in 1973, General J. N. Chowdhary, Chief of the Indian Army and a cavalryman, was visiting London when, at a social gathering, he met a lady wearing what he recognised was the badge of the 18th Cavalry. Enquiring, she told him she was Martha, Cowan's daughter, and confirmed how much pleasure her father had taken in being colonel-in-chief. For many years she sent the officer's mess, which has a portrait of Cowan on its walls, a New Year's card.

Rodney M. Bennett

APPENDICES

SOURCES and BIBLIOGRAPHY

ACKNOWLEDGMENTS

INDEX

APPENDIX A

The Price of Admiralty

THE FOLLOWING figures are a measure of the price which the Royal Navy was required to pay from November 1918 until the end of December 1919, to restore peace in the Baltic and to bring freedom to the States bordering its eastern shores.

British warships and auxiliaries employed in the area:

Light cruisers	23
Aircraft carrier	1 (and 55 aircraft)
Destroyers	85
Monitor	1
Minelayers	2
Minesweepers	18
Submarines	20
C.M.B.s	10
Depot ships	4
Auxiliaries	74
Total	238

Of these the daily average number in the area was:

Up to 30th June, 1919	29
From 1st July to 31st December, 1919	88

Allied warships employed in the area, of which only the French worked in close co-operation with the British force, totalled:

French	26
Italian	2
U.S.A.	14

British ships lost by enemy action, mining and stress of weather:

Light cruiser	1
Destroyers	2
Minesweepers	2
Submarine	1
C.M.B.s	8
Auxiliaries	3
Total	**17**

British ships damaged by mining, grounding, collision etc. (not including minor damage which did not curtail availability for operations):

Light cruisers	7
Minelayer	1
Destroyers	18
Minesweepers	5
Submarines	4
C.M.B.	1
Auxiliaries	25
Total	**61**

Aircraft lost:

Shot down	3
By forced landings	14
From other causes	20
Total	**37**

British casualties:

Royal Navy:	Officers	Men
Killed	16	107
Wounded	8	50
Taken prisoner	3	6
Royal Air Force		
Killed	4	1
Wounded	2	—

Soviet ships which were active in the area:

Battleships	2	
Cruiser	1	
Destroyers	8	
Minelayer	1	
Minesweepers	8	(*approx.*)
Submarines	6	
Miscellaneous	4	(*approx.*)
Total	30	(*approx.*)

Soviet ships lost and damaged:

Sunk:		Seriously damaged:	
Cruiser	1	Battleships	2
Destroyers	3	Submarine	1
Depot ship	1	Oiler	1
Surrendered:		Totals:	
Destroyers	2	Sunk	5
Patrol vessel	1	Surrendered	3
		Damaged	4

APPENDIX B

Notes on the Principal Warships which were employed in the Baltic, 1918–1920

BRITISH

THE MAJORITY of British warships employed in the Baltic were designed immediately before or during the First World War for working with or in support of the Grand Fleet in the North Sea. All were oil-fired except where otherwise stated.

Light Cruisers

Galatea, Inconstant, Phaeton and *Royalist* were 3500-ton lightly armoured ships of the "Arethusa" class completed in 1914–15. Armed with three 6-inch, four 4-inch and two 3-inch A.A. guns plus eight 21-inch torpedo tubes, they were designed for a maximum speed of 28.5 knots.

Cleopatra was a slightly larger vessel of 3750 tons belonging to the "Caroline" class completed in 1915. Except that her armament included four 6-inch guns instead of a mixture of 6-inch and 4-inch weapons, she was similar to the *Galatea*.

Caledon was the name ship of a class completed in 1917 which included the *Calypso, Caradoc* and *Cassandra*. Displacing 4120 tons, armed with five 6-inch guns and designed for a maximum speed of 29 knots, they were similar to the *Cleopatra*, except for two funnels instead of three.

Ceres was the name ship of a class commissioned in 1917–18 which included the *Cardiff* and *Curacoa*. These only differed significantly from the *Caledon* in having two of their five 6-inch guns mounted before the bridge, one superimposed a deck higher than the other.

Danae, Dauntless, Delhi, Dragon and *Dunedin* were larger ships of 4650 tons completed in 1918–19. Armed with six 6-inch and two 3- inch A.A. guns plus twelve tubes, they were designed for a maximum speed of 29 knots.

NOTES ON WARSHIPS EMPLOYED IN THE BALTIC

Aircraft Carrier

Vindictive was laid down as one of a class of five cruisers of 9750 tons, armed with seven 7.5-inch guns, for working with the battlefleet or for dealing with commerce raiders, for which they were given a maximum speed of 29 knots. But before completion she was converted to carry and operate 12 aircraft, when her armament was reduced to four 7.5-inch and four 3-inch A.A. guns plus six torpedo tubes, so that a flying-off deck and hangar could be fitted before her bridge and a landing-on deck installed abaft her after funnel.

Monitor

Erebus, like her sister-ship, the *Terror,* displaced 8000 tons and was completed in 1916. A member of her crew recalls that she was "built to bombard the Belgian coast and had just about enough engine power for that purpose (12 knots). To counteract her shallow draught and huge blisters, she had three rudders astern and one in the bow. Her armament was one twin 15-inch turret and eight 4-inch guns. Off the North Cape the bow rudders went out of action and (she) could not make enough steerage way to answer the helm. This difficulty was overcome by raising the 15-inch guns to full elevation and hoisting an awning from them as a sail. While in Murmansk the shipwrights stepped a mast which carried a jib and a flying jib, but in the first storm the unseasoned mast snapped and for the rest of the commission the raised guns did (this) duty."

Flotilla Leaders

Abdiel, of 1600 tons, was equipped to carry 72 mines, her armament being reduced to three 4-inch guns and no torpedo tubes. Completed in 1916 and capable of a speed in excess of 30 knots, she was unusual in having as many as four funnels.

Bruce, Mackay, Shakespeare, Spenser and *Wallace* were 1800-ton vessels designed for 32 knots and completed in 1917-18. They were armed with five 4.7-inch guns and six 21-inch torpedo tubes.

Destroyers

The "S" class (some of whose names began with T) were ships of 1070 tons completed in 1918–19. Capable of more than 30 knots they were armed with three 4-inch guns and four 21-inch tubes.

The "V and W" class were larger vessels of 1300 tons completed in 1917–18. Designed for 31 knots, the majority were armed with four 4-inch guns and six 21-inch tubes, but a proportion carried four 4.7-inch guns whilst some had only four torpedo tubes. A small number could also carry 72 mines if they sacrificed one gun and their torpedo tubes.

Submarines

The "E" class, completed between 1913 and 1917, displaced 660 tons (800 submerged), could proceed at 15 knots (10 knots submerged), and were equipped with five 18-inch torpedo tubes.

The smaller "H" class, which displaced 440 tons (550 submerged) were completed in 1917–19. With four 21-inch tubes their speed was limited to 13 knots (10 knots submerged).

Most of the larger "L" class, displacing 890 tons (1070 submerged), which were completed in 1918 and later years, could proceed at 17 knots (10 knots submerged) and were armed with one 4-inch gun in addition to four 21-inch and two 18-inch torpedo tubes. But the *L51* and higher numbers were armed with two 4-inch guns and six 21-inch torpedo tubes, which increased their displacement to 960 tons (1150 tons submerged).

C.M.B.s

More than sixty of these were completed in the latter half of the First World War for "tip and run" raids across the southern North Sea, for which they were equipped with petrol engines to drive them at 35 knots. The first were only 40 feet long and carried a single 18-inch torpedo. Later ones were 55 feet long, the majority carrying two 18-inch torpedoes.

Minelayer

Princess Margaret was a liner taken over by the Admiralty in 1914 and converted to lay 400 mines. Armed with two 4.7-inch guns, she could achieve 22 knots.

Minesweepers

Myrtle, Gentian, etc. were single screw, coal-fired vessels of the "Flower" class, displacing 1200 tons. Completed during the First World War they were armed with two 4-inch guns, and had a maximum speed of 17 knots.

Banbury, Lanark, Hexham, etc., also built during the First World War, were smaller (810 tons) paddle-driven, 15-knot ships, likewise coal-fired, which proved more useful in the Baltic than the "Flower" class.

FRENCH

Cruisers

Gueydon and *Montcalm* were obsolescent sister-ships of 9100 tons completed ten years before the First World War. Armed with two 7.6-inch and eight 6.5-inch guns, they were designed for 21 knots (coal-fired).

Destroyers, etc.

Gamier was a destroyer of 730 tons completed in 1911; with two 4.1-inch guns and four 18-inch torpedo tubes she could attain 31 knots.

Lestin was a similar, slightly larger (790 tons) destroyer completed in 1913.

Aisne, Ancre, Marne, etc., were small escort vessels of 650 tons completed in 1917–18. Armed with four 3.9-inch guns, they were designed for 21 knots (oil-fired).

Dunois was a torpedo gunboat of 900 tons completed at the turn of the century to carry six 9-pounder guns. Her effective maximum speed was 19 knots (coal-fired).

ESTONIAN

Destroyers

Wambola (ex-Russian *Spartak*) was a sister-ship of the *Gavriil* (see below).

Lennuk (ex-Russian *Avtroil*), completed in 1917, displaced 1800 tons and could steam at 32 knots (oil-fired). Armed with five 4-inch guns and nine 18-inch torpedo tubes, she could also lay 80 mines.

Gunboat

Lembit (ex-Russian *Bobr*), completed seven years before the First World War, displaced 875 tons. Armed with two 4.7-inch and four 11-pounder guns, her speed was limited to 12 knots (coal-fired).

FINNISH

The Finnish torpedoboats which worked from Biorko with Cowan's force were small ex-Russian vessels of 150 tons completed in 1904. Armed with two 3-pounder guns and two 15-inch torpedo tubes, they had a maximum speed of 29 knots (coal-fired).

RUSSIAN (BOLSHEVIK)

Battleships

Andrei Pervozvanni was the last pre-dreadnought completed for the Russian Navy (1910). A well-armoured vessel, she displaced 17,680 tons. Armed with four 12-inch, fourteen 8-inch and twelve 4.7-inch guns, plus two 18-inch torpedo tubes, she was designed for a maximum speed of 18 knots (coal-fired).

Petropavlovsk and *Sevastopol* were sister dreadnoughts completed in 1914–15. Well armoured, each displaced 23,370 tons. Their armament included twelve 12-inch guns in four triple centre-line turrets and sixteen 4.7-inch guns, plus four 18-inch tubes. They could steam at 23 knots (oil-fired and coal-fired).

Cruisers

Oleg, which displaced 6650 tons, was designed for 23 knots (coal-fired) and completed in 1903. She was armed with twelve 6-inch and twelve 12-pounder guns, plus four 18-inch tubes.

Avrora, a similar vessel except that she carried only ten 6-inch guns, her speed being limited to 20 knots, may still be seen at Leningrad where she is preserved as a reminder of the October Revolution. The gunlayer of her forecastle gun, whose shots enabled the Bolsheviks to seize the Winter Palace, had achieved the (equivalent) rank of commander and was serving as her Executive Officer when the author visited her in 1954.

Destroyers

Avtroil (see *Lennuk* under Estonian vessels above).

Azard, Gavriil, Konstantin, Spartak and *Svoboda* were sister-ships of 1260 tons completed in 1918. Armed with four 4-inch guns and twelve 18-inch torpedo tubes, each could also lay 80 mines. They were designed for a maximum speed of 35 knots (oil-fired).

NOTES ON WARSHIPS EMPLOYED IN THE BALTIC

Gaidamak and *Vsadnik* were small vessels of only 570 tons designed for 25 knots and completed about 1905. Armed with two 4-inch guns and three 18-inch tubes, they could also lay 25 mines.

Submarines

Pantera, Tigr, Tur, Volk and *Vyepr,* completed in 1916–17, displaced 500 tons (840 submerged) and were capable of 10 knots (9 submerged). They were armed with two 6-pounder guns and four 18-inch tubes, plus dropping gear for eight more torpedoes.

Minelayer

Narova was some fifty years old. Displacing 5030 tons and with a speed limited to 12 knots (coal-fired), she could lay 600 mines.

APPENDIX C

Geographical Glossary

GEOGRAPHICAL NAMES used in this book are those found in contemporary British documents and on British maps and charts of the same period. Many have been, or are now, commonly spelt in other ways (e.g. HELSINGFORS, the Swedish spelling, has been replaced by Helsinki, the Finnish version), whilst some have been, or are now, usually called by entirely different names (e.g. REVAL, the Swedish form, has been replaced by Tallinn, the Estonian, whilst PETROGRAD, formerly called St. Petersburg, has been renamed Leningrad). To assist the English reader to identify these places, etc., the name usually used in this book is given below followed by the variants (omitting the use of the German w instead of the Slav v, e.g. DVINA/Dwina). In all cases, accents (such as are used on many Latvian names) have been omitted, since few English readers know how these affect pronunciation.

BIORKO, Bolshoi Berezoviy
BREST-LITOVSK, Brest

CESIS, Wenden
CHRISTIANIA, Oslo
COURLAND, Kurland, Kurzeme

DAGO, Hiiumaa
DANZIG, Gdansk
DAUGAVPILS, Dunaborg
DOLGY NOS, Ustinsky
DORPAT, Tartu
DUNAMUNDE, Daugavgriva
DVINA, Daugava

ESTONIA, Esthonia

GREY HORSE, Seraya Loshad

HANGO, Hanko
HELSINGFORS, Helsinki

HARGEN ISLAND, Naissaar, Nayssar
NARVA, Narvskiy Zaliv, Narva-Joesuu, Narva Ygyesi

ORANIENBAUM, Lomonosov
OSEL, Saaremaa

PAPON BAY, Hara Laht
PEIPUS, LAKE, Peipsi, Lake, Chudskoye Ozero,
PERNAU, Parnu
PETERHOF, Leninsk, Petrodvorets
PETROGRAD, St. Petersburg, Leningrad

GEOGRAPHICAL GLOSSARY

PETSAMO, Pechenga
POLDISKI, Port Baltic,
  Roggervik

HOGLAND, Gogland,
  Suuarsaari, Sursaari

KAPORIA BIGHT, Kaporskaya
  Guba
KOIVISTO, Primorsk
KONIGBERG, Kaliningrad
KOVNO, Kaunas
KRASNAYA GORKA, Peredovoy
KUNDA, Kounda

LATGALE, Latgazia, Latgallia
LEMBURG, Lvov
LIBAU, Liepaja
LIVONIA, Vidzeme

MEMEL, Klaipeda
MITAU, Jelgava

MOON, Muhu

REVAL, Revel, Tallinn

SHAVLI, Siauliai
SHEPELEVSKY LT., Karavelda Lt.
STETTIN, Szczecin
STIRS PT., Stirsudden

TAUROGGEN, Taurage
TERRIOKI, Zelenogorsk
TILSIT, Sovietsk
TURKU, Abo
TYTERS ISLAND, Bolshoi Tyuters

VIBORG, Vyborg, Viipuri
VILNA, Vilno, Vilnius

WALK, Valka, Valga
WINDAU, Ventspils
WULF ISLAND, Aegna Saar

SOURCES AND BIBLIOGRAPHY

My MOST important source has been the relevant British Admiralty records now in the Public Record Office (ADM 137/1663–92). Valuable supplementary sources are the Cowan and Fremantle papers in the National Maritime Museum. The great majority of documents from which I have quoted are to be found in one or other of these collections.[1] Other unpublished sources consulted (in addition to the personal diaries, letters, etc. which have been made available to me by some of those who were in the Baltic at the time) include: *Naval Memories,* the autobiography of Admiral Sir Bertram Thesiger, and *The Adventure of Bermondt-Avalov* by Provost A. Gramatins. Published works which deal *inter alia* with some aspect of this story are listed below.

(*a*)　*Works in English (published in Great Britain or the U.S.A.)*

The files of *The Times, Naval and Military Record, Hansard* and other contemporary newspapers and journals.

AGAR, Captain A. W. S., *Baltic Episode. Footprints in the Sea. Naval Operations in the Baltic.* (*Journal of the Royal United Service Institution,* November 1928.)

ANDERSON, EDGAR, *British Policy towards the Baltic States, 1918–20.* (*Journal of Central European Affairs,* Volume XIX.) *The Undeclared Naval War: the British-Soviet Naval Struggle in the Baltic, 1918–20.* (*Journal of Central European Affairs,* April 1962.)

BELL, H. M., *Land of Lakes*

BILMANIS, A., *A History of Latvia*

BUSH, Captain E. W., *Bless our Ship*

CHALMERS, Rear-Admiral W. S., *Max Horton and the Western Approaches*

CHURCHILL, WINSTON S., *The World Crisis: The Aftermath*

COATES, W. P. and COATES, Z. K., *Armed Intervention in Russia, 1918–1922*

---

[1] Strict historians will wish to note that when quoting from documents, etc., I have in many cases abbreviated them for reasons of space without inserting ellipses. They are assured that the sense of such documents has not been distorted.

COWAN, Rear-Admiral Sir WALTER, *Baltic Despatch* (*London Gazette*, 6th April, 1920)

CUNNINGHAM, Admiral of the Fleet Lord, *A Sailor's Odyssey*

DAWSON, Captain LIONEL, *Sound of the Guns*[1]

DUKES, Sir PAUL, *The Story of S.T. 25*

DURANTY, WALTER, *I Write as I Please*

DZIEWANOWSKI, M. K., *Pilsudski's Federal Policy, 1919–1921* (*Journal of Central European Affairs*, Volume X)

EYCH, ERICH, *A History of the Weimar Republic*

FREMANTLE, Admiral Sir SYDNEY, *My Naval Career*

GADE, J. A., *All my Born Days: Experiences of a Naval Intelligence Officer in Europe*

GORDON H. J., *The Reichswehr and the German Republic, 1919–1926*

GOUGH, General Sir HUBERT, *Soldiering On*

HALE, R. W., *The Letters of Warwick Greene, 1915–1928*

JACKSON, J. H., *Estonia*

JURGELA, C. R., *History of the Lithuanian Nation*

LATVIAN DELEGATION, WASHINGTON, D.C., *Latvia, 1918–1958*

LLOYD GEORGE, D., *Memories of the Peace Conference*

LOCKHART, R. H., *Memoirs of a British Agent*

MANNERHEIM, Marshal, *Memoirs*

MERGER, Commander D., *The Baltic Sea Campaign, 1918–20* (*Proceedings of the U.S. Naval Institute*, September 1962)

PAGE, S. W., *The Formation of the Baltic States*

"PARAVANE," *With the Baltic Squadron, 1918–20* (*Fortnightly Review*, May 1921)

PICK, E. W., *The New Baltic Nations*

RUTTER, OWEN, *The New Baltic States*

SAUNDERS, M. G., *The Soviet Navy*

SCHWABE, A., *The Story of Latvia and her Neighbours*

SMITH, C. J., *Finland and the Russian Revolution*

TALLENTS, Sir STEPHEN, *Man and Boy*

TARULIS, A., *Soviet Policy towards the Baltic States, 1918–1920*

TEMPERLEY, H. M. V., *A History of the Peace Conference of Paris, 1919*

THORNEYCROFT, J., and Co., *A Short History of the Thorneycroft Coastal Motor Boats*

TORMA, A. and RAUD, V., *Estonia, 1918–1952*

WAITE, R. G. L., *The Freikorps Movement: Vanguard to Nazism*

WATSON, H. H. GRANT, *An Account of a Mission to the Baltic States*

WEMYSS, Lady WESTER, *The Life and Letters of Lord Wester Wemyss*

WOODWARD, Sir LLEWELLYN, *Documents on British Foreign Policy, 1919–1939*, First Series, Vol. III

[1] Cowan's Biography.

ANONYMOUS, *A Twist in the Lion's Tail—and its Results* (*The Navy*, Vol. XLIII)

(*b*)   *German Works*

BERMONDT-AVALOV, F. P. M., *Im Kamf gegen den Bolshewismus, Erinnerungen*
BISCHOFF, J., *Die Letzte Front, Geschichte der Eisernen Division im Baltikum, 1919*
GOLTZ, R. GRAF, v.d., *Als politischer General im Osten, Finnland und Baltikum, 1918 und 1919*
NOSKE, G., *Von Kiel bis Kapp*
OERTZEN, F. W. v., *Die Deutschen Freikorps, 1918–1923*
RABENAU, F. v., *Seeckt, aus seinem Leben, 1919–1936*
SCHMIDT-PAULI, E. v., *Geschichte der Freikorps, 1918–1924*
WINNIG, A., *Am Ausgang der Deutschen Ost-Politik, Personliche Erlebnisse und Erinnerungen*

(*c*)   *Works in Russian* (*published in the U.S.S.R.*)

ANDREEV, N. M., *Borba Litouskogo Naroda za Sovietskuyu Vlast 1918–1919 gg.*
BELOV, G. A. and others, *Istorii Grazhdanskoi Voina, SSSR: sbornik dokumentov i materialov*
BUROV, A. S., KAMENEV, S. S. and EIDEMAN, R. P., *Grazhdanskaya Voina, 1918–1921 gg.*
GRAUDIN, K. M. and STOROZHENKO, G., *Voina Interventsii; Latviya v 1918–1919 gg.*
GRECHANYUK, N. and others, *Baltiisky Flot*
IAKUSHKIN, E. E. and POLUNIN, S., *Angliskaya Interventsiya v. 1918–1920 gg.*
KHVOSHELINSKII, Y. A., *Zapiski shturmana "Pantera"*
KORNATOVSKII, N. A., *Borba za Krasny Petrograd 1919 g.*
KRASTIN, Y. P., *Sotsialisticheskaya Sovietskaya Respublika Latvii v 1919 g. inostrannaya interventsiya; dokumenty i materialy;* Vols. 1 and 2
MINTS, I. and GORODESTSKY, E., *Dokumenty po Istorii Grazhdanskoi Voiny v SSSR;* Vol. 1: *Pervy etap grazhdanskoi voiny*
PUKHOV, A. S., *Petrograd ne Zdavat: Kommunisty vo Glave Oborony Petrograda v 1919 g. Baltiisky Flot v Zashchite Petrograda 1919 g. kak Vozughalsya Petrograda, 1918–1919 gg.*
RYBAKOV, M. V., *Geroicheskaya Oborona Petrograda v 1919 g.*
SHAPOSHNIKOV, V. I., *Podvigi Baltiitsev v 1918 g.*
SOBELIEV, A. A., *Krasny Flot v Grazhdanskoi Voina Istorya Grazhdanskoi Voiny v SSSR, 1917–1922 gg.,* Vols. 3 and 4.
SOBELIEV, A. A., *Iz Istorii Grazhdanskoi Voiny v SSSR; sbornik dokumentov v treh tomah, 1918–1922 gg.,* Vols. 1 and 2.

TAIGRAO, J. J., *Borba Trudyashchikhsya Estonii za Sovietskuyu Vlasi i za Mir v Gody Grazhdanskoi Voiny, 1918–1920 gg.*

VISHNEVSKY, V. (Script) and DZIGAN, Y. (Director), *My iz Kronsthadta* (Mosfilm)

ZOFFE, V and others, *Piat Let Krasnogo Flota, 1917–1922 gg.*

(*d*) *Other Works*

ENCKELL, C., *Politiska Minnen*, Vol. 2 (Helsinki)

GAILLARD, G., *L'Allemagne et le Balticum* (Paris)

NIEDRA, A., *Ka tas Lietas tika Diratas* (Riga)

NIESSEL, H. C., *L'Evacuation des Pays Baltiques par les Allemands* (Paris)

PARQUET, Colonel DU, *L'Aventure Allemande en Lettonie* (Paris)

THOMAZI, A. A., *La Marine Française dans la Grande Guerre, 1918–1919; La Guerre Navale dans la zone des Armées du Nord* (Paris)

ACKNOWLEDGMENTS

No PREVIOUS account of the operations conducted in the Baltic by the British Navy from 1918 to 1920 has been published in book form. My foremost debt is therefore to the Lords Commissioners of the Admiralty for allowing me access to their records. The Trustees of the National Maritime Museum, Greenwich, have likewise helped by permitting me to use the papers of Admirals Sir Walter Cowan and Sir Sydney Fremantle.

For valuable assistance, especially for the loan of diaries, letters and other records, I am grateful to Captain A. W. S. Agar, Field-Marshal the Earl Alexander of Tunis, M. Bronius Balutis, Rear-Admiral M. G. Bennett, Mr. W. H. Blanshard, Commander M. S. Bradby, Mr. N. Cheshire, Captain J. Creswell, the late Admiral of the Fleet Lord Cunningham of Hyndhope, Vice-Admiral Berwick Curtis, Captain L. Dawson, Captain K. Dowding, Captain F. G. Glossop, the late General Sir Hubert Gough, Mr. J. C. Howard, Commander H. H. Kitson, Vice-Admiral Sir Richard Lane-Poole, Surgeon-Captain E. L. Markham, Herr J. Meister, Mr. E. B. Newman, Commander G. C. Pitcairn-Jones, Lieutenant-Commander A. B. Sainsbury, Admiral Sir Bertram Thesiger, Commander W. R. Titterton, M. August Torma, Captain H. S. P. Watch, Mr. D. C. Watt, Admiral Sir Lionel Wells, Admiral of the Fleet Sir Algernon Willis, Mr. A. C. Yeates, and the late M. Charles Zarine.

Others whom I have to thank are Lieutenant-Commander P. K. Kemp and the staff of the Admiralty Library, Brigadier J. Stephenson and the staff of the Royal United Service Institution, the Librarian of the House of Commons, Mr. A. W. H. Pearsall, Custodian of Manuscripts at the National Maritime Museum, Greenwich, the Librarian and the Photographic Librarian at the Imperial War Museum, Lambeth, Dr. Klink of the Federal German Armed Forces Historical Research Office, the Director of the Lenin Library, Moscow, and the Director of the Central Maritime War Museum, Leningrad.

I gladly record my debt to Miss J. Pemberton and Lieutenant-Commander J. Davidson for their help with translating Russian sources, to Miss Margaret Dyson and Miss Adrienne Edye for typing my manuscript, to Lieutenant-Commander A. B. Sainsbury for casting his eagle eye over the proofs and to Miss Mary Rundle for her assistance with the Index.

ACKNOWLEDGMENTS

The majority of the documents from which I have quoted are unpublished Crown-copyright material in the Public Record Office, and are reproduced by permission of the Controller of H.M. Stationary Office. For permission to reproduce similar material in the National Maritime Museum I am indebted to the Trustees. I am likewise grateful to the authors and publishers of the following works: *A Sailor's Odyssey* by Admiral of the Fleet Lord Cunningham, published by Messrs. Hutchinson and Co.; *Footprints in the Sea* by Captain Augustus Agar, published by Messrs. Evans and Co.; *Sound of the Guns* by Captain Lionel Dawson, published by the Pen-in-Hand Co.; and *The Undeclared Naval War* by Edgar Anderson in the *Journal of Central European Affairs* for April 1962, published by the University of Colorado.

INDEX